Law Beyond the State

Normative Orders

Publications of the Cluster of Excellence “The Formation of Normative Orders” at Goethe University Frankfurt am Main

Edited by Rainer Forst and Klaus Günther

Volume 18

Rainer Hofmann and *Stefan Kadelbach* both are Professors of Public Law, European Law and Public International Law at Goethe University Frankfurt am Main.

Rainer Hofmann, Stefan Kadelbach (eds.)

Law Beyond the State

Pasts and Futures

Campus Verlag
Frankfurt/New York

This publication is part of the DFG-funded Cluster of Excellence "The Formation of Normative Orders" at Goethe University Frankfurt am Main.

DFG

NORMATIVE ORDERS
Exzellenzcluster an der Goethe-Universität Frankfurt am Main

ISBN 978-3-593-50650-0 Print
ISBN 978-3-593-443492-6 E-Book (PDF)

Cover design: Campus Verlag GmbH, Frankfurt-on-Main
Printed on acid free paper.
Printed in the United States of America

For further information:
www.campus.de
www.press.uchicago.edu

Contents

Law Beyond the State—Pasts and Futures: An Introduction

Rainer Hofmann

I. Introduction

On 10 June 1914, Emperor Wilhelm II signed—albeit in his capacity as King of Prussia which had annexed Frankfurt in the aftermath of the Prussian-Austrian war of 1866 thus terminating its century-long status of *Freie Reichsstadt*—the decree granting the foundation of a university in Frankfurt am Main. The final step was taken on 1 August 1914 when Wilhelm II assented to the statutes of the university. Due to the ongoing war, the inauguration on 26 October 1914 is reported to have been more sober than originally planned; lectures began the following day thus successfully ending a long and often protracted process initiated and carried forward by a number of outstanding personalities such as *Franz Adickes*, long-time mayor of Frankfurt, and *Wilhelm Merton*, founder of *Metallgesellschaft* who had succeeded in mustering the political and above all very strong financial support of leading and affluent members of Frankfurt's traditionally cosmopolitan and liberal *bourgeoisie* characterized by its very high percentage of Jews; their very substantial endowments made Frankfurt University a true citizens' university, financially independent from any Prussian state support.[1] The Faculty of Law[2], one of the five initial faculties, comprised seven full professors (*Ordinarien*) among whom

1 For an account of the history of the foundation of Frankfurt University see Ludwig Heilbrunn, Die Gründung der Universität Frankfurt am Main, Frankfurt 1915.

2 For a presentation of the history of the Faculty of Law see Bernhard Diestelkamp, Kurzer Abriss einer Geschichte der Fakultät/des Fachbereichs Rechtswissenschaft der Johann Wolfgang Goethe-Universität zu Frankfurt am Main bis zum Ende des 20. Jahrhunderts, in: Fachbereich Rechtswissenschaft (ed.), 100 Jahre Rechtswissenschaft in Frankfurt. Erfahrungen, Herausforderungen, Erwartungen, Frankfurt 2014, 11–104.

Friedrich Giese[3] who was tasked to teach Public Law, including Public International Law.

Commemorating the 100st anniversary of its foundation, Frankfurt University and a number of its institutions organized workshops and other academic events throughout 2014. Considering the eminent role usually accorded to Frankfurt scholars for the development of international law, the Faculty of Law convened, on 11 June 2014, in cooperation with the Cluster of Excellence "The Formation of Normative Orders", a workshop analyzing the role of Frankfurt in the past development of both Public International Law and European (Union) Law as well as looking into the futures of these branches of law as essential components of a "Law Beyond the State": *Michael Bothe* discussed, from a historic point of view, *Public International Law in Frankfurt*; *Martti Koskenniemi* shared his thoughts on *International Law's Futures—Yesterday, Today, Tomorrow*; *Ingolf Pernice* presented his project on *Global Constitutionalism and the Internet. Taking People Seriously*; and *Joseph H.H. Weiler* developed his vision on *Taking (Europe's) Values Seriously*.

These papers, some of them substantially enlarged and revised, and complemented by an article by *Stefan Kadelbach* on *Frankfurt's Contribution to European Law*, are assembled in this publication in order to make them available to the public-at-large.

II. The Pasts

While German-speaking scholars always had played an important role in the development of international law, both as concerns its inter-state aspects as *Völkerrecht* as well as its conflict-of-laws aspects as *Internationales Privatrecht*, this situation was not reflected in any institutional academic settings until the years immediately preceding and following World War I: 1914 saw the foundation of the Kiel *Institute for International Law* headed by *Theodor Niemeyer*; the separation between Public and Private International Law was well reflected in the foundations of the Berlin-based Kaiser-Wilhelm-Institutes for Comparative and International Public Law, under

3 See Michael Stolleis, Friedrich Giese, in: Bernhard Diestelkamp/Michael Stolleis (eds.), Juristen an der Universität Frankfurt am Main, Baden-Baden 1989, 117–127.

the directorship of *Viktor Bruns*, in 1924 and for Comparative and International Private Law, under the directorship of *Ernst Rabel*, in 1926, respectively. The strongly increasing relevance of Public International Law in Germany, not the least as a result of the Versailles Peace Treaty, was reflected, as concerns Frankfurt, in the fact that already in 1920, *Karl Strupp* began its teaching activities, first as *Privatdozent*, later (1926) as *Extraordinarius* but only in 1932 as *Ordinarius*, about one year before he—because of his being a Jew—lost his position and had to emigrate, first to Turkey, then to Denmark and France where he died in 1940—never able to take up a professorship at Columbia University which had been offered to him in 1939.[4] His and his Frankfurt successors' contribution to the development of Public International Law are presented and analyzed in the pertinent contribution by *Michael Bothe*.

The aftermath of World War II saw, among other developments, the advent of serious integration efforts in the non-communist part of Europe, resulting in the foundation of the Council of Europe in 1949 as a traditional inter-national organization, on the one hand, and of the European Coal and Steel Community (ECSC) in 1951/1952 as the first supranational organization, on the other hand. The ECSC formed the nucleus of what became, subsequent to the entry into force of the treaties establishing the European Economic Community and the European Atomic Energy Community in 1957 and later developments such as the treaties of Maastricht, Amsterdam, Nice and Lisbon the European Union as we know it today. These developments also resulted in the establishment of a specific branch of International Law, European (Union) Law which was to a large extent influenced by Frankfurt-based scholars such as, in particular *Walter Hallstein*, the first post-war *Rektor* of the University (1946 1948) and, as of 1958, the first President of the European Economic Community as which he served until 1967.[5] His and his successors' contribution to the development of European (Union) Law are presented and discussed in the pertinent contribution by *Stefan Kadelbach*.

4 See Michael Bothe, Karl Strupp, in: Diestelkamp/Stolleis, ibid., 161–170.

5 See Friedrich Kübler, Walter Hallstein, in: Diestelkamp/Stolleis, ibid., 268–281.

1. Public International Law in Frankfurt

In order to cover his topic, i.e. public international law in Frankfurt, *Michael Bothe* chose to tell "three different, but intricately intermingled tales: A tale about persons who shaped teaching, research and outreach of international law in Frankfurt during a century; a tale about the history of Germany and the world at large which has had a marked impact on the life and work of these persons; and a tale about the development of legal thought to which these persons have contributed". [6]

The persons who figure most prominently in these tales are *Karl Strupp*, *Walter Hallstein*, *Heinrich Kronstein* and *Hermann Mosler. Bothe* considers them—and rightly so—as initiators of developments which became eventually significant for public international law at Frankfurt. These developments or aspects are the documentation of international law, the role of international economic law, and the international system as a legal community.

Strupp's strong international reputation was well reflected in, *inter alia*, his membership in the *Institut de Droit International*, first (1927) as associated member, then (in 1932) as ordinary member, and the three invitations to give lectures at the Hague Academy, in 1924 ("L'intervention en matière financière"), 1930 ("Le droit du juge international de statuer selon l'équité") and 1934 ("Les règles génèrales du droit de la paix"). In addition to publishing his important monographs such as *Das völkerrechtliche Delikt* (1920) and *Die völkerrechtliche Haftung des Staates* (1927), he initiated what became a true Frankfurt tradition: the documentation of international law as reflected in his *Wörterbuch des Völkerrechts* (published in three volumes between 1924 and 1929).

This approach, i.e. the understanding that the effectiveness of international law depends to a large extent on its being known by all relevant actors and, therefore, requires its documentation in an easily accessible, encyclopedic format was continued by *Hans-Joachim Schlochauer*, *Strupp's* former assistant who being himself a Jew, had fled to Oxford from where he returned to Frankfurt in 1951 to take up a professorship in public international law which he held until 1974. Between 1960 and 1962, he was responsible for the second edition of the *Wörterbuch*, again in three volumes. Two decades later, it was understood that such a compilation

6 Michael Bothe, Public International Law in Frankfurt (in this book), 35.

needed the administrative support of a larger unit—and it was *Rudolf Bernhardt*, a disciple of *Hermann Mosler* and former professor of public law at Frankfurt, who having assumed his position as co-director of the Heidelberg Max-Planck Institute for Comparative and International Public Law, set out to edit the *Encyclopedia of Public International Law* (the four volume library edition was published in the nineties) to be succeeded by the *Max-Planck Encyclopedia of Public International*, edited since 2006 under the aegis of *Rüdiger Wolfrum*, available also in electronic form. Notwithstanding the fact that thanks to the internet, the real problem might no longer be to have actual access to international law documents, but consists in having access to information on international law presented in a "digestable" way, which imposes on editors of any encyclopedia an increased responsibility carefully to select the essentials of any international law aspect while strictly separating facts from assessment—the need for any encyclopedia fulfilling such requirements might be greater than ever.[7]

Although neither *Walter Hallstein* nor *Heinrich Kronstein* might be considered as engaged in public international law but rather comparative and private international law (conflict of laws), they were clearly instrumental, together with *Schlochauer*, in establishing international economic law as a subject of research and teaching in Frankfurt, notably by founding, in 1951, the *Institute of Foreign and International Economic Law*. While is activities were focused in its early years mainly on issues connected with the legal integration of European economies and competition law, it later became in the seventies, under the leadership of *Günther Jaenicke*, home for a new area of international economic law: the law of commodities (*Rohstoffrecht*) which, in recent years, has seen quite a strong renaissance, lately also in Frankfurt due to the research conducted by *Isabel Feichtner*. After *Jaenicke's* retirement the Institute was dissolved in the nineties and it took some time until, in the framework of the *Wilhelm-Merton Centre for European Integration and International Economic Order*, research and teaching activities in this field have gained again some weight after 2004, in particular in the field of investment law; a "Frankfurt specificity" is the strong interest in questions relating to the interrelationship between general international law and investment law

7 Ibid., 41.

as reflected in the topics dealt with in the annual Frankfurt Investment Law Workshops (*Rainer Hofmann*).[8]

Obviously, Frankfurt based scholars have always addressed such fundamental questions of public international law as the use of force and humanitarian law (suffice to mention the ground-breaking work of *Michael Bothe*), environmental law (again *Michael Bothe*), Law of the Seas (*Günther Jaenicke*), and more recently human rights law, including the rights of national minorities and refugees (*Rainer Hofmann* and *Stefan Kadelbach*). In addition to that, there has always been a very keen interest in dealing with more general issues concerning the (legal) structure of the international community. This clearly dates back to the writings of *Karl Strupp* and, in particular, to the post-war period when *Hermann Mosler* held the chair of public international law. Although he already left Frankfurt in 1954 to become director of the Heidelberg Max Planck Institute (thus setting the ground for a truly impressive personal linkage between Frankfurt and Heidelberg as described by *Bothe*[9]) and published his seminal works when he was Judge at the International Court of Justice[10], he left behind the strong interest in these questions as reflected in the academic work of all his successors, in particular *Michael Bothe*, *Armin von Bogdandy* and currently *Stefan Kadelbach*. This interest ranges from more practical issues such as remedies in international law and procedural aspects of human rights protection to truly general issues such as positivism vs. value orientation. And, as *Michael Bothe*, shows there has always been a Frankfurt trend not to accept a pure positivism as the fundamental basis of international law but to integrate values: This can be found, albeit in a somewhat embryonic expression, in *Strupp's* approach, before it becomes quite important in *Mosler's* seminal articles in the mid- seventies and more recently in what *Bothe* calls *Stefan Kadelbach's* school on "International Law as a Normative Order"; and indeed: an international legal system which would not be based on fundamental values and the quest for an international system

8 See Rainer Hofmann/Christian Tams (eds.), International Investment Law and General International Law (2011); Rainer Hofmann/Christian Tams (eds.), International Investment Law and its Others (2012); Rainer Hofmann/Stephan Schill/Christian Tams (eds.), Preferential and Trade and Investment Agreements (2013); Stephan Schill/Christian Tams/Rainer Hofmann (eds.), International Investment Law and Development (2015).

9 See Michael Bothe, Public International Law in Frankfurt (in this book, 35).

10 Ibid., 44.

based on the unambiguous prohibition of the use of force and the strict respect for human rights would run counter to the deeply held convictions of all those who have been and are teaching and doing research on public international law in Frankfurt.

2. Frankfurt's Contribution to European Law

Noting that, in contrast to public international law, the history of European law only begins to attract scholarly attention, *Stefan Kadelbach* sets out to show that there is a specific Frankfurt contribution to the development of European law. In order to do so, he starts by sketching the four phases through which European legal scholarship has gone: the founding phase of the fifties and early sixties was characterized by writings, authored by persons involved in the treaty-making process, on the founding treaties themselves; the second phase, starting with the *van Gend & Loos* and *Costa ./. ENEL* cases in the mid- sixties and lasting until the end of the eighties, was marked by the unfolding of the norm programme enshrined in the treaties, supported and put forward by an increasingly important role of the ECJ as the *engine of integration* and accompanied by doctrinal debates in which the federal ideal provided the *leitmotiv* for the scholarly discussion on the process of European integration; the third phase began with the foundation of the European Union and ended with what *Kadelbach* rightly describes as "the failure of the treaty on a Constitution for Europe which was supposed to improve the political legitimacy of the Union by a new constitution-making process (Convent procedure) and, above all, by more parliamentary say in law-making"[11]—a phase during which scholars addressed issues such as the (alleged) need for limiting the development of judge-made law or for increasing the democratic legitimacy of public power in Europe while at the same time dealing with the 'Europeanization' of wide aspects of private, administrative and criminal law; the present phase is indeed characterized by a widespread and strong feeling of a crisis of European integration notwithstanding (or closely related to?) the enlargement process of the previous decade, the consequences of the problematic entry into force of the *Lisbon Treaty* accompanied by the *Lisbon Judgment* of the *Bundesverfassungsgericht* and the still on-going "Euro crisis"—

11 Stefan Kadelbach, Frankfurt's Contribution to European Law (in this book) 49.

to which one might add the profoundly shattered idea of European solidarity as witnessed in the context of the current "refugee crisis" or the various scenarios envisaged as a result of a possible *BREXIT*.

During the initial phase of European integration, members of the Frankfurt faculty were closely involved in this process: While the essential role of *Walter Hallstein* (professor for civil and trade law 1946–1954) as secretary of state in the Chancellor's Office and later in the Ministry of Foreign Affairs and leader of the German delegation during the negotiations of the Treaty on the European Coal and Steal Community (ECSC) (from 1958–1967 he served as the first President of the European Commission) is public knowledge, the substantial contributions made, during the early stages of European integration, by *Hermann Mosler* who, in addition of being professor of public law from 1949–1954 served as head of the legal department of the Ministry of Foreign Affairs in the crucial years 1951–1953, *Carl Friedrich Ophüls*, *Hans-Jürgen Schlochauer* and *Ernst Steindorff* are much lesser known and deserve to be stressed.[12] They, and *Günther Jaenicke* who joined the Frankfurt faculty in 1959, sought to find categories for the new structure of the EC which, at first sight, seemed to be part of international law as flowing from an international treaty but the introduction of supranational powers indicated the existence of a somewhat different body of law. In contrast to the ECJ which saw the ground for the normativity of supranational law on the domestic plane in the autonomy of European law, they found its basis in the founding treaties and parliamentary assent thereto—and, thus, conceived the EC as a new public power with features of a federal entity. Such a power, however, must be subject to constitutional constraints: the rule of law—and that is why the EC was (and remains to be) conceived as a *Rechtsgemeinschaft*.[13]

During the second phase, scholarly interest focused on the consequences of this new legal order for the domestic legal system. In the Frankfurt context, this approach was personified by *Manfred Zuleeg* who served as professor from 1977–2003 (and as judge at the ECJ from 1988–1994) and analyzed these effects of EC/EU law on most areas of (domestic) law. Fully in the tradition of *Hallstein* and others, he conceived the EC/EU as a *Rechtsgemeinschaft* with federal features based on treaties serving

12 Ibid., 53.

13 Ibid., 54.

as their "constitution" while being in need for further steps to complete a true constitutional setting.

This idea of the need for a further *constitutionalization* of Europe was taken up and further developed, in the nineties and onwards, by *Ingolf Pernice* with his theory of multi-level constitutionalism, a model in which the constitutional orders of the Member States and of the EU are closely intertwined; the federal construction of the EU is built on a legitimacy of its own, a genuine kind of *contrat social* among the peoples of Europe. Also *Armin von Bogdandy* who succeeded *Pernice* in 1997 but left Frankfurt already in 2002 (to assume a directorship at the Heidelberg Max-Planck Institute and was succeeded by *Stefan Kadelbach*) developed his own theory of a *supranational federalism.* Both approaches result in a kind of 'Europeanization` of constitutional law, a process which, as *Kadelbach* rightly points out[14], could have been observed in many branches of domestic law such as labour and economic law, data protection law, environmental law, social law, and general administrative law, to be later followed by asylum and immigration law.

As most striking common characteristic among the various Frankfurt contributions to European law, *Kadelbach* identifies what he describes as "a pro-European idealism rooted in constitutional law thinking".[15] The EC/EU is considered to be a "compound of public authority complementary to the member states" which explains the need to search for ways and means to counter its constitutional deficits and the answer found in its quality as *Rechtsgemeinschaft* with a strong reliance on federal paradigms. This approach might indeed contribute to overcoming the present crisis of European integration; or, as *Kadelbach* puts it: "The contractually agreed pluralism, free of national obstinacy, among equals in a community of law with safeguards against abuses of power of all sorts, as it was sketched out by different generations of European constitutionalists and economic lawyers, can still serve as the guiding idea".[16]

14 Ibid., 56.
15 Ibid., 61.
16 Ibid., 63.

III. The Futures

While the contributions in the first section of this publication are concerned with the past, and more precisely with the past of public international law and European law in Frankfurt, the second section assembles contributions looking into the future of these branches of law—and necessarily not in Frankfurt but worldwide: *Martti Koskenniemi* presents, on the basis of a short and concise history of public international law theories, his very own ideas on the future of public international law for which he sees an urgent need to overcome its instrumentalization within the process of globalization as a tool of "global wealth extraction" instead of an instrument for shaping a "better future for all—not then, but now"[17]; he is followed by *Joseph H.H. Weiler* who develops, modifying the title of his famous critique on the European Court of Justice's jurisprudence on human rights[18], his thoughts on Europe's future by looking at Europe's values, at the "spiritual condition of Europe and the role law plays in shaping it."[19] Finally, *Ingolf Pernice* is concerned with the Internet—obviously a most essential factor in the current development of the international political (and legal) order—and the impact it might have on the future of international law: He sees it as a means to develop a system which would eventually allow for the participation of all persons actually affected by global decision-making in that decision-making process and would, thus, contribute to the establishment of a system "taking people seriously".[20] While all three of them look at different aspects of international and European law from different perspectives—one thing they have in common is that they all deal with the (potential) role of international law beyond the (boundaries of national) state(s) and, thus, with the actual future of international law as "law beyond the state".

17 Martti Koskenniemi, The International Law's Futures—Yesterday, Today, Tomorrow (in this book), 71.

18 See J.H.H. Weiler/Nicolas Lockhart, "Taking rights seriously" seriously: The European Court and its fundamental human rights jurisprudence, 32 (1995) Common Market Law Review, 51–94,579–627; it goes without saying that this title is referring to Ronald Dworkin's seminal book Taking Rights Seriously (1977).

19 J.H.H. Weiler, Taking (Europe's) Values Seriously (in this book), 93.

20 Ingolf Pernice, Global Constitutionalism and the Internet. Taking People Seriously (in this book), 151.

1. International Law's Future—Yesterday, Today, Tomorrow

In his contribution, *Martti Koskenniemi* wants to "examine the historical dynamic that lawyers have presumed underlies the process towards future unity" including a study on the "views about the international world involved", and the "legal theory and the institutional mechanism assumed to bring about that future".[21]

As one would expect *Koskenniemi* to do, he looks at the history of international law the emergence of which he dates back to the "European encounter with indigenous communities in the context of 16th century colonial expansion".[22] The first phase of international law development, starting with Spanish theologians-lawyers such as *Francisco de Vitoria* adapting *Thomas Aquinas'* doctrinal thoughts to the current needs of Spanish colonialism, encompassing the later fundamental additions and modifications to the theoretical foundations of international law by such eminent lawyers as *Hugo Grotius* and *Samuel Pufendorf*, and ending with *Immanuel Kant's* "influential teleology on peace and republicanism", remained dominated by the "weight of natural law".[23] The second phase, beginning with the French Revolution and ending with the outbreak of World War I, was characterized by the "Rise of Professional International Law"[24] which meant that "international law was not about realizing contested futures but about coordinating state behaviour through diplomacy"[25], or, as *Lassa Oppenheim* wrote, that international law was a law "between, not above, the single states", a regulatory technique available to nations; nonetheless there were, as *Koskenniemi* rightly observes, some authors who, while accepting that international law emanated from the will of states, thought that such will was determined by "an underlying progresssive history pointing to an increasingly united world".[26]

However, the outbreak of World War I, and the horrors it implied, led to the abandonment of the previously predominant idea of international law as a mere tool for diplomacy among states. There was a widespread

21 Martti Koskenniemi, The International Law's Futures—Yesterday, Today, Tomorrow (in this book), 71.

22 Ibid., 72.

23 Ibid., 72 f.

24 Ibid., 74.

25 Ibid., 74.

26 Ibid., 76.

understanding of the need for permanent institutions with appropriate institutional design.[27] And so there was a "turn to institutions", notably the League of Nations with its Covenant which was seen by some as some kind of "higher law" but then, as *Koskenniemi* rightly points out, politicians wanted "a system of international organization to facilitate international co-operation but failed to give it powers independent from the ambitions of members".[28] Still, the weakness of the institutions, the (perceived) failure of the League in the thirties turned many away from an international law of the Geneva-based institutions into fascination for an unending struggle for power, for the rise and falls of empires, away from an international law of co-operation between states back to an international law of mere coordination of national interests.[29]

This failure of the third phase, often attributed to an excessive reliance on legal rules and institutions, opened the way for a "realistic" approach to international relations: Law was no longer conceived as a means to express any shared values of a future world, but as a tool to maintain peace in the cold-war era for which it needed the great powers.[30] Notwithstanding the advent of strongly integrationist movements in Europe (Council of Europe and European Economic Community) which eventually imagined international law's future as a larger version of itself, on the global level the cold war prevented international lawyers from being too clear about international law's *telos*. It was sufficient that it helped containing conflicts and assisted in "peaceful coexistence". However, legal thinking on progressive modernization persisted and resulted in the changes of the sixties when the "international community" was increasingly assigned with tasks in social, environmental and humanitarian fields; this paved (again) the way for ideas of international law as "law of cooperation" as a means to solve global problems. This development was soon reflected in the rise of human rights with individuals as subjects of international law, the reduction of areas considered to be purely "domestic affairs" and the perception of the UN system as producer and administrator of international law. The ideal of future was seen, as *Koskenniemi* points out, as a public-law governed international community of states, "collaborating to resolve common problems with the view of just distribution of the fruits of progressive

27 Ibid., 76.

28 Ibid., 77.

29 Ibid., 78.

30 Ibid., 79.

modernization across the world."[31] But these expectations were not met as poverty and conflict persisted, mainly in the Southern hemisphere. By the early eighties, the kind of state and public administration existing in the Third World (and in the socialist countries), was seen as the main obstacle to progressive development and resulted in a renaissance of liberalism (or the advent of neo-liberalism) with the prevailing idea that "regulatory solutions and state-centrism had to give room to free markets as an instrument of change".[32]

So, "in the eighties international law's welfarism and public law orientation began to crumble. State-driven modernization was put to question […] The policies of the IMF and the World Bank were now directed to combating inflation, supporting private investment and opening access to the markets".[33] *Koskenniemi* also notes that "while diplomacy oriented itself towards dismantling of institutions designed to advance global redistribution, novel optimism arose with respect to the security system".[34] And indeed, the demise of socialism and the ensuing end of the Cold War opened new possibilities for the Security Council to act, first in its quite successful reaction to the occupation of Kuwait by Iraq, and later on with respect to the armed conflict in Yugoslavia, the genocide in Rwanda and other crises—albeit less successful, these actions resulted in a new belief in the possibility of a rule-based security system and an increased rhetoric of the rule of law, most strikingly reflected in the strong advances made by international criminal jurisdictions such as ICTY, ICTR and ICC. In *Koskenniemi's* view, the preferred institutions were "those of the market, courts and arbitral tribunal plus private-public relationships".[35] This trend towards a *judicialization* of solving conflicts was seen in the establishment of the WTO dispute settlement system or the increasing reliance on investor-state arbitration under rules such as ICSID, or UNCITRAL. The then prevailing social theory of a methodological individualization resulted in the spread of human rights activism as witnessed by the expansion of the Council of Europe human rights protection system into Central and Eastern Europe, in new or increasingly effective human rights treaty monitoring both under the UN and regional auspices in

31 Ibid., 80.

32 Ibid., 81.

33 Ibid., 81.

34 Ibid., 82.

35 Ibid., 82.

Africa, Europe, and the Americas. The "Kosovo crisis of 1999 demonstrated the willingness of Western actors to undertake a military operation even against the UN Charter if only a conflict could be depicted as a humanitarian crisis or 'state failure', a kind of systemic collapse that would be dealt with through regime change and transformation occupation"[36]—an approach which, it might be added, failed later on both in Afghanistan and Iraq. *Koskenniemi* rightly observes that "lawyers began to learn the languages of global governance and regulation"[37], and to think in international relations categories such as strategic choices and optimal efficiency while there was a strongly increasing trend to establish specialized legal sub-regimes. Interests of members of specific groups started to be seen as 'rights' which, in turn, prompted a "ubiquitous process of rights balancing in authoritative institutions" applying "indicators, standards, and criteria for benchmarking and assessment […] The technical aspects of legal work were stressed at the expense of openly normative ones".[38] However, by the end of the millennium, this era, termed by *Koskenniemi*, as the *Washington Consensus*, was over as it had been dismantled in view of the havoc which restructuring had wreaked in developing countries. "The result was a kind of 'restructuring with a human face' in which the institutions of the state were enlisted to provide the rule of so as to guarantee the security of private rights and the proper operation of the market and where democracy would operate as a channel to deal with political conflict".[39]

In the first years of the new millennium, named by *Koskenniemi* as the 'post-neoliberal future', international lawyers were greatly concerned by the challenges which its (perceived) "fragmentation" brought to the role of international law in global governance: In the presence of an ever increaseing number of specialized legal sub-regimes such as trade, human rights, humanitarian and environmental law, many lawyers felt the absence of an "overarching objective, public ethos or vision of the future".[40] Lawyers were also busy dealing with regime-conflicts or mechanisms to integrate norms from an 'alien regime'. Nonetheless, the concern over "fragmentation" gradually dissipated, not the least as a result of the effects of the world-wide 'fight against terrorism' in the aftermath of 9/11:

36 Ibid., 83.

37 Ibid., 84.

38 Ibid., 84.

39 Ibid., 85.

40 Ibid., 85.

"Domestic security agencies were empowered and secret operations conducted in ways that few attempted to justify under international law. The widely accepted 'illegality' of the US-UK war against Iraq […]"[41], the widespread practice of extraordinary renditions or torture as a means of interrogation strongly damaged the perception of law as a means to shape the future—although the global human rights system and the global security system were able to create a *modus vivendi* in which such violations of fundamental norms of international law were, as 'exceptions', integrated into the new normality of a post-liberal age.[42] In line with this development, the prevailing social theory of the post-neoliberal period (re-)turned to political realism a resurgence of geopolitics with institutional decision-making and increased recourse to secret or otherwise 'exceptional' measures thus highlighting the role of the executive—not the law-makers'![43] The neo-liberal idea that competition of projects and agendas would result in a kind of 'equilibrium' was replaced by the feeling that the "peaceful normality of the law could not be trusted; stronger executive rule was needed"[44]—coupled with a clear shift towards the acceptance of (more) authoritarian rule.

According to *Koskenniemit*, the present situation of international law might be well discussed taking as example the debates concerning TTIP, or more specifically, the public interest in Investor-State arbitration (ISDS). He sees this as a conflict between international law targeted to produce 'wealth' against international law to protect, inter alia, the environment, human rights and security. In this situation, the "optimal realization of conflicting interests is allocated to the state understood as a 'regulator' whose operations are checked and supervised by groups of impartial international 'experts'.This is an image there is little reason to share".[45] This is a very clear statement which is explained by the argument that such bodies are not part of—what *Koskenniemi* calls—"our institutions, set up and operating in accordance with our constitution, by virtue of the compact we have made".[46] Instead, he sees ISDS as a prime example of the "re-definition, within the fluid process of 'globalization', of political com-

41 Ibid., 86.

42 Ibid., 86.

43 Ibid., 87.

44 Ibid., 87.

45 Ibid., 88.

46 Ibid., 88.

munities as no longer masters of their own lives, but turned into localized 'regulators' of global wealth extraction".[47]

Against this background, *Koskennemi* turns to thoughts about the future and, more precisely to *Kant*, who supposed that the fact that we cannot objectively know the future and that the past is not available as an impartial verification, "has no bearing on our duty to work in order to make the future better than the present, and not just for ourselves but for all. This would be to think not of a future 'then' (to which intermediate generations would be sacrificed), but now".[48] While this is clearly a conclusion to which many would want to subscribe, as it ascribes international law the objective of contributing to the creation of a 'better world for all', again something one would not like to disagree with—still, there seem to remain fundamental questions such as who defines in which procedure what constitutes a better future and by which means such a better future might be achieved.

2. Taking (Europe's) Values Seriously

At the very outset of is contribution, *Weiler* states that he is interested "in the spiritual condition of Europe and the role law plays in shaping it" as forming part of his interest in three interrelated themes: "The way in which legal norms and practices reflect and shape political culture; a more general interest in non-instrumental and non-functionalist dimensions of law; and the spiritual dimensions of legal regimes generally and the European legal order more specifically".[49]

In the first section of this contribution, simply entitled "Values—History and Historiography", *Weiler* sets out by showing that European integration had, since its very inception, always combined two strands, a functionalist and an idealist, or pragmatism and values, and stating that, in addressing (European) values, he wants to identify the "content of values discourse as a matter of fact, situating it conceptually and then examining it critically".[50] He starts out by showing that the (historically) first trilogy of

47 Ibid., 90.

48 Ibid., 90.

49 J.H.H. Weiler, Taking (Europe's) Values Seriously (in this book), 93.

50 Ibid., 96.

values, i.e. peace prosperity and supra-nationalism, has lost, for the present "Schengen generation", its mobilizing force but has been replaced by a second trilogy of values, i.e. democracy, human rights and rule of law, as constituting the basis for Europe's self-understanding as a "Community of Values".[51] The ensuing historiography of these values and their conceptualization and (intended) implementation in the process of European integration explain, in *Weiler's* view, "deep-seated habits and practices" characterizing the European Union: Its perception as a project of things to be done and to be achieved, and, at least as regards the second trilogy, its problems in grafting values such as democracy and human rights.[52] But what essentially remains is the "centrality of value speak as part of general European Union discourse".[53] This leads to a truly fascinating conclusion concerning the input of these two value trilogies into European law which is said to have transformed classical international law in three successive waves:[54] "In Wave I State obligations were converted into enforceable Community rights—turning […] the indi-vidual from Object to Subject" (with obvious reference to the *van Gend & Loos* case); "In Wave 2 Human Rights opposable against the Community and Union Institutions (and in some cases against the Member States directly) were articulated *ex nihili* injecting a human centered core into the market instrumentalities" (a process initiated in the *Stauder*, *Internationale Handelsgesellschaft*, *Nold* and *Hauer* cases); "In Wave 3 … Citizen rights are being fleshed out, destined in the rhetoric of the European Court to constitute the fundamental status of Individuals in the Union" (here reference is made to cases such as *Grzelczyk*, *Baumbast* or *Garcia Avello*): The common thread is indeed the Individual, with the European Union as a polity in which the individual is in the center—"a very efficient way of summarizing the two trilogies of values the underlying etrhos of which is, indeed, a deep humanist commitment".[55]

The second section is going beyond history and historiography and devoted to laying the ground for *Weiler's* central thesis dealing with the resurrection of virtue—as distinct from values. A central part of this thesis is the argument that "upholding or believing in a value, has replaced virtue

51 Ibid., 100.

52 Ibid., 103 f.

53 Ibid., 104.

54 Ibid., 106 ff.

55 Ibid., 106.

or rather has become the virtue" or, putting it differently, "believing in the importance of honesty counts as practicing the virtue of being honest".[56] In bringing the distinction between values and virtues to European Integration, *Weiler* follows Aristotle, Maimonides and Aquinas in two respects, i.e. that virtue is a personal characteristic, a habit, and that this habit is acquired, perfected through practice—and in that sense law is affecting "our virtuous disposition".[57] *Weiler* differs, however, from the three thinkers insofar as he profoundly believes that the "resurrection of virtue theory requires an understanding that virtues cannot stand alone from values and that values cannot stand alone from virtues—but nonetheless, the two are distinct".[58] On this basis, *Weiler* formulates his thesis which he will try to illustrate in the major part of his essay, i.e. that the "habits and practices of European integration, and some of its foundational legal structures and processes, militate against those noble values" (of European integration)[59], or, putting it differently, "the corrupting tendency of European practices on both values and virtues which are central to the realization of the deepest objectives of European Integration".[60]

This means that in the larger part of his essay, *Weiler* is examining whether the actual practices of European integration actually militate against—instead of supporting—the realization of the core values of European integration, i.e. prosperity and solidarity,[61] democracy,[62] peace,[63] the rule of law,[64] protection of fundamental human rights,[65] and, finally, European citizenship.[66] For obvious reasons, it is impossible to give, in the framework of this introduction, a detailed account of the arguments put forward and discussed by *Weiler*—even more so as these pages are absolutely worth reading in detail! Nonetheless, a number of issues should be referred to—the choice being made obviously a very subjective one.

56 Ibid., 108.
57 Ibid., 109.
58 Ibid., 110.
59 Ibid., 110.
60 Ibid., 112.
61 Ibid., 112–116.
62 Ibid., 116–124.
63 Ibid., 124–128.
64 Ibid., 128–133.
65 Ibid., 133–140.
66 Ibid., 140–143.

Weiler rightly asserts that there was an idealistic dimension to the quest for *prosperity*: When set against the destruction and poverty prevailing in the early fifties Europe, individual and social prosperity meant personal and collective dignity, absence of the embarrassment of dependence on others.[67] The principal motor towards prosperity is based on ordo-liberalism, is self-interest and competition which produces prosperity—and winners and losers.[68] Taking the central pillars of European integration, the four fundamental freedoms, it is clear that they are at the center, they are the norm—and competing values such as public order are the exception which must be interpreted narrowly: "The free market we interpret expansively, the competing values restrictively".[69] Then there might be need for solidarity—with the losers. But this solidarity is mainly left to government, "social solidarity is almost entirely through agency".[70] So, while "individual self-interest will produce prosperity, public agency at national and infranational level will take care of the less fortunate. As we strive for prosperity, we forget about the virtues of compassion, generosity and responsibility".[71]

When it comes to *democracy*, *Weiler* obviously has to turn to the proverbial 'democratic deficit' of the European integration process which, as he argues, will not go away (that easily) as the "two primordial norms of democracy, the principle of accountability, and the principle of representtation, are compromised in the actual practices of the Union".[72] Still, notwithstanding this democratic deficit on the European level, the European construct has been democratically approved over and over again—on the Member States level. This is explained with the "invasion of a market mentality into the sphere of politics whereby citizens become consumers of political outcomes rather than active participants in the political process".[73] This again impacts on the understanding of (democratic) legitimacy of political decision-making: "Legitimation through accomplishment, professionalism and results instead of through process becomes,

67 Ibid., 113.

68 Ibid., 114.

69 Ibid., 114.

70 Ibid., 115.

71 Ibid., 116.

72 Ibid., 118.

73 Ibid., 119.

thus, the surrogate for democratic process and democratic legitimation".[74] The citizen, reduced to a consumer of political results rather than a participant in a process, is subtly encouraged "to make choices based on non-ideological grounds."[75] In the end, we have "a legal system which places the individual in the center but renders him a self-centered individual—in strong tension with the spiritual ideal of human integration".[76]

The establishment of lasting *peace* in Europe, overcoming the constant threats of tensions between the archenemies France and Germany, was clearly one of the major (initial) goals of European integration. But, as *Weiler* very strongly argues, the very success of Europe has sapped commitment to the values for which peace seemed so important with the result that "Today we want peace in a Leave-me-in-peace mode" and that "Europe has eschewed the responsibility for peace".[77] Telling again the story of Bosnia and Kosovo, of the Srebrenica massacre, of the need eventually to have to rely on US forces to impose the end of hostilities in parts of Europe, *Weiler* concludes that these events show "the growing gap between social mores and personal virtue".[78]

Turning to the *rule of law*, he turns to the Court presenting his thesis that the Court is implicated in the democratic deficit. Returning to *van Gend & Loos*, to the direct effect of EC law and its supremacy over national law, questions whether the poor "level of democratic representation and accountability, seen through the lenses of normative political theory, can truly justify the immense power of direct government which the combined doctrines of direct effect and supremacy placed in the hands of the then Community institutions?".[79] Clearly: No! In an interesting perspective of the system of preliminary references/rulings he concludes that this system is "ingenious for two reasons: First, it deploys individuals, vindicating their own rights as the monitors and enforcers of Community obligations vis-à-vis the Member States... And second, it deploys national courts. The judgment is spoken through the mouths of Member State courts. The habit of obedience associated with nation al law is, thus, attached to European law. "The gap between the rule of law and the rule of international law is

74 Ibid., 120.
75 Ibid., 123.
76 Ibid., 124.
77 Ibid., 126.
78 Ibid., 126.
79 Ibid., 131.

narrowed, even closed".[80] But this situation always posits an individual vindicating a "private interest against the public good, That is why it works, that is part of its genius, but that is also why this wonderful value also constitutes another building block in that construct which places the individual in the center but turns him into a self-centered individual."[81]

Clearly, there can be no doubt that the protection of *fundamental human rights* is a central feature of modern constitutions as well as the judicial review activity of supreme courts in Western countries. Still, there was a total absence of any reference to human rights in the founding treaties of the Communities. This was soon seen as an impediment to European integration and protecting human rights became a joined legal and political imperative. Having told the human rights narrative of the Communities culminating in the entry into force of the Fundamental Rights Charter, *Weiler* addresses some of the issues connected with the "iconographical position"[82] of human rights in the European culture, such as its contribution to the ever increasing role of courts and judges in public discourse, the essential relevance attached to the judicial protection of human rights, and its role as (the) core value of European integration. But, as he strongly advocates, the

"real problem is the absence of a human rights policy [...] The point is that there is something significant about the fact that the value placed higher than any other in the inventory of European integration, is precisely the one that is structured on the responsibilization of the other, of public authorities, and one that demands so little of those who, in good faith, profess such. The way human rights play out in the broader matrix of political culture resembles the critique offered in relation to solidarity—it is constitutive of the culture of Agency which itself is not conducive to the virtues and sensibilities necessary for real community and solidarity".[83]

Finally, there is *European* or *Union Citizenship*. Admitting that the pertinent jurisprudence of the Court is often hailed as having cut off the free movement from its market rationale *Weiler* holds that this is not (entirely) true: In his view, this

"jurisprudence precisely fails to make the conceptual transition from a market based free movement to a citizenship based concept [...] as it militates against the

80 Ibid., 132.
81 Ibid., 133.
82 Ibid., 136.
83 Ibid., 140.

integration of migrants into their host communities [...] The ideal type 'free movement' is not one in which the host country embraces the migrant and the migrant embraces the host country [...] instead it puts in place a model in which the migrant is forever to regard himself or herself, and even their children as such, as migrants, and for the host society to regard them as migrants albeit, with very special rights, at times exceeding that which citizens enjoy".[84]

Weiler concludes that the European Union has been quite successful in bringing Europe's states together but has been much less successful in pursuing its underlying spiritual rationale; in such a situation, the discussion would normally turn to policy investigating which steps should be taken in order to overcome this situation. But it is here where *Weiler* differs fundamentally: For him, the 'turn to policy' itself is

"part of the problem—of responsibilizing others, of addressing the issue in technocratic governance terms. The redress, if any, may be found in greater attention to the spiritual dimensions to our lives and that of our children; the way we think of ours and educate, and cultivate theirs. Education to the necessary virtues of decency and true human solidarity, if achieved, can easily enough counteract the almost inevitable impact of the structure and process of governance. If achieved".[85]

3. Global Constitutionalism and the Internet. Taking People Seriously

Pernice begins his extensive contribution by clarifying what he will address—and what not: He will not enter (again) the debate as to whether the concept of constitution is applicable only to states but also conducive to understanding and describing processes of establishing, legitimizing and limiting public authority beyond the state; instead, he wants to emphasize the "role of the individual in constitutional thinking beyond the state; this approach, therefore, focuses on people as individuals, not *the* people as a political unity".[86]

---

84 Ibid., 143.

85 Ibid., 144.

86 Ingolf Pernice, Global Constitutionalism and the Internet. Taking People Seriously (in this book), 151.

He continues by re-stating that from the perspective of the (European) individual, constitutionalism is to be understood as encompassing several levels of legitimate public authority for different purposes and serving the interest of persons who have decided to define themselves as citizens of local, national, regional (European) and, arguably, global communities. This system is not conceived as hierarchical, but as

"a pluralistically integrated legal system composed of political shells around the individual [...] this concept of multilevel constitutionalism is driven by the basic understanding that what ultimately matters is the individual, not legal or political constructs like the states [...] Law serves the individuals and the protection of their rights, not less and not more."[87]

This fundamental concept also applies to the political community at global level in which the perspective of the individual remains the key aspect; this leads to the central ambition of *Pernice's* paper:

"Global constitutionalism is about rethinking constitutional law from the perspective of global citizens. Despite the major challenges that democratic participation and activism are facing online, the Internet has still certain potential of empowering people. To a new extent there is a chance to actively participate in political processes and to legitimize regulation at all levels, including the global level".[88]

Taking up *Hasso Hofmann's* theory of the state as a community of solidarity, *Pernice* proposes to study to what extent ... this approach of 'dignity as mutual promise' among individuals (people) defining themselves as citizens of a political community can be beneficially harnessed with regard to the global community emerging as a 'constitutional community': "The Internet, it is submitted, could play a crucial role in catering to this mutual promise".[89] Or, in other words: *Pernice* wishes to explore

"whether and under what conditions globally available information and communication through the internet and emerging social networks across borders amalgamates people of the existing local, regional, national communities progresssively to constitute a global community 'on top' of a multilevel global constitutional system".[90]

87 Ibid., 152.
88 Ibid., 154.
89 Ibid., 155.
90 Ibid., 155.

However, as is rightly observed, presently people do not consider themselves as origin and owners of legal instruments such as the UN Charter or international human rights treaties which indeed are "laws or institutions among states, not among citizens".[91] Now, can the internet change this situation, could it "emerge as an instrument through which the mutual promise of dignity […] might reach a global dimension?"[92] *Pernice* sets out to address this question by showing that there is an increasing democratic deficit and a need for new forms of democratically legitimate and binding regulation at the global level;[93] this is to be followed by examples for arrangements established to meet these challenges allowing to identify some principles guiding the constitutional foundations of such regulation;[94] current concepts for the construction of legitimacy rooted in the individual as discussed under the heading of global constitutionalism[95] will be further developed to discuss some critical elements for a global constitutional arrangement sustaining democratically legitimate regulation at the global level.[96]

As to the first issue, *Pernice* refers first to what is called 'external effects of national policies which might negatively impact on people who had no say in the adoption of the underlying decisions; then there are global challenges which individual states acting unilaterally or by taking recourse to traditional means of inter-state cooperation simply cannot solve. Therefore, he argues, we need global regulation and gives as an example the global protection of private data in the internet: "Thus, if a globally open Internet were considered in the common global interest, only a global regulatory framework on privacy […] would effectively protect the fundamental rights of the individual users".[97]

In order to be able to outline what he considers as "elements of a constitution of global governance", *Pernice* sketches some 'models of governance beyond the state' such as the European Union with its attempt to establish supranational legitimacy, the United Nations with its serious institutional flaws relating to the powers of the Security Council, the

91 Ibid., 156.
92 Ibid., 157.
93 Ibid., 159–163.
94 Ibid., 163–175.
95 Ibid., 175–183.
96 Ibid., 183–196.
97 Ibid., 163.

WTO-system still lacking any provision for legislative power and democratic participation, the Rio Process seeking to establish a system of 'multistakeholderism' to enhance its legitimacy, and finally internet-governance characterized by what is often called 'private-public ordering, i.e. a system the rules of which are developed by private actors to be endorsed subsequently by public authorities—a system in which a 'multistakeholder' approach as reflected in the Internet Governance Forum is of particular relevance. In the end, what is needed is a system allowing for the institutionalization of a

"meaningful global public discourse on what is in the global public interest […] there is a need for common institutions for democratically legitimate rule-making and compliance-control, a system of judicial review and dispute settlement as provision for the participation in the decision-making process of the relevant stakeholders, if not the (global) citizens, and for the effective protection of fundamental rights".[98]

So, what about "global constitutionalism and legitimacy"? Here, *Pernice* sets out by describing, under the heading 'from bourgeois to citizen', *Anne Peter's* two-track model of global democracy as an example for the re-discovery of the individual for constituting legitimacy at the global level[99] in which also the judiciary is accorded a specially important role, as clearly reflected in the pertinent publications of *Sabino Cassese* and *Armin von Bogdandy* with *Ingo Venzke*.[100] But is really the internet which has the potential for an effective empowerment of the citizens: Taking up *Anne-Marie Slaughter's* concept of an internet-based 'network of constitutional courts' allowing for the emergence of common principles in accordance with fundamental rights, facilitated by all forms of communication vie the internet, *Pernice* stresses that such communication will not be limited to the actual judges but open to all (interested) stakeholders:

"though in an un-coordinated way, common principles and, if so, a *ius commune globale* will emerge through the jurisprudence of the global network of courts communicating, thorough the internet, not only among each-other but also with—and under the control of—all relevant stakeholders including the general public".[101]

98 Ibid., 174.
99 Ibid., 177–185.
100 Ibid., 180–185.
101 Ibid., 183.

This brings *Pernice* to the final section of his paper where, under the heading 'Enabling global constitutionalism', he identifies the "seven constitutive elements of an internet-driven global constitutional framework"[102]: These are (1) internet-based equal, free and open access to knowledge, information, and education as the 'enabling' basis for meaningful participation in political processes at the global level; (2) such access presupposes the existence of an appropriate space where to pursue the necessary public discourse, i.e. a transnational public sphere as a prerequisite for effective political participation at the global level; (3) such sphere would not emerge without an appropriate institutional framework at the operative level where all the diverse opinions and interests would be channeled and transformed into manageable propositions; (4) following the method of a consensus-based process involving all relevant stakeholders non-binding standards might be set which could serve as a referential normative framework for the policies of states, undertakings, civil society as well as for private enterprises and individuals; (5) such (legally non-binding) standards might then be validated as binding law through pertinent references in binding international agreements, in decisions of international organisations, in supranational or national legislation or in judicial decisions; (6) oversight through judicial institutions would ensure compliance, settlement of disputes and the protection of individual rights as preconditions for the effectiveness of such standards and trust among people in such standards; (7) finally, there should be an inclusive review mechanism providing for control by all people concerned and the possibility to initiate reform ensuring adaptation to changed circumstances.

By respecting these seven constitutive elements the effective implementtation of which clearly requires widespread recourse to, and use of, the Internet would allow to

> "locate decision-making power on matters of common global interest at the global level [...] Common regulation for all people concerned, by ensuring that all who are possibly affected can actually participate in the process of decision-making on equal terms, means self-rule of these people and, thus, taking people seriously."[103]

102 Ibid., 183.
103 Ibid., 197.

IV. Concluding Remarks

Attempting to embark on a truly comprehensive and critical assessment of all the arguments put forward and discussed in the three particularly rich and thought-inspiring contributions devoted to the future of international law, a future for which all three authors see the necessity to discuss the potential situation of an 'international law beyond the state', would clearly exceed the framework of this introduction. Instead, I take the liberty to permit myself to focus on one aspect dealt with all three authors which is also of central relevance for my approach to international law: the individual and his and her position within the international legal order.

In this context, it is evident that all three authors accept the essential role which the individual is being accorded in present general international law and, even more so, in European law. But all three of them seem, albeit possibly to a slightly varying degree which, however, might also be due to the quite different focus of their respective contributions, to be truly concerned about a development which is most clearly described by *Weiler* according to whom the fact that the individual has been put in the center of the law made him or her a self-centered (if not selfish) individual who is mainly interested in his or her (financial) individual well-being while, at the same time, shifting all responsibilities for the common good onto institutions of public authority. All three of them are strongly concerned about identifying ways and means to change this situation: Be it by increasing our (i.e. the present generation's) sense of responsibility for future generations, be it by a return to respecting virtues instead of possibly superficial values, or by empowering individual people in the process of global decision-making.

A final and, thus, concluding remark: The need to ensure the respect for human dignity, or the dignity of all human beings, is like a thread through all three contributions concerned with the future of international law beyond the state. And that, I think, is a most appropriate approach to any exchange of views on international law in Frankfurt where researching and teaching law was, if not always but most of the times, and hopefully continues to be, focused on the individual as a member of society—and not as an individual in pursuit of his or her individual well-being in neglect of his or her responsibilities for the common good.

Public International Law in Frankfurt

Michael Bothe

This contribution is tasked to present the history of teaching and research in public international law in Frankfurt over the last 100 years. Speaking about the task in this context is not equivalent to a funeral speech. History never ends as long as there is human life on Earth. Thus, there is a past, a present and a future for international law in Frankfurt. Speaking about the past, one has to set the stage for the future. Doing so, I have to tell three different, but intricately intermingled tales: A tale about persons who shaped teaching, research and outreach of international law in Frankfurt during a century, a tale about the history of Germany and the world at large which has had a marked impact on the life and work of these persons, and a tale about the development of legal thought to which these persons have contributed.[1]

I.

The first person to be mentioned is Karl Strupp, a Jew born in 1886.[2] He had studied law in Heidelberg, then lived in Frankfurt as a private international legal scientist, financially independent as he was. His first encounter with the history of Germany was in 1914, when the conscience of German international lawyers was challenged by the violation of the neutralized status of Belgium by the German armed forces. Strupp did research on the law of State responsibility,[3] which later founded his reputation, lasting until well after the Second World War. In 1917, he wrote that this breach was

1 See also Bothe, "Internationales Recht in Frankfurt", 119–132.

2 See Bothe, "Karl Strupp", 161–170.

3 Strupp, Das völkerrechtliche Delikt; idem, Die völkerrechtliche Haftung des Staates, insbesondere bei Handlungen des Staates.

justified by a state of necessity.[4] After the War, he revoked, not by changing his mind on the theory of necessity, but due to a different assessment of the facts, on the famous question of how necessary is necessary. This revocation, to say the least, was not helpful after his second encounter with history: he lost his money in the inflation of the early 20ies and now depended on some kind of a job to gain his living. Although he enjoyed, at that time, a great international renown and prestige, his position in the German academic establishment was somewhat problematic. The revocation just mentioned was one, but apparently not the only reason for this. His frequent writings in French, for a number of his German colleagues still being the language of the "enemy", was another. In Frankfurt, he thus had difficulties both with his "Habilitation" and with getting the position of an "ordinary" professor.[5] Finally, he was appointed in 1932 after some kind of change of mind of the Prussian ministry (at the time still a social-democratic government). It was not to last very long, due to his third encounter with history: together with a large part of the German intellectual elite assembled in the universities, he lost this job in 1933 as a Jew pursuant to the Gesetz zur Wiederherstellung des Berufsbeamtentums—as did many other brilliant spirits in the Faculty and in universities ll over Germany.[6] He first emigrated to Turkey, then to Denmark and France and finally received a professorship in the United States. He died in 1940 before he could take up this job. His wife and family continued to live in the U.S.

His assistant, Hans-Jürgen Schlochauer, shared Strupp's fate being removed from the University for the same racial reasons. He went to the Netherlands, later to Oxford, came back to Germany after the war, and got a chair of international law in Frankfurt in 1951 where he taught until his retirement in 1974.[7]

But by 1951, the story of the impact of Frankfurt's law faculty on the international position of Germany and on the practice and theory of international law in Germany and beyond had already started. 1945 was the end of a nightmare and a window of opportunity for a new start. The challenge was both the reintegration of Germany in the community of

4 Strupp, "Die Neutralisation und die Neutralität Belgiens"; on Strupp's arguments see Link, "Ein Realist mit Idealen – Der Völkerrechtler Karl Strupp", 72 et seq., 151 et seq.

5 See Bothe (supra note 2), 163.

6 Stolleis, Geschichte des öffentlichen Rechts in Deutschland, 265.

7 See von Münch, "Hans-Jürgen Schlochauer zum 75. Geburtstag", IX et seq., XIII.

decent nations and the shaping of a new international order having to deal with new problems. To explain Frankfurt's role in meeting these challenges, three other persons must be introduced, two of them not specialists in international law. The first one is Walter Hallstein.[8] He had been an assistant at the Kaiser Wilhelm Institute for Comparative and International Private Law in Berlin, where he received his habilitation, then was professor in Rostock and since 1941 in Frankfurt. He returned to Frankfurt from American captivity in 1945 and became the first elected rector after the war. He was a visiting professor at Georgetown University a year later, where he met Heinrich Kronstein, a lawyer originally from Mannheim who had emigrated to the U.S. and came back to Germany as an advisor in 1945. Hallstein invited Kronstein to Frankfurt, where Kronstein then taught private law, in particular economic and competition law for years to come. This laid the basis for two important developments: first the exchange between Frankfurt and Georgetown, and secondly, perhaps more importantly, for a tradition of research and teaching of economic law, including international economic law, based on the principles of a modern ordo-liberal market economy.[9]

Yet quite a different event accounted for the historic role of Walter Hallstein as international and European lawyer, as diplomat and politician. When the deliberations of the Schuman Plan which envisaged the creation of a European Coal and Steel Community started, Chancellor Adenauer consulted a highly respected economist, Wilhelm Röpke, then teaching in Zurich. It was Röpke who drew Adenauer's attention to Walter Hallstein.[10] Adenauer soon gained confidence in Hallstein. Adenauer made him the head of the delegation which negotiated German accession to UNESCO, then Secretary of State in the Chancellor's Office, later in the newly created Foreign Office (Adenauer also being the first foreign minister of the newly created Federal Republic of Germany) and also head of the German delegation in the negotiations of the European Coal and Steel Community. These were creative moments to meet the two challenges just mentioned. It was a personal achievement of Adenauer at the top and Hallstein on the next lower level that Germany became a respected partner in the construction of a new European order. This new order was based on the rule of

8 See Piela, Walter Hallstein – Jurist und gestaltender Europapolitiker der ersten Stunde, 27 et seq.

9 More on this aspect see below IV.

10 Piela, op.cit. note 7, at 34.

law. The ECSC became an unprecedented organization not only due to its "supranational" powers, but also because of an institutional set-up which provided for a powerful court and legal remedies for all those actors whose rights were at stake in the activities of the Community, in other words an organization based on the rule of law. This can to a large degree be credited to the German delegation, reacting to the unhappy memory of Germany's recent past of disregard for the law.

At this point, the third actor of these early creative years has to be introduced, the international lawyer *stricto sensu*, namely Hermann Mosler.[11] In the thirties, he had been an assistant at the Kaiser Wilhelm Institute for Comparative Public Law and International Law, received his habilitation in Bonn 1946 and a chair of public law in Frankfurt 1949. Yet he soon followed Hallstein to Bonn where he became (1951–1953) the head of the legal department of the newly created German Foreign Office. In this capacity, he was thoroughly involved in the negotiations just described. Like Hallstein he was formally on leave, but also like Hallstein, he continued teaching in Frankfurt, sometimes together with Hallstein (this is at least what the *Vorlesungsverzeichnis* tells). Yet in 1954, he became the director of the Max Planck Institute[12] for Comparative Public Law and International Law, now in Heidelberg,[13] and also professor at that university. He thus took over a position which has been central in the German science of public international law. Following the traditions of the former Kaiser Wilhelm Institute founded in 1924, he cultivated a close connection between the science and the practice of international law, in particular the practice of the Foreign Office. In 1959, he was elected as the first German judge at the European Court of Human Rights, and in 1976, as the first German judge at the International Court of Justice.[14] He

11 On Mosler see "Frowein, Nachruf Hermann Mosler", 725 et seq.

12 After the unconditional surrender of Germany in 1945, the Kaiser Wilhelm Gesellschaft, the central institution of cutting edge research in Germany, was not dissolved, but renamed "Max Planck Gesellschaft" by the British Authorities, as the seat of the society happened to be in the British Occupation Zone, see Lange, "Carl Bilfingers Entnazifizierung und die Entscheidung für Heidelberg. Die Gründungsgeschichte des völkerrechtlichen Max-Planck-Instituts nach dem Zweiten Weltkrieg", at 700.

13 Originally, the Kaiser Wilhelm Institut für ausländisches öffentliches Recht und Völkerrecht was located in Berlin. The transfer of its activities to Heidelberg was somewhat controversial, see Lange (supra note 11) at 719 et seq.

14 The only German Judge at the ICJ's predecessor, the Permanent court of International Justice, had been Walter Schücking from Kiel.

became the internationally most respected and most influential German international lawyer in the decades after the Second World War.

His position in Frankfurt proved to be only transitional. His influential legal writings, to which I will return in a moment, were written after his Frankfurt years. But the practical achievement of his Frankfurt years were considerable, and it is fair to state that his relation with Hallstein and the functions he obtained through it provided a starting opportunity which was essential for his further success. I personally know that he appreciated his Frankfurt years as an important step in his life.

Hallstein, Kronstein, Mosler and Schlochauer were the actors in a creative moment imposed by history. They reinstituted the science of international law and a practice based on international law in Germany after the black hole of twelve years of disregard for the law. Those who followed them could navigate in calmer waters. Nevertheless, these following years saw fundamental changes in the international system to which legal responses had to be found.

Mosler's move from Frankfurt to Heidelberg also was the beginning of a then unpredictable exchange and relationship between the Max Planck Institute in Heidelberg and the Frankfurt Law Faculty,[15] which led Michael Stolleis to call Frankfurt a kind of international legal suburb ("eine Art völkerrechtlicher Vorort")[16] of Heidelberg: In addition to the criminal lawyer Wolfgang Preiser who also taught international law and specialized in its history, the next international lawyer appointed in Frankfurt, Günther Jaenicke, who taught in Frankfurt from 1959 to 1982, came from Heidelberg. So did Rudolf Bernhardt, who had studied in Frankfurt, then worked in Heidelberg nd came back to Frankfurt in 1965, where he taught until 1970, when he became the co director of the Max Planck Institute in Heidelberg. In 1979, Manfred Zuleeg joined the Faculty coming from Cologne, but this author and his successor Rainer Hofmann joined Frankfurt, after a relatively short detour to the North, coming from Heidelberg. Ingolf Pernice came to Frankfurt from Brussels, but soon left for Berlin. His successor Armin von Bogdandy only stayed for a relatively short while and became the third member of the Frankfurt law faculty to be appointed director in Heidelberg. But he remains connected with our

15 Before the decision to re-establish the former Kaiser Wilhelm-Institute in Heidelberg, there had been a debate to establish it at other locations, inter alia in Frankfurt with Mosler as director; Lange, loc.cit. note 11, at 715 et seq.

16 Stolleis, op.cit note 5, at 210.

law school as a honorary professor and with the university at large as chair of the Advisory Board of the Cluster of Excellence "Formation of Normative Orders". His successor in the chair of international law, Stefan Kadelbach, is a disciple of Manfred Zuleeg.

II.

After this review of personalities, let me turn to the substance of research and publications on international law in Frankfurt since the times of Karl Strupp to the present days. I will select three items: the documentation of international law, international economic law and, last not least, the international system as a legal community.

III.

The effectiveness of international law depends to a large extent on the internalization of its norms by relevant actors. Its first prerequisite is knowledge. Therefore, a comprehensive presentation of international law in encyclopedic form is important. This was the idea behind Karl Strupp's *Wörterbuch des Völkerrechts*, which he published after some hesitations in three volumes between 1924 and 1929.[17] A new edition was then published, still in three volumes, by his disciple and former assistant Schlochauer between 1960 and 1962, the Strupp-Schlochauer, "Wörterbuch des Völkerrechts". It contained over 1000 entries. In 1964, the ASIL awarded it the "Certificate of Merit for a most Important Work in the Field of International Law". The work this implied could still be done in the framework of a university chair. This is no longer possible. The following comprehensive documentation of international law therefore moved from Frankfurt to Heidelberg as well, the Encyclopedia of Public International Law edited by Rudolf Bernhardt. Its Library Edition was published 1992 to 2003[18] and needs about twice the shelf space of the

17 Hatschek/Strupp, Wörterbuch des Völkerrechts und der Diplomatie.

18 Bernhardt, Encyclopedia of Public international Law.

Strupp-Schlochauer. As this type of publication needs a global market, it had to be done in English. Still more extensive is the following edition, the Max Planck Encyclopedia of Public International Law, edited by Rüdiger Wolfrum, paper version published in 2012, but all of us use the online version on our computers.[19] To make international law known: Strupp's basic idea is still alive, but the technical means to achieve it have dramatically changed. And they keep changing. We are exposed to an over-offer of information, where the main question no longer is access to information, but the selection of the relevant one. The role of an encyclopedia is thereby enhanced: it is not only to provide information, but also to screen it, concentrate on essentials and make it digestible—a great responsibility for modern editors.

IV.

The cooperation between Hallstein, Kronstein and Schlochauer resulted in the establishment of an Institute for Foreign and International Economic Law. It was established in 1951 and in 1954 transformed into a foundation with the participation of the Federal Government, the State of Hessen, the City of Frankfurt and the University. The first directors were Schlochauer, Hallstein and Helmut Coing, Mosler was co-editor of the Institute's first publication series. The Institute was dissolved in the 1990ies, yet the Merton Center for European Integration and International Economic Order, founded as an Institute for European Studies in 1998, bearing the new name since 2004, has taken over the task of fundamental research on the legal framework of the international economic order. The new Institute for Law and Finance has a somewhat different mandate.

The first publications of the Institute in the fifties concentrated very much on the then new phenomenon of European integration, but also on competition law and approximation of laws. Transgressing the boundaries of traditional legal disciplines became the distinctive mark of the Institute. This was in particular the innovation which characterized the extensive research project on primary commodities, the "Rohstoffprojekt", which the Institute undertook in the seventies under the guidance of Günther

19 See www.mpepil.com.

Jaenicke. The project looked at different forms of production of primary materials (mining, including deep sea mining, tropical agriculture) not only from the point of view of international law, but went into the analysis of the relevant contractual relations. The eleven volumes of publications[20] do not only constitute an impressive collection of materials, but also open up new ways of the analysis of complex legal relationships in a multilevel context. After a long pause, these issues are taken up again in the work on investment regimes undertaken by Rainer Hofmann, Stefan Kadelbach[21] and a number of younger researchers in the Merton Center. It includes a moot court on investment law.

The approach of transgressing the boundaries of traditional legal disciplines was also pursued in the eighties by a project concerning legal questions of the debt crisis.[22] It dealt with general international legal questions of default on debts, with the different fora of debt rescheduling (public debts in the Paris Club and the more complicated procedures of rescheduling of private debts, often called the London Club) and with the ensuing problems of national law. This comprehensive approach opened the way to fresh looks, for instance an analysis of the "Agreed Minutes" of the Paris Club, which for all practical purposes constitute a comprehensive regulation of specific cases of debt rescheduling, in the light of the evolving theory of non-legal obligations. The analysis also led to a question which still constitutes a kind of taboo, namely that of a legal responsibility of the IMF for its measures relating to the rescheduling process which are far-reaching and decisive, meaning gain or loss of billions of dollars for the affected States or banks.

It is not possible in the present context to analyze a number of projects concerning specific questions relating to the international economic order in one way or the other, for instance in the fields of environmental law, telecommunications or the law of the sea. Frankfurt research in international economic law, and not only in economic law, has tried to meet (allow me to add: successfully so) the basic challenge relating to the capacity of the law to govern the growing complexity of transnational relations. The vertical and horizontal fragmentation of the law (including the horizontal fragmentation of international law) is a fact, and it is even

20 Jaenicke et al., Studies in Transnational Law of Natural Resources, 11 volumes.

21 See e.g. Hofmann/Tams, International Investment Law and General International Law.

22 Bothe/Brink/Kirchner/Stockmayer, Rechtsfragen der internationalen Verschuldungskrise.

necessary. But in order to give meaningful answers to the legal questions posed in a globalized world, a reasonable integration of the fragments has to be elaborated on case-by-case basis. Notions like "praktische Konkordanz"[23] or "mutual supportiveness" are helpful in this regard.

V.

Let me finally turn to the fundamental characteristics of the international legal order as a subject of research in Frankfurt. It is an often heard banality that the rule of law in international relations has to be strengthened. When it comes to a necessary ingredient of this postulate, namely the availability of adequate remedies for persons or entities affected by decisions taken at the international level, one leaves, however, the domain of banality and enters that of controversy.

It has been pointed out that one of the unprecedented achievements of the European integration institutions was the availability of judicial remedies for all actors affected by the decisions of these institutions, an achievement to which Hallstein and Mosler had actively and effectively contributed. In the first volume of the publication series of the Institute for Foreign and International Economic Law, Schlochauer analyzed this new system of judicial remedies.[24] The intensification of activities of international organizations has lifted this problem to a global level: legal responsibility of, and legal remedies against, international organization or other international institutions are required, but rarely available. The issue of a legal responsibility of the IMF in the framework of the rescheduling process has been mentioned. The subject has become a scientific hobby horse of this author, who some years ago published a study on remedies against decisions of the Security Council in the field of sanctions,[25] just before a very good doctoral dissertation on this question was published in

23 Casting some doubt on this notion: Fischer-Lescano, "Kritik der praktischen Konkordanz", 166–178. A.F.L. was assistant at the Frankfurt Law School and received his PhD and Habilitation in Frankfurt.

24 Schlochauer, Der Rechtsschutz gegenüber der Tätigkeit internationaler und übernationaler Behörden.

25 Bothe, "Security Council's Targeted Sanctions against Presumed Terrorists. The Need to Comply with Human Rights Standards", 541–555.

Heidelberg.[26] Yet the issue remains on the agenda. We organized a colloquium on procedural questions of remedies against decisions taken by institutions created under the Kyoto Protocol which affect private actors—where millions of dollars are at stake. You will soon be able to read a good Frankfurt doctoral dissertation on these questions, and I hope we will be able to publish in not too distant a future another dissertation on remedies before the quasi-judicial institution created by the World Bank, namely the Inspection Panel.

Thus, the work begun by Hallstein, Mosler and Schlochauer is not finished yet. Frankfurt keeps it on the agenda, inter alia by Stefan Kadelbach's participation in the Heidelberg project on the exercise of public authority by international institutions which is directed by Armin von Bogdandy.

VI.

Last but not least, let me address another fundamental problem of the international legal order, namely the issue of positivism v. value orientation.

Karl Strupp was so to say a positivist by training, and he still expressly confessed it in 1934.[27] Yet he has rightly been described a "a realist with ideals".[28] When he changed his view on the violation of the neutralized status of Belgium at the start of the First World War, he was not claiming an interpretation of necessity based on values. From a formal point of view, he just modified his assessment of the facts. But was this not inspired by values? In his Hague general course on the general rules of the law of peace, he cautiously moved closer to natural law: "Mais point de droit positif qui ne soit pas en harmonie avec le droit naturel. Si cette harmonie existe, le 'fiat iustitia, pereat mundus' se change en un 'fiat iustitia, vivat mundus".[29] Also a positivist may have dreams.

26 Feinäugle, Hoheitsgewalt im Völkerrecht.

27 Les règles générales du droit de la paix, RdC 47 (1934) 261–595, at 581: "je suis positiviste".

28 See the title of the book by Link, supra note 3.

29 Loc.cit. note 27, at 585 et seq.

A centerpiece of the scientific writings of Mosler is his general course at the Hague Academy of International Law 1974 "The International Society as a Legal Community"[30] and the article "Völkerrecht als Rechtsordnung"[31] published in 1976. The basic approach of his legal argument still is that of positivism, as is rightly pointed out by Stefan Kadelbach.[32] International law is the legal order governing the relationship between the sovereign States, and its content is to be ascertained by observing the behaviour of these States. The existence of international organization on the one hand, and the need to integrate rights of individuals into the system of international law does not really affect that basic structure. Nevertheless, Mosler, following the teachings of Verdross, recognizes elements of a "constitution" in the international system, namely in two respects: a procedural one, as there are rules on the creation of legal norms, and a substantive one, the recognition of certain basic values. This latter admission is a consequence of the concept of *ius cogens* which had become positive law at the latest by its recognition in the Vienna Convention on the Law of Treaties of 1966. Among these values Mosler mentions the core of human rights.[33]

All this is, so to say, post-Frankfurt Mosler. But it has inspired fundamental thinking on the nature of the international order in Frankfurt, too, in particular in the project of Stefan Kadelbach and, shall I say, his school on "International Law as a normative order", which is related to the new interdisciplinary Center of Excellence "Formation of Normative Orders". An essential part of this project has been the work by Kadelbach and Kleinlein on "Überstaatliches Verfassungsrecht: Zur Konstitutionalisierung im Völkerrecht".[34] There is, however, a long way from Mosler's short reflections on an international constitution to the thorough conceptual scrutiny of the very concept. Like Mosler, Kadelbach and Kleinlein derive their results from an observation of current international reality. What is a concept of constitution which corresponds to these realities? Does the system need a constitution in this sense? Their answer to the latter

30 H. Mosler, The International Society as a Legal Community, RdC 140 (1974 IV), 1–320.

31 Mosler, "Völkerrecht als Rechtsordnung", 6–49.

32 Kadelbach, "Völkerrecht als Verfassungsordnung? Zur Lage der Völkerrechtswissenschaft in Deutschland", 606 et seq.

33 Mosler, "Ius Cogens im Völkerrecht", 12 et seq.

34 Kadelbach/Kleinlein, "Überstaatliches Verfassungsrecht – zur Konstitutionalisierung im Völkerrecht", 235–266.

question is a nuanced "yes". For me, the most convincing argument is the need of legitimacy. A constitutional order provides legitimacy. Legitimacy nowadays is a prerequisite of the effectiveness of international law. Where international institutions exercise public authority, the need for legitimation is most pressing. In this respect, these reflections also relate to the question of remedies just mentioned. On that basis, Kadelbach and Kleinlein cautiously show a "plurality of constitutionalization phenomena": the reduction of the *domaine reservé,* the primacy of the UN Charter, the recognition of a *ius cogens* and of *erga omnes* norms, and last not least general principles.[35]

It is not possible within the framework of this overview to do justice to the richness of theoretical analysis of these current research projects. My purpose has only been to show how the quest for an international law which meets the needs of the international community at a particular moment in history is a never ending story.

VII.

In the pursuit of this quest, there has not been a Frankfurt School of international law like the Frankfurt School of political philosophy. But over the last hundred years, or more precisely: the last 90 years with a break of 12 years, international lawyers in Frankfurt have tried to deliver a meaningful contribution to the effectiveness of international law as the "gentle civilizer of nations".[36] That effectiveness makes legal procedures a valuable alternative to the use of force, an important subject of research at the Frankfurt Law School which cannot be addressed in the present context.

Works Cited

Bernhardt, Rudolf (ed.) (1992–2003): *Encyclopedia of Public international Law*, 5 volumes Amsterdam.

35 Loc. cit. at 246 et seq.

36 Koskenniemi, The Gentle Civilizer of Nations: the Rise and Fall of International Law 1870–1960, Koskenniemi is a doctor honoris cause of the Frankfurt Law School.

Bothe, Michael/Brink, Josef/Kirchner, Christian/Stockmayer, Albrecht (1988): *Rechtsfragen der internationalen Verschuldungskrise*, Frankfurt et al.

Bothe, Michael (1989): "Karl Strupp", in: Bernhard, Diestelkamp/Michael Stolleis (eds.), *Juristen an der Universität Frankfurt am Main*, Baden-Baden, 161–170.

Bothe, Michael (2008): "Security Council's Targeted Sanctions against Presumed Terrorists. The Need to Comply with Human Rights Standards", in: *Journal of International Criminal Justice* 6, 541–555.

Bothe, Michael (2014): "Internationales Recht in Frankfurt", in: Fachbereich Rechtswissenschaft der Goethe-Universität Frankfurt am Main (ed.), 100 Jahre Rechtswissenschaft in Frankfurt: Erfahrungen, Herausforderungen, Erwartungen, Frankfurt am Main, 119–132.

Feinäugle, Clemens A. (2011): *Hoheitsgewalt im Völkerrecht: Das 1267-Sanktionsregime der UN und seine rechtliche Fassung*, Heidelberg et al.

Fischer-Lescano, Andreas (2008): "Kritik der praktischen Konkordanz", in: *Kritische Justiz* 2, 166–178.

Frowein, Jochen Abr. (2011): "Nachruf Hermann Mosler", in: *Zeitschrift für ausländisches öffentliches Recht und Völkerrecht* (ZaöRV), 61, 725 *et seq.*

Hatschek, Julius/Strupp, Karl (eds.): *Wörterbuch des Völkerrechts und der Diplomatie* vol. 1 1924, vol. 2I 1925, vol. 3 1929, Berlin et al.

Hofmann, Rainer/Tams, Christian J. (eds.) (2011): *International Investment Law and General International Law*, Baden-Baden.

Jaenicke, Günther et al. (1979 et seq.): *Studies in Transnational Law of Natural Resources*, 11 volumes, Deventer.

Kadelbach, Stefan/Kleinlein, Thomas (2006): "Überstaatliches Verfassungsrecht – zur Konstitutionalisierung im Völkerrecht", in: *Archiv des Völkerrechts* (AVR) 44, 235–266.

Kadelbach, Stefan (2007): "Völkerrecht als Verfassungsordnung? Zur Lage der Völkerrechtswissenschaft in Deutschland", in: *Zeitschrift für ausländisches öffentliches Recht und Völkerrecht* (ZaöRV) 67, 599–621.

Koskenniemi, Martti (2001): *The Gentle Civilizer of Nations: the Rise and Fall of International Law 1870 1960*, Cambridge.

Les règles générales du droit de la paix, RdC 47 (1934) 261–595, at 581: "je suis positiviste".

Link, Sandra (2003): *Ein Realist mit Idealen – Der Völkerrechtler Karl Strupp (1886–1940)*, Baden-Baden.

Lange, Felix (2014): "Carl Bilfingers Entnazifizierung und die Entscheidung für Heidelberg. Die Gründungsgeschichte des völkerrechtlichen Max Planck Instituts nach dem Zweiten Weltkrieg", in: *Zeitschrift für ausländisches öffentliches Recht und Völkerrecht* (ZaöRV) 74, 697–731.

Mosler, Hermann (1968): "Ius Cogens im Völkerrecht", in: *25 Schweizerisches Jahrbuch für Internationales Recht*, 1–20.

Mosler, Hermann: The International Society as a Legal Community, RdC 140 (1974 IV), 1–320.

Mosler, Hermann (1976): "Völkerrecht als Rechtsordnung", in: *Zeitschrift für ausländisches öffentliches Recht und Völkerrecht* (ZaöRV) 36, 6–49.

Piela, Ingrid (2012): "*Walter Hallstein – Jurist und gestaltender Europapolitiker der ersten Stunde*", Berlin.

Schlochauer, Hans-Jürgen (1952): *Der Rechtsschutz gegenüber der Tätigkeit internationaler und übernationaler Behörden*, Frankfurt.

Stolleis, Michael (1999): *Geschichte des öffentlichen Rechts in Deutschland*, vol. 3, München.

Strupp, Karl (1917): *Die Neutralisation und die Neutralität Belgiens*, Gotha.

Strupp, Karl (1920): *Das völkerrechtliche Delikt*, Stuttgart et al.

Strupp, Karl (1927): *Die völkerrechtliche Haftung des Staates, insbesondere bei Handlungen des Staates*, Kiel.

Von Münch, Ingo (1981): "Hans-Jürgen Schlochauer zum 75. Geburtstag", in: von Münch, Ingo (ed.), *Staatsrecht-Völkerrecht-Europarecht. Festschrift für Hans-Jürgen Schlochauer zum 75. Geburtstag*, Berlin, IX *et seq.*, XIII.

Frankfurt's Contribution to European Law

Stefan Kadelbach

A

The roots of international legal scholarship in history have found much attention, particularly so in the past years.[1] By contrast, the discipline of European Law has been described rarely in a historical perspective.[2] This may be due to the relatively short period of time passed from the beginnings until today, but perhaps also a result of the fact that European Law cuts through the disciplines of public and private economic law. This observation contrasts in a certain way with the history of European integration itself,[3] for which the time in which we mostly depended on memoires and testimonies of the acting personnel[4] has been left behind long ago. The archives of the EC were opened only in 1983 to the

1 For accounts of the history of public international law and its theory see Nussbaum, A Concise History of the Law of Nations; Reibstein, Völkerrecht – Eine Geschichte seiner Ideen in Lehre und Praxis; Grewe, Epochen der Völkerrechtsgeschichte; Ziegler, Völkerrechtsgeschichte; for academic history Koskenniemi, The Gentle Civilizer of Nations; for public international law in Frankfurt Bothe, "Karl Strupp", 161 ff. and his contribution in this volume; Link, Ein Realist mit Idealen – der Völkerrechtler Karl Strupp (1886–1940).

2 A historical perspective is staken in Stolleis, "Europa als Vorstellung und Arbeitsgebiet der westdeutschen Staatsrechtslehre seit 1945", 237 ff.; id., "Geschichte des öffentlichen Rechts in Deutschland", 609 ff.; Mangold, Gemeinschaftsrecht und deutsches Recht, 243 ff.; in a thematic order von Bogdandy, "Beobachtungen zur Wissenschaft vom Europarecht", 3 ff.

3 Lipgens, A History of European Integration; Loth, Der Weg nach Europa; Gerbet, La construction de l'Europe; Gilbert, "Narrating the Process: Questioning the Progressive Story of European Integration", 641 ff.

4 Schumann, Pour l'Europe; Spaak, Combats inachevés; Monnet, Mémoires, dt. Erinnerungen eines Europäers; Küsters, Die Gründung der Europäischen Wirtschaftsgemeinschaft; von der Groeben, Aufbaujahre der EG; id., Deutschland und Europa in einem unruhigen Jahrhundert; Hirsch, Ainsi va la vie; Uri, Penser pour l'action, un fondateur de l'Europe.

historians of European law.[5] Since then, a research field of its own has developed, first in private,[6] then in constitutional law.[7] Who studies the history of European legal scholarship will note soon that European law has been a subject of special interest for the Frankfurt law faculty for more than sixty years. The following sections try to assess what the specific contribution of Frankfurt has been and if it displays characteristics which make it unique.

B

In order to approach such an assessment, it is useful to recapitulate briefly the separate phases through which European legal scholarship has gone and to grasp the general weather conditions in which the Frankfurt climate has come about. Apart from utopian concepts of the time before and during the Second World War,[8] four phases may be discerned which partly overlap.

In the founding phase of European integration, the main issues were description and assessment of the work on the founding treaties.[9] These pioneer writings of the fifties and early sixties were to a considerable degree provided by the participants of the treaty-making process. They were concerned with the negotiation, drafting and contents of the central instruments[10] and referred to categories of constitutional law in order to

---

5 Official Journal of the European Union (OJ EC) 1983 No. L 43, 1 (EEC and Euratom) and 14 (ECSC).

6 See the overview by Schulze/Hoeren, "Einleitung", XXI ff.

7 Cf. Schorkopf, Der Europäische Weg; Thornhill, "The formation of a European constitution: an approach from historical-political sociology", 354 et seq.

8 See, on one hand, on ideas in exile and resistance movements Lipgens (ed.), Europa-Föderationspläne der Widerstandsbewegungen 1940–1945, 1968; on the other hand Joerges, "Europe a Großraum? Shifting Legal Conceptionalisations of the Integration Project", 167 et seq.

9 Cf. Mosler, "Die europäische Integration aus der Sicht der Gründungsphase", 911, 915 et seq.

10 See e.g. Reuter, "Le Plan Schuman", 519 et seq.; the first commentaries to the treaties have to be seen against this background, see von der Groeben/von Boeckh, Kommentar zum EWG-Vertrag, 2 vols., 1958 and 1960; Wohlfarth/Everling/Glaesner/Sprung, Die Europäische Wirtschaftsgemeinschaft, 1960.

grasp what was new about the European organizational structure, given the fact that a European federation was the vanishing point of the integrationist perspective.[11]

The second phase, which can be placed in the period from the mid sixties to the late eighties, is marked by the unfolding of the norm programme empowered by the founding treaties. This process of consolidation was accompanied by the early jurisprudence of the European Court of Justice (ECJ) by which it defined the operating conditions of European law as a distinct legal order, such as direct effect as a result of a transformation of what initially was formulated as state obligations into subjective rights,[12] the supremacy of Community Law,[13] the adaptation of *effet utile*, originally a tool of treaty interpretation, to the needs of application of EC law[14] and a construction of competencies of the European institutions later criticized as expansive.[15] Legal subjects of a specific European brand came about such as agricultural law and competition law,[16] complemented by further fields like external trade law, European labour law, environmental law etc. In 1961, the first congress of the *Fédération Internationale de Droit Européen* (FIDE) took place in Brussels, where aspects of merger control and other topics were discussed,[17] and the most common of the journals of European law still published today were founded.[18] European law found its

11 Jaenicke, "Bundesstaat oder Staatenbund. Zur Rechtsform einer europäischen Staatengemeinschaft", 71 ff.

12 Case 26/62, van Gend & Loos, [1963] ECJ 1.

13 Case 6/64, Costa/ENEL, [1964] ECJ 1141; a similar construction of supremacy is found in Ipsen, "Das Verhältnis des Rechts der europäischen Gemeinschaften zum nationalen Recht", 1 ff. This so-called Bensheim speech at the first meeting of the German Society for European Law in 1964 was held a few days before the Costa judgment was handed down.

14 An analysis of the case-law since the 1950s is found in von Oettingen, Effet utile und individuelle Rechte im Recht der Europäischen Union, 47 ff.

15 Cf. Case 22/70, ERTA, [1970] ECR 263.

16 Jaenicke, "Das Verhältnis zwischen Gemeinschaftsrecht und nationalem Recht in der Agrarmarktorganisation der Europäischen Wirtschaftsgemeinschaft", 485 ff.; Mestmäcker, Europäisches Wettbewerbsrecht, 1974.

17 Centre interuniversitaire de droit comparé, Rapport au Colloque international de droit européen organisé par l'association belge pour le droit européen, Bruxelles, 12–14 Oct. 1961, 1962.

18 The oldest, Sociaal-economische wetgewing—Tijdschrift voor Europees en economisch wet (SEW), had been founded in 1952, Revue du Marché Commun in 1958; in 1961,

place in German public law,[19] it has belonged to the academic curriculum since 1963,[20] and in the seventies, the first textbooks were published[21]. During this time, characterized by conflict on the autonomy of the Communities (as evidenced by the French *chaise vide* policy) and a standstill in European politics ("eurosclerosis"), the law was the principal force of integration.[22] This observation was also the initial hypothesis of the *Integration through Law* project, a central enterprise of the European University Institute founded in Florence in 1976, which was based on a federal analogy to the United States.[23] The steadfastness of the federal ideal provides the *leitmotiv* in European history as a narrative of continuous approximation to an ideal state of affairs against which progress and setbacks are measured.

The ECJ's function as the "engine of integration",[24] the increasing amount of competencies of the EC and finally the foundation of the European Union ensued in the third phase, which was marked by the general topic of the consolidation and legitimacy of supranational authority.[25] Legal publications of the nineties were concerned with the limits of progressive development of judge-made law of the ECJ[26] and democratic

---

Rivista di diritto europeo, was started, in 1963 Common Market Law Review followed; Cahiers de droit européen and Revue trimestrielle de droit européen exist since 1965, the German journal Europa-Recht since 1966.

19 Kaiser/Badura, "Bewahrung und Veränderung demokratischer und rechtsstaatlicher Verfassungsstruktur in den internationalen Gemeinschaften", 1 et seq.; see Stolleis, Geschichte (note 2), 612.

20 Ipsen, "Europäisches Gemeinschaftsrecht im Hochschulstudium", 961 ff.; thoroughly dealt with in Mangold (note. 2), 254 ff.

21 P. Kapteyn/P. VerLoren van Themaat, Inleiding tot het recht van de Europese Gemeenschappen; Ipsen, Europäisches Gemeinschaftsrecht; Bleckmann, Europarecht; Constantinesco, Das Recht der Europäischen Gemeinschaften; Nicolaysen, Europäisches Gemeinschaftsrecht; since 1976, the 15 volume Commentaire Mégret, Le droit de la CEE, is being published.

22 VerLoren van Themaat, "Die Rechtsangleichung als Integrationsinstrument", 243 ff.; Pescatore, The Law of Integration.

23 Cappelletti/Seccombe/Weiler, Integration Through Law.

24 This concept is further analysed by Mangold (note 2), 86 ff.; as to the role of the ECJ see the classic text by Weiler, "The Transformation of Europe", 2403 ff.

25 Cf. Huber, Maastricht-ein Staatsstreich?.

26 Rasmussen, On law and politics in the European Court of Justice, 62 and passim; for representatives of the German debate see Kirchhof, "Deutsches Verfassungsrecht und Europäisches Gemeinschaftsrecht", 11 ff.; one of the consequences of this critique is

legitimacy of public power in Europe on the one hand,[27] on the other hand, critically or systematically, they took note of the Europeanization[28] of many areas of the domestic realm such as private law,[29] administrative law[30] and criminal law.[31] The subsequent debate on the constitutionalization of Europe[32] was paralleled by the demand to tame the European bureaucracy, to set limits to their powers and to provide for better parliamentary participation. The central events of that period were the launching and, finally, the failure of the Treaty on a Constitution for Europe which was supposed to improve the political legitimacy of the Union by a new constitution-making process (Convent procedure) and, above all, by more parliamentary say in law-making.

Today, we witness the fourth phase. Not only has the constitutional project not resulted in a politicization of European governance, it has contributed to de-legitimize the Union as it is. The Lisbon Treaty, which has transformed the essence of the Constitutional Treaty into the form of a classic revision of the Founding Treaties, raised the question which powers should and could be transferred to the Union at all. The Lisbon judgment of the German Federal Constitutional Court has a considerable share in this debate in that it modeled the protection of the state against unconstitutional transfer of competencies as a fundamental right to state identity which can be invoked by individuals before court.[33] The reaction of the

---

the ultra vires review claimed by the Federal Constitutional Court, a reservation vis-à-vis the supremacy of European Union law directed to the ECJ, see 89 Entscheidungen des Bundesverfassungsgerichts (hereinafter BVerfGE) 155, at 209 f.

27 Grimm, "Braucht Europa eine Verfassung?", 581 ff.; Weiler/Haltern/Mayer, European Democracy and its Critique—Five Uneasy Pieces; Scharpf, Regieren in Europa – Effektiv und demokratisch?; Lübbe-Wolff, "Europäisches und nationales Verfassungsrecht", 246 ff.

28 Wahl, Europäisierung: "Die miteinander verbundenen Entwicklungen von Rechtsordnungen als ganzen", 869 ff.

29 Cf. Ulmer, "Vom deutschen zum europäischen Privatrecht?", 1 ff.; Blaurock, "Europäisches Privatrecht", 270 ff.

30 Hatje, Die gemeinschaftsrechtliche Steuerung der Wirtschaftsverwaltung; in a sceptical tone von Danwitz, Verwaltungsrechtliches System und europäische Integration; from a systematic perspective Schmidt-Aßmann, Das Allgemeine Verwaltungsrecht als Ordnungsidee.

31 Tiedemann, "Europäisches Gemeinschaftsrecht und Strafrecht", 23 ff.

32 Cf. Oeter, "Europäische Integration als Konstitutionalisierungsprozess", 901 ff.

33 123 BVerfGE 267, at 331 f.

states of the Euro group to the ongoing finance crisis was organized outside the EU Treaties and dealt with as an intergovernmental affair, which triggered further doubts as to the suitability of the Union's powers and the legitimacy of European governance.[34]

C

Turning to the contribution of Frankfurt faculty members, their intensive involvement in the drafting of the founding treaties is conspicuous. There is no doubt that *Walter Hallstein* must be named first; a professor for civil and trade law (1946–54), he was appointed secretary of state and lead the German delegation during the negotiations of the Treaty on the European Coal and Steel Community (ECSC).[35] But also others played an important role: *Hermann Mosler*, professor of public law 1949–54, who was also the head of the legal department of the foreign office between 1951 and 1953;[36] *Carl Friedrich Ophüls*, since 1949 honorary professor for civil law and intellectual property law, head of a department in the Federal ministry of justice who conceived parts of the ECSC treaty, in particular those on legal constraints of the High Authority (the predecessor of the Commission today); *Hans-Jürgen Schlochauer*, who likewise had been an official in the ministry of justice before having become a professor in Frankfurt;[37] and *Ernst Steindorff*, a PhD candidate of *Hallstein's*, who be-

34 Habermas, "Die Krise der Europäischen Union im Lichte einer Konstitutionalisierung des Völkerrechts", 39 ff.

35 Because of his governmental functions, Hallstein, who had joined the faculty in 1941, was only to a limited degree an active University teacher, see Kübler, "Walter Hallstein (1901–1982)", (note 1), 268, 271 f.; since 1948, together with Franz Böhm and Fritz Neumark, he was a member of the advisory council of the federal ministry of economy, 1950 he became secretary of state first in the Chancellor's office, then in the foreign office; from 1958 to 1967, he was the first president of the Commission; see Loth, "Europäische Politik mit Walter Hallstein", 28 ff.

36 Mosler became director of the Heidelberg Max Planck Institute for Public International Law in 1954, served from 1959 onwards for three terms as a judge to the European Court of Human Rights and was a judge to the International Court of Justice between 1976 and 1985; s. Frowein, "Nachruf Hermann Mosler", 725 ff.

37 von Münch, "Hans-Jürgen Schlochauer", 473 f.

longed to the German delegation as a secretary of the Schuman Plan.[38] Like *Hallstein*, *Ophüls* was also a member of the German delegations of the Treaty of the European Defence Community (which did not come about) and of the Rome Treaties, since 1952 he was responsible for supranational organizations in the foreign office and since 1960 he functioned as Permanent Representative to the European Communities in Brussels.[39] The involvement of faculty members in these tasks was so intensive that it apparently caused difficulties in the organization of the curriculum at Frankfurt University's law school. The problem is witnessed by a letter from the then dean *Erler* to *Hallstein* in 1952 in which he asks to refrain from entrusting *Schlochauer* with a new "substantial political mandate".[40] *Adenauer* is quoted with the remark "now virtually all better posts are taken by Frankfurt professors".[41]

This experience provided for ample material for scholarly work. Before his appointment at Frankfurt University in 1959, *Günther Jaenicke* was charged at the Heidelberg Max Planck Institute for Public International Law with an expertise for the Federal Chancellery on the Schuman Plan which also formed the core of his PhD thesis (*habilitation*).[42] Just like the writings of the others mentioned, this work stands for the effort to find categories for the new structures of the Communities. Their descent from treaty law at first sight pointed at public international law as the pertinent discipline, but the peculiarities of supranational order seemed to have left

38 Steindorff later became a professor at universities of Tübingen (1959–64) and Munich (since 1964); for biographical data see Baur/Hopt/Mailänder, "Vorwort", in: FS Ernst Steindorff, V f.

39 See entry Ophüls, Carl Friedrich, in: Munzinger Online/Personen—Internationales Biographisches Archiv, URL http:/munzinger.de/document/00000006828 (3 March 2015).

40 Hammerstein, Die Johann Wolfgang-Goethe-Universität Frankfurt am Main, 61 f.

41 It is hard to do justice to the Cologne accent ("Jetzt haben wir aber nachjerade alle bessere Stelle mit Frankfurter Professore besetzt"), see the letter of Böhm to Edgar Bonjour of 26 September 1953, cited by Wiethölter, "Franz Böhm (1895–1977)", (note 1), 208, 239.

42 Jaenicke, "Die Sicherung des übernationalen Charakters der Organe internationaler Organisationen", 14 ff.; id., "Die Europäische Gemeinschaft für Kohle und Stahl – Struktur und Funktionen ihrer Organe", 727 ff.; id., "Die übernationale Gemeinschaft – eine neue Form der völkerrechtlichen Staatenverbindung"; id., "Der übernationale Charakter der Europäischen Wirtschaftsgemeinschaft", 153 ff.; as to his biography see Wolfrum, "Nachruf Prof. Dr. Günther Jaenicke", 1 f.

traditional concepts of the law of international organizations behind.[43] Already with regard to the ECSC, the question of control of the newly established High Authority by parliamentary and judicial institutions had arisen.[44] That a constitutional perspective took European law as a special branch of public international law became apparent in contributions to the debate of the early sixties on the ground for the normativity of supranational law on the domestic plane; for they did not see that basis in an autonomy of European law as perceived by the European Court of Justice,[45] but, in a traditional fashion, in the founding treaties and parliamentary assent thereto within the member states.[46] Yet, since the Schuman Plan, the federal state served as the model to which the communities are related, and it is used as an analytical tool and a source of inspiration to explain the special features of the constitutional elements of the Community.[47] The EC is not conceived as an institution with functional limits (*Zweckverband*) whose autonomy is restricted to these very functions,[48] but as a prototype of a new public power with features of a federal entity. For civil law authors, the transactional nature, as it were, of the transfer of powers to the Communities entails the invalidity of all law the enactment of which is no longer within the competencies of the member states,[49] similar to the rights of the former owner after having transferred

43 Jaenicke (note 11), 78 ff.; Ophüls, "Juristische Grundgedanken des Schuman-Plans", 289 ff.; Schlochauer, "Der übernationale Charakter der Europäischen Gemeinschaft für Kohle und Stahl", 289 f.; id., "Rechtsformen einer europäischen Ordnung", 40 ff.; id., "Zur Frage der Rechtsnatur der Europäischen Gemeinschaft für Kohle und Stahl", 361 ff.; Steindorff, "Schuman-Plan und Europäischer Bundesstaat", 3955 ff.; id., "Europäische Gemeinschaft für Kohle und Stahl", 458 ff.

44 Schlochauer, Rechtsschutz gegen die Tätigkeit internationaler und übernationaler Behörden, 1952; in retrospect Mosler, "Die Entstehung des Modells supranationaler und gewaltenteilender Staatenverbindungen in den Verhandlungen über den Schuman-Plan", 357, 362 ff.

45 Note 13.

46 Jaenicke (note 16), 518 ff.; Schlochauer, "Das Verhältnis des Rechts der Europäischen Wirtschaftsgemeinschaft zu den nationalen Rechtsordnungen der Mitgliedstaaten", 1 ff.

47 Ophüls, "Zur ideengeschichtlichen Herkunft der Gemeinschaftsverfassung", 387 ff.

48 Ipsen (note 13), 17 ff.; id., Europäisches Gemeinschaftsrecht, 61 ff.

49 Ophüls, "Quellen und Aufbau des Europäischen Gemeinschaftsrechts", 1697 ff.; Steindorff, Rechtsschutz und Verfahren im Recht der Europäischen Gemeinschaften, 47; Hallstein, "Zu den Grundlagen und Verfassungsprinzipien der Europäischen Gemeinschaften", 1, 14 ff.

property to someone else. Whereas, for an administrative union confined to a few limited functions the independence of executive expertise might have sufficed,[50] a comprehensive public authority apparatus called for constitutional constraints. Such a constraint is the rule of law, and this is why the EC was conceived as a community of law (*Rechtsgemeinschaft*)[51] with checks and balances.[52] However, if the federal state is the ideal, this balancing mechanism is not sufficient to compensate for the unsatisfactory democratic legitimacy.[53]

A different, but nonetheless important contribution to this concept of an economic order beyond the nation state based on individual freedom and to the solution of the ubiquitous problem of the balancing out of powers was made by private law authors. They were adherents to the idea of an economic liberalism in the tradition of the Freiburg school, but saw the necessity to equip competent authorities with the power to intervene in cases of market failure. The most prominent representative of this group was *Franz Böhm*, a friend of *Hallstein's* and an exceptional scholar who belonged to the Frankfurt faculty from 1946 until he retired in 1962.[54] During this time, he was the head of the delegation during the negotiations of the agreement between Germany and Israel and a directly elected member of the German Parliament between 1955 and 1961.[55] In this function, he prepared the law against restrictions of the competition (*Gesetz gegen Wettbewerbsbeschränkungen*)[56] which entered into force on 1 January

50 Kaiser, "Bewahrung und Veränderung demokratischer und rechtsstaatlicher Verfassungsstruktur in den internationalen Gemeinschaften", 1, 23 ff.; cf. also Ipsen, Gemeinschaftsrecht (note 48), 1044 f.

51 In a threefold sense, in that it is (1) founded by law, (2) acting with, and subject to review by, the means of law and (3) answerable to the idea of law, see Hallstein, "Die EWG – Eine Rechtgemeinschaft", speech on the occasion of the honorary doctorate at the university of Padova 12 March 1962, 341 ff.

52 Mosler (note 44).

53 Mosler, "Internationale Organisation und Staatsverfassung", 273, 289; Hallstein, "Zu den Grundlagen und Verfassungsprinzipien der Europäischen Gemeinschaften", 1, 5; id., Der unvollendete Bundesstaat, 66 ff.

54 See e.g. Böhm, Die Aufgaben der freien Marktwirtschaft; id., "Wettbewerbsfreiheit und Kartellfreiheit", 167 ff.; id., "Demokratie und ökonomische Macht", (note 60), 3 ff.

55 For details of this impressive personality see Wiethölter (note 41), 208 ff.; Boehm's ground breaking Freiburg habilitation is still of interest, see Wettbewerb und Monopolkampf, 1933, unaltered reprint 1964.

56 Bundesgesetzblatt 1957 I, 1081.

1958, on the same day like the EC Treaty with its provisions on cartels and monopolies which had been incorporated on German initiative.[57] Around *Franz Böhm*, *Helmut Coing* and *Heinrich Kronstein*,[58] the successor of *Hallstein*, an intellectual environment was created in which many works on fundamental questions of the economic order came about, essentially based on liberal economic theory and comparative analysis.[59] The institutional framework was the institute of comparative and international economic law (*Institut für Ausländisches und Internationales Wirtschaftsrecht*, AIW), which conducted studies on private and public economic law since 1953.[60] The historical dimensions of private law in Europe were the declared research programme of the Max Planck-Institute of European History founded by *Helmut Coing* in 1964 which was designated to promote a common legal scholarship for the countries of the EC.[61]

At this time, European legal science had already left behind the founding phase. The interest in the principal foundations of this new legal order had moved to a concentration on its consequences on the domestic plane. This topic, in all breadth, was the scholarly interest of *Manfred Zuleeg* who, in a large number of books and articles, analyzed the effects of Community law in virtually all subject matters, ranging from administrative

57 As to the negotiations see von der Groeben, Deutschland und Europa (note 4), 342 ff.; Schulze/Hoeren (note 6), vol. 3: Kartellrecht (until 1957), Doc. 45 ff.

58 Like Hallstein, Kronstein had worked with Martin Wolff in Berlin before his exile in the United States, see Rehbinder, "Heinrich Kronstein (1897–1972)", (note 1), 253 ff.

59 Cf. the PhD theses and other studies supervised by Böhm (Mestmäcker, Konzerngewalt und Rechte der Aktionäre; Biedenkopf, Vertikale Wettbewerbsbeschränkung und Wirtschaftsverfassung) and Kronstein (Rehbinder, Extraterritoriale Wirkungen des deutschen Kartellrechts, 1965; id., Konzernaußenrecht und allgemeines Privatrecht); see also Biedenkopf (ed.), Recht und wirtschaftliche Macht – ausgewählte Schriften von Heinrich Kronstein; Kronstein, Das Recht der internationalen Kartelle; Götz, Das Recht der Wirtschaftssubventionen; for impressions from this time see Mestmäcker and Rehbinder, "Die Grundlagen einer europäischen Ordnungspolitik an der Universität Frankfurt am Main", 12 ff. and 21 ff.

60 Under the guidance of Kronstein, the AIW was transformed into a foundation of the Federal state, the state of Hesse and the city of Frankfurt in 1956; in 2002, it was closed, due to constraints to public budgets; the private law section was succeeded in 2002 by the Institute of Law and Finance, stock and agenda of the public international and European law sections were taken over in 2004 by the Wilhelm Merton-Centre for European Integration and Economic Order.

61 Coing, "Gemeines Recht und Gemeinschaftsrecht in Europa", 116 ff.; id., "Europäisierung der Rechtswissenschaft", 937 ff.

law to civil law and from social law to migration law. Between 1988 and 1994, he also served as a judge to the ECJ.[62] *Zuleeg's* theory of Community law rested on public international law categories, but advocated a strict view on domestic reservations to its supremacy, as did the generation before.[63] Like *Hallstein*, he conceived the EC as a legal community with federal features, resting on treaties which served as their constitution, even though it would take further steps to make this constitutional framework complete.[64]

Such thoughts were taken up and further elaborated in the debate on the constitutionalization of Europe. One of the first topics of this general debate was the protection of fundamental rights in the Community, to which *Rudolf Bernhardt* and *Ingolf Pernice* contributed early.[65] *Pernice,*[66] with his theory of multi-level constitutionalism, developed a multi-layer model in which the constitutional orders of the member states and of the Union

---

62 Upon habilitation in Cologne in 1968, and a first professorship in Bonn, Zuleeg came to Frankfurt in 1977 and retired in 2003; for the span of his work see, among many other contributions, id., "Die Bedeutung des europäischen Gemeinschaftsrechts für das Ausländerrecht", 2193 ff.; id., "Der Beitrag des Strafrechts zur europäischen Integration", 761 ff.; id., "Die Rolle des Arbeitsrechts in der europäischen Integration", 133 ff.

63 Zuleeg, Das Recht der europäischen Gemeinschaften im innerstaatlichen Bereich; id., "Der Schutz der Menschenrechte im Gemeinschaftsrecht", 937, 942; similarly, Bernhardt, "Das Recht der EG zwischen Völkerrecht und innerstaatlichem Recht", 229, 231 ff., see also note 65.

64 Zuleeg, "Die Entwicklung des Verfassungsrechts im europäischen Raum", 1 ff.; id, "Der Verfassungsgrundsatz der Demokratie und die Europäischen Gemeinschaften", 27 ff.; id., "Die Europäische Gemeinschaft als Rechtsgemeinschaft", 545 ff.; id., Der rechtliche Zusammenhalt der Europäischen Union, 165 ff.

65 Cf. Bernhardt, "Der Schutz der Grundrechte bei der Schaffung und Fortentwicklung des Gemeinschaftsrechts"; Bernhardt was in Frankfurt from 1965 to 1970, before he changed to the Max-Planck-Institute in Heidelberg; until 1978, he was an honorary professor in Frankfurt; he succeeded Mosler as a judge to the ECtHR 1981 to 1998; see Beyerlin et al., Festschrift Rudolf Bernhardt, VII ff.; see also Pernice, Grundrechtsgehalte im Europäischen Gemeinschaftsrecht.

66 Pernice took his habilitation in Bayreuth in 1987 and served in the EU Commission until 1992 before he came to Frankfurt. Having changed to the Humboldt University in Berlin, he founded the Walter Hallstein Institute for European Constitutional Law in 1996.

are closely intertwined.[67] This approach, which is also open for comparative impulses,[68] builds the federal construction of the Union on a basis of legitimacy of its own which consists of a genuine type of a social contract between the peoples of Europe. Also *Pernice's* successor, *Armin von Bogdandy*, adheres to a European constitutionalism with federalist characteristics.[69] Such approaches result in a "Europeanization" of constitutional law, a process which had been observed in many areas before and which is accompanied by Frankfurt research projects of the eighties and nineties in the fields of labour and economic law,[70] data protection,[71] environmental law,[72] social law[73] and general administrative law.[74]

---

67 Pernice, "Maastricht, Staat und Demokratie", 449 ff.; id., "Die Dritte Gewalt im europäischen Verfassungsverbund", 27 ff.; id., "Europäisches und nationales Verfassungsrecht", 148 ff.

68 See the contributions to the Frankfurt-Columbia Symposium on Comparative Law, part 1 was published as I. Pernice (ed.), Harmonization of Legislation in Federal Systems, 1996, part 2 in the Columbia Journal of European Law 2 (1996), with an introduction by G.A. Bermann, ibid. 395 ff.

69 von Bogdandy was appointed at Frankfurt University in 1997 and, like others, later (2002) became a director of the Heidelberg Max Planck Institute; he still is an honorary professor in Frankfurt; see his Supranationaler Föderalismus als Wirklichkeit und Idee einer neuen Herrschaftsform; von Bogdandy/Bast, "The Constitutional Approach to EU Law", 1 ff.; id., "Founding Principles", 13 ff.

70 Kübler, "Die Transformation des Europäischen Gesellschaftsrechts", 559 ff.; Weiss, "Die Europäisierung des Arbeitsrechts", 589 ff., with further reference.

71 Simitis, "Datenschutz und Europäische Gemeinschaft", 3 ff.

72 As to the "principle of best environmental protection" Zuleeg, "Vorbehaltene Kompetenzen der Mitgliedstaaten auf dem Gebiete des Umweltschutzes", 280 ff.; Pernice, "Kompetenzordnung und Handlungsbefugnisse der Europäischen Gemeinschaft auf dem Gebiet des Umwelt- und Technikrechts", 4 ff.; the—inevitably Europeanized—environmental law is a field of its own, as reflected in the research centre on environmenal law (Forschungsstelle Umweltrecht) founded by Michael Bothe, Eckard Rehbinder and Rudolf Steinberg and presently directed by Indra Spiecker.

73 Ebsen, "Social Policy in the European Community", 421 ff.; research in social law resulted in the foundations of the institute for European health law and social law in 2003 (Institut für europäische Gesundheitspolitik und Sozialrecht) it was initially directed by Ingwer Ebsen and is now led by Astrid Wallrabenstein.

74 Kadelbach, "Der Einfluß des EG-Rechts auf das nationale Allgemeine Verwaltungsrecht", 131 ff.; id., Allgemeines Verwaltungsrecht unter europäischem Einfluß; Zuleeg, "Deutsches und europäisches Verwaltungsrecht – Wechselseitige Einwirkungen", 153 ff.; Pernice/Kadelbach, "Verfahren und Sanktionen im Wirtschaftsverwaltungsrecht", 1100 ff.

Can it now be said, with a view at this complex picture, that there is something unique about European law in Frankfurt? Taking into account the various approaches as to the understanding of the European legal order, historical contingencies, the ubiquity of some of the views taken and the diversity of the participating disciplines, it is probably not appropriate to speak of a "Frankfurt School". However, there are some common characteristics among the authors.

The most striking one is a pro-European idealism rooted in constitutional law thinking.[75] Accordingly, the Union is not a utilitarian enterprise with merely functional purposes, but a compound of public authority complementary to the member states. This is why there was a concern from the beginning how its constitutional deficits could be countered. The emphasis on the legal character of integration is an important part of that approach. This does not simply express the obvious, i.e. that the European Communities and European Union have to act in accordance with law, as any other authority; more importantly, law is the source, the means and the limit of integration itself.[76] Thus, it was a guiding premise that not only states can have a constitution, long before this question became a dominant topic in the literature of the nineties in what was called above the third phase.[77] For this thinking, a federal paradigm is characteristic, irrespective of whether the Union is called an "incomplete federal state", a "federal democracy", a "multi-level constitutional compound" or a system of "supranational federalism".[78] This perspective may not be a Frankfurter speciality, but it allows us to draw a line from *Walter Hallstein* to the Humboldt speech of former foreign minister *Joschka Fischer* and the constitutional project of *Jürgen Habermas.*[79]

---

75 A caveat is in place with respect to criminal law, where the transfer of powers to the Union encounters fundamental reservations; see Lüderssen, "Europäisierung des Strafrechts und gubernative Rechtsetzung", 71 ff.; Albrecht, Der Weg in die Sicherheitsgesellschaft, 191 ff.

76 Hallstein (note 51); Zuleeg (note 64); Pernice, "Begründung und Konsolidierung der Europäischen Gemeinschaft als Rechtsgemeinschaft", 56 ff.

77 Ophüls (note 47); Hallstein, Bundesstaat (note 53), 39 ff.

78 Hallstein (note 53); Zuleeg, Zusammenhalt (note 64), S. 133 f.; also id., "Der unvollendete Bundesstaat: Vision oder Realität", in: id. (note 35), 97 ff.; Pernice (note 67); von Bogdandy (note 69); Kadelbach, "Autonomie und Bindung der Rechtsetzung in gestuften Rechtsordnungen", 7, 10 ff.

79 Fischer, "Vom Staatenverbund zur Föderation: Gedanken über die Finalität der europäischen Integration", speech of 12 May 2000, reprinted in: Joerges/Mény/Weiler (eds.),

Under these auspices, the idea is that an economic constitution based on personal liberty and competition is to develop in which economic power is kept in check by interventions democratically accounted for, so that the affairs of the market citizens may unfold for the common good.[80] A conservative element of many members of the Frankfurt group is that the reform and harmonization of European economic law should be not such much a matter of day-to-day politics but of profound knowledge of its history and the diversity of its sources.[81]

D

In the end the question remains what the Frankfurt spirit could contribute to the present fourth phase of European legal science. One of the most important projects since the founding era ought to be to find a way out of the deadlock into which a general tendency of intergovernementalism on the one hand,[82] and recent decisions by the Federal Constitutional Court insisting on restricted powers of the European Parliament on the other hand have taken us, since immanent options to enhance legitimacy thus appear to have been reduced substantially.[83]

Unaffected by this eurosceptic turn in the jurisprudence of the FCC, functional differentiation of European law and its diffusion into the various fields of law continue. The topics of labour, social and migration law, public and private economic law and many harmonization projects which reach into core components of civil and criminal law offer ample

What Kind of Constitution for What Kind of Polity, 5 ff.;as to the "federal bias" from Hallstein to Fischer see Majone, Dilemmas of European Integration, 204 f.

80 Hallstein, Wirtschaftliche Integration als Faktor politischer Einigung, Festgabe Alfred Müller-Armack, 267 ff.; see also references on the circle around Böhm and Kronstein above note 59.

81 For Coing see note 61.

82 Habermas (note 34); an effort to translate this critique into the terms of institutional law is made in Kadelbach, "Lehren aus der Finanzkrise – Ein Vorschlag zur Reform der politischen Institutionen der Europäischen Union", 489 ff.; as to the domestic plane see von Bogdandy/Ioannidis, "Systemic deficiency in the rule of law", 59 ff.

83 The decision on the 5 and 3 per cent hurdles for a party's representation in Parliament are particularly conspicuous in that respect, see 129 BVerfGE 300; also jgt. of 26 Feb. 2014, case 2 BvE 2/13 et al.; this is a departure from 51 BVerfGE 222.

subjects for a legal science informed by comparative study and economic theory; it should be given, and take the opportunity, to anticipate initiatives with a view at unification of the law which are often seen as imposed by a self-empowered bureaucracy.[84] The contractually agreed pluralism, free of national obstinacy, among equals in a community of law with safeguards against abuses of power of all sorts, as it was sketched out by different generations of European constitutionalists and economic lawyers, can still serve as the guiding idea.

Works Cited

Albrecht, Peter-Alexis (2010): *Der Weg in die Sicherheitsgesellschaft*, Berlin.

Baur, Jürgen F./Hopt, Klaus J./Mailänder, K. Peter (1990): "Vorwort", in: Jürgen F. Baur (ed.) *Festschrift für Ernst Steindorff*, Berlin, New York.

Bernhardt, Rudolf (1980): "Das Recht der EG zwischen Völkerrecht und innerstaatlichem Recht", in: Emanuel Diez (ed.), *Festschrift für Rudolf Bindschedler*, Bern.

Bernhardt, Rudolf: "Der Schutz der Grundrechte bei der Schaffung und Fortentwicklung des Gemeinschaftsrechts", in: *Bulletin der EUROPÄISCHEN GEMEINSCHAFTEN* (Bull EG) Beilage 5/76.

Bermann, George A. (1996): "Regulatory Federalism: A Reprise and Introduction", in: *Columbia Journal of European Law* (Colum J Eur L) 2, 395–402.

Beyerlin, Ulrich, et al. (eds.) (1995): *Festschrift Rudolf Bernhardt*, Berlin, VII ff.

Biedenkopf, Kurt (1958): *Vertikale Wettbewerbsbeschränkung und Wirtschaftsverfassung*, Heidelberg.

Biedenkopf, Kurt (ed.) (1962): *Recht und wirtschaftliche Macht – ausgewählte Schriften von Heinrich Kronstein*, Karlsruhe.

Blaurock, Uwe (1994): "Europäisches Privatrecht", in: *Juristenzeitung* (JZ), 1994, 270–276.

Bleckmann, Albert (1976): *Europarecht: das Recht der Europäischen Wirtschaftsgemeinschaft*, Köln et al.

von Bogdandy, Armin (1999): *Supranationaler Föderalismus als Wirklichkeit und Idee einer neuen Herrschaftsform*, Baden-Baden.

von Bogdandy, Armin (2001): "Beobachtungen zur Wissenschaft vom Europarecht", in: Der Staat 40, 3–43.

von Bogdandy, Armin/Bast, Jürgen (2010): "Founding Principles", in: id. (eds.), *Principles of European Constitutional Law*, 2nd ed. 2010, Oxford, München.

84 See Rehbinder, "Die Grundlagen einer europäischen Ordnungspolitik an der Universität Frankfurt am Main", 27.

von Bogdandy, Armin/Bast, Jürgen (2010): "The Constitutional Approach to EU Law", in: id. (eds.), *Principles of European Constitutional Law*, 2nd ed. 2010, Oxford, München.

von Bogdandy, Armin/Ioannidis, Michael (2014): "Systemic deficiency in the rule of law", in: *Common Market Law Review* (CML Rev) 51, 59–96.

Bothe, Michael (1989): "Karl Strupp", in: Bernhard Diestelkamp/Michael Stolleis (eds.), *Juristen an der Universität Frankfurt am Main*, Baden-Baden.

Böhm, Franz (1951): *Die Aufgaben der freien Marktwirtschaft*, München.

Böhm, Franz (1958): "Wettbewerbsfreiheit und Kartellfreiheit", in: *Jahrbuch für die Ordnung von Wirtschaft und Gesellschaft* (ORDO) 10, 167–203.

Böhm, Franz (1961): "Demokratie und ökonomische Macht", in: Ausländisches und Internationales Wirtschaftsrecht (AIW) (ed.), *Kartelle und Monopole im modernen Recht*, Vol. I, Karlsruhe.

Boehm, Franz (1933, unaltered reprint 1964): *Wettbewerb und Monopolkampf*, Berlin.

Cappelletti, Mauro/Seccombe Monica/Weiler, Joseph H (1986): *Integration Through Law*, Vol. I, Books 1–3, Berlin et al.

Coing, Helmut (1966): "Gemeines Recht und Gemeinschaftsrecht in Europa", in: Ernst von Caemmerer et al. (eds.), Probleme des europäischen Rechts, in: *Festschrift für Walter Hallstein zu seinem 65. Geburtstag*, Frankfurt am Main.

Coing, Helmut (1990): "Europäisierung der Rechtswissenschaft", in: *Neue Juristische Wochenschrift* (NJW), 937–941.

Constantinesco, Léontin-Jean (1977): *Das Recht der Europäischen Gemeinschaften*, Baden-Baden.

von Danwitz, Thomas (1996): *Verwaltungsrechtliches System und europäische Integration*, Tübingen.

Ebsen, Ingwer (1996): "Social Policy in the European Community", in: *Columbia Journal of European Law* (Colum J Eur L), 2, 421–441.

Fischer, Joschka (2000): "Vom Staatenverbund zur Föderation: Gedanken über die Finalität der europäischen Integration", in: Christian Joerges/Yves Mény/H. Weiler (eds.), *What Kind of Constitution for What Kind of Polity*, San Domenico.

Frowein, Jochen Abr. (2001): "Nachruf Hermann Mosler", in: *Zeitschrift für ausländisches öffentliches Recht und Völkerrecht* (ZaöRV) 61, 725–727.

Gerbet, Pierre (2007): *La construction de l'Europe*, 4th ed., Paris.

Gilbert, Mark (2008): "Narrating the Process: Questioning the Progressive Story of European Integration", Journal of Common Market Studies 45, 641–647.

Grewe, Wilhelm (1984): *Epochen der Völkerrechtsgeschichte*, 1st ed., Baden-Baden.

Grimm, Dieter (1995): "Braucht Europa eine Verfassung?", in: *Juristenzeitung* (JZ) 1995, 581–591.

von der Groeben, Hans/von Boeckh, Hans (1958 and 1960): *Kommentar zum EWG-Vertrag*, 2 vols., Baden-Baden.

von der Groeben, Hans (1982): *Aufbaujahre der EG*, Baden-Baden.

von der Groeben, Hans (1995): *Deutschland und Europa in einem unruhigen Jahrhundert*, Baden-Baden.

Götz, Volkmar (1966): *Das Recht der Wirtschaftssubventionen*, München, Berlin.

Habermas, Jürgen (2011): "Die Krise der Europäischen Union im Lichte einer Konstitutionalisierung des Völkerrechts", in: id., *Zur Verfassung Europas*, Berlin.

Hammerstein, Notker (2012): *Die Johann Wolfgang Goethe-Universität Frankfurt am Main*, vol. II, Göttingen.

Hallstein, Walter (1961): *Wirtschaftliche Integration als Faktor politischer Einigung, Festgabe Alfred Müller-Armack*, Berlin.

Hallstein, Walter (1965): "Zu den Grundlagen und Verfassungsprinzipien der Europäischen Gemeinschaften", in: Walter Hallstein (ed.), *Festschrift Carl Friedrich Ophüls*, Karlsruhe.

Hallstein, Walter (1965): "Zu den Grundlagen und Verfassungsprinzipien der Europäischen Gemeinschaften", in: *Festschrift für Carl Friedrich Ophüls.*

Hallstein, Walter (1969): *Der unvollendete Bundesstaat: europäische Erfahrungen und Erkenntnisse*, Wien.

Hallstein, Walter (1979): "Die EWG – Eine Rechtgemeinschaft", in: Thomas Oppermann (ed.), *Walter Hallstein – Europäische Reden*, Stuttgart.

Hatje, Armin (1997): *Die gemeinschaftsrechtliche Steuerung der Wirtschaftsverwaltung*, Baden-Baden.

Hirsch, Étienne (1988): *Ainsi va la vie*, Lausanne.

Huber, Peter M. (1993): *Maastricht – ein Staatsstreich?,* Stuttgart.

Ipsen, Hans Peter (1964): "Europäisches Gemeinschaftsrecht im Hochschulstudium", in: *Neue Juristische Wochenschrift* (NJW), 961–967.

Ipsen, Hans Peter (1965): "Das Verhältnis des Rechts der europäischen Gemeinschaften zum nationalen Recht", in: *Aktuelle Fragen des europäischen Gemeinschaftsrechts*, 1–27.

Ipsen, Hans Peter (1972): *Europäisches Gemeinschaftsrecht*, Tübingen.

Jaenicke, Günther (1951/52): "Die Sicherung des übernationalen Charakters der Organe internationaler Organisationen", in: *Zeitschrift für ausländisches öffentliches Recht und Völkerrecht* (ZaöRV) 14, 46–117.

Jaenicke, Günther (1951/52): "Die Europäische Gemeinschaft fur Kohle und Stahl – Struktur und Funktionen ihrer Organe", in: *Zeitschrift für ausländisches öffentliches Recht und Völkerrecht* (ZaöRV) 14, 727–788.

Jaenicke, Günther (1954): "Bundesstaat oder Staatenbund. Zur Rechtsform einer europäischen Staatengemeinschaft", in: Georg Schreiber/Hans Ballreich (eds.), *Völkerrechtliche und staatsrechtliche Abhandlungen: Carl Bilfinger zum 75. Geburtstag am 21. Januar*, Köln et al.

Jaenicke, Günther (1957): "Die übernationale Gemeinschaft – eine neue Form der völkerrechtlichen Staatenverbindung", unpublished.

Jaenicke, Günther (1958): "Der übernationale Charakter der Europäischen Wirtschaftsgemeinschaft", in: *Zeitschrift für ausländisches öffentliches Recht und Völkerrecht* (ZaöRV) 19, 153–196.

Jaenicke, Günther (1963): "Das Verhältnis zwischen Gemeinschaftsrecht und nationalem Recht in der Agrarmarktorganisation der Europäischen Wirtschaftsgemeinschaft", in: *Zeitschrift für ausländisches öffentliches Recht und Völkerrecht* (ZaöRV) 23, 485–535.

Joerges, Christian (2003): "Europe a Großraum? Shifting Legal Conceptionalisations of the Integration Project", in: Christian Joerges/ Navraj Singh Ghaleigh (eds.), *Darker Legacies of Law in Europe – The Shadow of National Socialism and Fascism over Europe and its Legal Traditions*, Oxford et al..

Kadelbach, Stefan (1993): "Der Einfluß des EG-Rechts auf das nationale Allgemeine Verwaltungsrecht", in: von Danwitz, Thomas et al. (eds.), *Auf dem Wege zu einer europäischen Staatlichkeit*, Stuttgart.

Kadelbach, Stefan (1999): *Allgemeines Verwaltungsrecht unter europäischem Einfluß*, Tübingen.

Kadelbach, Stefan (2007): "Autonomie und Bindung der Rechtsetzung in gestuften Rechtsordnungen", in: *Veröffentlichungen der Vereinigung der Deutschen Staatsrechtslehrer* (VVDStRL) 66, 7, 9–44.

Kadelbach, Stefan (2013): "Lehren aus der Finanzkrise – Ein Vorschlag zur Reform der politischen Institutionen der Europäischen Union", in: *Zeitschrift Europarecht* (EuR), 489–503.

P. Kapteyn/P. VerLoren van Themaat (1970): *Inleiding tot het recht van de Europese Gemeenschappen*, Deventer.

Kaiser, Joseph H. (1966): "Bewahrung und Veränderung demokratischer und rechtsstaatlicher Verfassungsstruktur in den internationalen Gemeinschaften", in: *Veröffentlichungen der Vereinigung der Deutschen Staatsrechtslehrer* (VVDStRL), 1–33.

Kirchhof, Paul (1991): "Deutsches Verfassungsrecht und Europäisches Gemeinschaftsrecht", in: *Zeitschrift Europarecht* (EuR) Supp. 1, 11 et seq.

Koskenniemi, Martti (2001): *The Gentle Civilizer of Nations: the Rise and Fall of International Law 1870–1960*, Cambridge.

Kronstein, Heinrich (1967): *Das Recht der internationalen Kartelle*, Berlin.

Kübler, Friedrich (1989): "Walter Hallstein (1901–1982)", in: Bernhard Diestelkamp/Michael Stolleis (eds.), *Juristen an der Universität Frankfurt am Main*, Baden-Baden.

Kübler, Friedrich (2005): "Die Transformation des Europäischen Gesellschaftsrechts", in: *Festschrift für Manfred Zuleeg*, Baden-Baden.

Küsters, Hanns Jürgen (1982): *Die Gründung der Europäischen Wirtschaftsgemeinschaft*, Baden-Baden.

Link, Sandra (2003), *Ein Realist mit Idealen – Der Völkerrechtler Karl Strupp (1886–1940)*, Baden-Baden.

Lipgens, W. (1982): *A History of European Integration 1945–194. The Formation of the European Unity Movement*, Oxford.

Lipgens, Walter (ed.) (1968): *Europa-Föderationspläne der Widerstandsbewegungen 1940–1945*, München.

Loth, Wilfried (1996): *Der Weg nach Europa: Geschichte der europäischen Integration* 1939–1957, 3rd ed., Göttingen.

Lübbe-Wolff, Gertrude (2001): Europäisches und nationales Verfassungsrecht, *Veröffentlichungen der Vereinigung der Deutschen Staatsrechtslehrer* (VVDStRL) 60, 246–289.

Loth, Wilfried (2003): "Europäische Politik mit Walter Hallstein", in: M. Zuleeg (ed.), *Der Beitrag Walter Hallsteins zur Zukunft Europas*, Baden-Baden.

Lüderssen, Klaus (2003): "Europäisierung des Strafrechts und gubernative Rechtsetzung", in: *Goltdammer\'s Archiv für Strafrecht* (GA), 71–84.

Majone, Giandomenico (2005): *Dilemmas of European Integration*, Oxford.

Mangold, Anna Katharina (2001): *Gemeinschaftsrecht und deutsches Recht*, Tübingen.

Mestmäcker, ErnstJoachim/Rehbinder Eckard (2003): "Die Grundlagen einer europäischen Ordnungspolitik an der Universität Frankfurt am Main", in: Manfred Zuleeg (ed.), *Der Beitrag Walter Hallsteins zur Zukunft Europas*, Baden-Baden.

Mestmäcker, Ernst Joachim (1958): *Konzerngewalt und Rechte der Aktionäre*, Karlsruhe.

Mestmäcker, Ernst-Joachim (1974): *Europäisches Wettbewerbsrecht*, München.

Monnet, Jean (1976): *Mémoires*, Paris.

Monnet, Jean (1978): *Erinnerungen eines Europäers*, München.

Mosler, Hermann (1956): "Internationale Organisation und Staatsverfassung", in: Walter Schätzel (ed.), *Festschrift für Hans Wehberg*, Frankfurt am Main.

Mosler, Hermann (1966): "Die Entstehung des Modells supranationaler und gewaltenteilender Staatenverbindungen in den Verhandlungen über den Schuman-Plan", in: Ernst von Caemmerer (ed.), *Festschrift Walter Hallstein*, Frankfurt am Main.

Mosler, Hermann (1995): "Die europäische Integration aus der Sicht der Gründungsphase", in: Ole Due/Marcus Lutter/Jürgen Schwarze (eds.), *Festschrift für Ulrich Everling*, Baden-Baden.

von Münch, Ingo (1991): "Hans Jürgen Schlochauer", in: *Neue Juristische Wochenschrift* (NJW), 473–474.

Nussbaum, Arthur (1947): *A Concise History of the Law of Nations*, New York, Berlin.

Nicolaysen, Gert (1979): *Europäisches Gemeinschaftsrecht*, Stuttgart.

Oeter, Stefan (1999): "Europäische Integration als Konstitutionalisierungsprozess", in: *Zeitschrift für ausländisches öffentliches Recht und Völkerrecht* (ZaöRV) 59, 901–917.

von Oettingen, Anna (2010): *Effet utile und individuelle Rechte im Recht der Europäischen Union*, Baden-Baden.

Ophüls, Carl Friedrich (1951): "Juristische Grundgedanken des Schuman-Plans", in: *Neue Juristische Wochenschrift* (NJW), 289–292.

Ophüls, Carl Friedrich (1963): "Quellen und Aufbau des Europäischen Gemeinschaftsrechts", in: *Neue Juristische Wochenschrift* (NJW), 1697–1701.

Ophüls, Carl Friedrich (1966): "Zur ideengeschichtlichen Herkunft der Gemeinschaftsverfassung", in: *Festschrift Walter Hallstein*, Frankfurt am Main.

Ophüls, Carl Friedrich, in: *Munzinger Online/Personen – Internationales Biographisches Archiv,* URL http:/munzinger.de/document/00000006828 (3 March 2015).

Pescatore, Pierre (1974): *The Law of Integration*, Leiden.

Pernice, Ingolf (1979): *Grundrechtsgehalte im Europäischen Gemeinschaftsrecht*, Baden-Baden.

Pernice, Ingolf (1989): "Kompetenzordnung und Handlungsbefugnisse der Europäischen Gemeinschaft auf dem Gebiet des Umwelt- und Technikrechts", in: *Die Verwaltung* (DV), 22, 1–54.

Pernice, Ingolf (1993): "Maastricht, Staat und Demokratie", in: *Die Verwaltung* (DV) 26, 449–488.

Pernice, Ingolf (1996): "Die Dritte Gewalt im europäischen Verfassungsverbund", in: *Zeitschrift Europarecht* (EuR), 27–43.

Pernice, Ingolf (ed.) (1996): *Harmonization of Legislation in Federal Systems*, Baden-Baden.

Pernice, Ingolf/Kadelbach, Stefan (1996): "Verfahren und Sanktionen im Wirtschaftsverwaltungsrecht", in: *Deutsches Verwaltungsblatt* (DVBl.), 1100–1114.

Pernice, Ingolf (2001): "Europäisches und nationales Verfassungsrecht", in: *Veröffentlichungen der Vereinigung der Deutschen Staatsrechtslehrer* (VVDStRL) 60, 148–193.

Pernice, Ingolf (2003): "Begründung und Konsolidierung der Europäischen Gemeinschaft als Rechtsgemeinschaft", in: Zuleeg, Manfred (ed.), *Der Beitrag Walter Hallsteins zur Zukunft Europas*, Baden-Baden.

Pernice, Ingolf (2003): "Der unvollendete Bundesstaat: Vision oder Realität", in: Manfred Zuleeg (ed.), *Der Beitrag Walter Hallsteins zur Zukunft Europas*, Baden-Baden.

Reibstein, Ernst (1958 and 1963): *Völkerrecht – Eine Geschichte seiner Ideen in Lehre und Praxis*, 2 vols, Freiburg, München.

Rasmussen, Hjalte (1986): *On law and politics in the European Court of Justice*, Dordrecht et al., 62 and passim.

Rehbinder, Eckard (1965): *Extraterritoriale Wirkungen des deutschen Kartellrechts*, Baden-Baden.

Rehbinder, Eckard (1969): *Konzernaußenrecht und allgemeines Privatrecht,* Frankfurt am Main.

Rehbinder, Eckard (1989): "Heinrich Kronstein (1897–1972)", in: Bernhard Diestelkamp/Michael Stolleis (eds.), *Juristen an der Universität Frankfurt am Main*, Baden-Baden.

Reuter, Paul (1952): "Le Plan Schuman", in: Recueil des Cours 81.

Scharpf, Fritz W. (1999): *Regieren in Europa – Effektiv und demokratisch?*, Frankfurt am Main, New York.

Schlochauer, Hans-Jürgen (1951): "Der übernationale Charakter der Europäischen Gemeinschaft für Kohle und Stahl", in: *Juristenzeitschrift* (JZ) 1951, 289–290.

Schlochauer, Hans-Jürgen (1952): *Rechtsschutz gegen die Tätigkeit internationaler und übernationaler Behörden,* Frankfurt am Main.

Schlochauer, Hans-Jürgen (1955/56): "Rechtsformen einer europäischen Ordnung", in: *Archiv des Völkerrechts* (AVR) 5, 40–62.

Schlochauer, Hans-Jürgen (1956): "Zur Frage der Rechtsnatur der Europäischen Gemeinschaft für Kohle und Stahl", in: Walter Schätzel (ed.), *Festschrift für Hans Wehberg*, Frankfurt am Main.

Schlochauer, Hans-Jürgen (1963/64): "Das Verhältnis des Rechts der Europäischen Wirtschaftsgemeinschaft zu den nationalen Rechtsordnungen der Mitgliedstaaten", in: *Archiv des Völkerrechts* (AVR) 11, 1–34.

Schmidt-Aßmann, Eberhardt (1998): *Das Allgemeine Verwaltungsrecht als Ordnungsidee*, Berlin et al.

Schorkopf, Frank (2010): *Der Europäische Weg*, Tübingen.

Schulze, Reiner/Hoeren, Thomas (1999): "Einleitung", in: id. (eds.), *Dokumente zum Europäischen Recht*, vol. 1: Gründungsverträge, Berlin, XXI ff.

Schulze, Reiner/Hoeren, Thomas (2000): in: id. (eds.), *Dokumente zum Europäischen Recht*, vol. 3: Kartellrecht (until 1957), Berlin, Heidelberg, Doc. 45 ff.

Schumann, Robert (1963): *Pour l'Europe*, Paris.

Simitis, Spiros (1990): "Datenschutz und Europäische Gemeinschaft", in: *Recht der Datenverarbeitung* (RDV) 6, 3–23.

Spaak, Paul-Henri (1969): *Combats inachevés*, Paris.

Steindorff, Ernst (1964): *Rechtsschutz und Verfahren im Recht der Europäischen Gemeinschaften*, Baden-Baden.

Steindorff, Ernst (1951): Schuman-Plan und Europäischer Bundesstaat, in: *Europa-Archiv* (EA) 6, 3955–3960.

Steindorff, Ernst (1960): "Europäische Gemeinschaft für Kohle und Stahl", in: Karl Strupp/Hans-Jürgen Schlochauer (eds.), *Wörterbuch des Völkerrechts*, vol. I, Berlin.

Stolleis, Michael (2010), "Europa als Vorstellung und Arbeitsgebiet der westdeutschen Staatsrechtslehre seit 1945", in: *Festschrift für Heinz Duchardt.*

Stolleis, Michael (2012), "Geschichte des öffentlichen Rechts in Deutschland", in: id. *Staats- und Verwaltungsrechtswissenschaft in West und Ost: 1945 – 1990*, vol. IV.

Thornhill, Christopher (2012): "The formation of a European constitution: an approach from historical-political sociology", in: *International Journal of Law in Context 8*, 354–393.

Tiedemann, Klaus (1993): "Europäisches Gemeinschaftsrecht und Strafrecht", in: *Neue Juristische Wochenschrift* (NJW) 1993, 23–31.

Ulmer, Peter (1992): Vom deutschen zum europäischen Privatrecht?, in: *Juristenzeitung* (JZ), 1–8.

Uri, Pierre (1991): *Penser pour l'action, un fondateur de l'Europe*, Paris.

VerLoren van Themaat, Pieter (1965): "Die Rechtsangleichung als Integrationsinstrument", in: Walter Hallstein (ed.), *Festschrift für Carl Friedrich Ophüls aus Anlaß seines 70. Geburtstages*, Karlsruhe.

Wahl, Rainer (2008): "Europäisierung: Die miteinander verbundenen Entwicklungen von Rechtsordnungen als ganzen", in: *Festschrift Eberhard Schmidt-Aßmann*, Tübingen.

Weiler, Joseph (1991): "The Transformation of Europe", in: Yale L Rev 100 (1991), 2403–2483.

Weiler, Joseph/Haltern, Ulrich/Mayer, Franz (1995): *European Democracy and its Critique – Five Uneasy Pieces*, EUI Working Paper No. 95/11.

Weiss, Manfred (2005): "Die Europäisierung des Arbeitsrechts", in: *Festschrift für Manfred Zuleeg*, Baden-Baden.

Wiethölter, Rudolf (1989): "Franz Böhm (1895–1977)", in: Bernhard Diestelkamp/Michael Stolleis (eds.), *Juristen an der Universität Frankfurt am Main*, Baden-Baden.

Wohlfarth, Ernst (1960): *Die Europäische Wirtschaftsgemeinschaft*, Berlin.

Wolfrum, Rüdiger (2008): "Nachruf Prof. Dr. Günther Jaenicke", in: *Zeitschrift für ausländisches öffentliches Recht und Völkerrecht* (ZaöRV) 68, 1–2.

Ziegler, Karl-Heinz (2007): Völkerrechtsgeschichte, 2nd ed., München.

Zuleeg, Manfred (1969): *Das Recht der europäischen Gemeinschaften im innerstaatlichen Bereich*, Köln.

Zuleeg, Manfred (1970): "Die Entwicklung des Verfassungsrechts im europäischen Raum", *Jahrbuch des öffentlichen Rechts der Gegenwart* (JöR NF) 20, 1–64.

Zuleeg, Manfred (1978): "Der Verfassungsgrundsatz der Demokratie und die Europäischen Gemeinschaften", in: *Der Staat* 17, 27–47.

Zuleeg, Manfred (1987): "Vorbehaltene Kompetenzen der Mitgliedstaaten auf dem Gebiete des Umweltschutzes", in: *Neue Zeitschrift für Verwaltungsrecht* (NVwZ), 280–286.

Zuleeg, Manfred (1987): "Die Bedeutung des europäischen Gemeinschaftsrechts für das Ausländerrecht", in: *Neue Juristische Wochenschrift* (NJW), 2193–2199.

Zuleeg, Manfred (1992): "Der Schutz der Menschenrechte im Gemeinschaftsrecht", in: *Die öffentliche Verwaltung* (DöV), 937–944

Zuleeg, Manfred (1992): "Die Rolle des Arbeitsrechts in der europäischen Integration", in: *Recht der Arbeit* (RdA) 1992, 133–141.

Zuleeg, Manfred (1992): "Der Beitrag des Strafrechts zur europäischen Integration", *Juristenzeitung* (JZ), 761–769

Zuleeg, Manfred (1994): "Die Europäische Gemeinschaft als Rechtsgemeinschaft", *Neue Juristische Wochenschrift* (NJW), 545–549

Zuleeg, Manfred (1994): "Deutsches und europäisches Verwaltungsrecht – Wechselseitige Einwirkungen", in: *Veröffentlichungen der Vereinigung der Deutschen Staatsrechtslehrer* (VVDStRL) 53, 154–201.

Zuleeg, Manfred (2004): *Der rechtliche Zusammenhalt der Europäischen Union*, Baden-Baden.

International Law's Futures—Yesterday, Today, Tomorrow

Martti Koskenniemi

In his posthumously edited *Realizing Utopia* Antonio Cassese invited many colleagues to speculate about the legal forms that the future "international community" might take. The need for such speculation, he stressed, was prompted by "the dramatic tensions between the old society of states hinging on self-interest, reciprocity and 'a parochial spirit', on the one side, and emerging community values, on the other".[1] The formulation repeated international lawyers' favoured normative teleology—the contrast between a present of sovereign egoism and a future of shared values, solidarity and "a modicum of community institutions". This language is familiar from many texts where we have seen jurists step back from daily work to reflect on its meaning within a larger historical frame. We have tended to distinguish them as "realists" or "idealists" by reference to how distant they feel the coming "community" and its "values" are. In an essay in Cassese's volume I focused on what Freud once called the "oceanic feeling", a psychological sense of unity with humankind that seemed operative in such teleology.[2] Here I want to examine the historical dynamic that lawyers have presumed underlies the process towards future unity. What kinds of views about the international world are involved? What is the legal theory and the institutional mechanism assumed to bring about that future? How specific is the view of "international community" waiting in the future? As always, my interest is not purely historical, but inspired by an effort to think critically about the futures proposed to us by present legal projects and institutions.

1 Cassese, "Introduction", xx.

2 Koskenniemi, "Projects of World Community", 3–13.

The Weight of Natural Law

International law emerged from the European encounter with indigenous communities in the context of 16th century colonial expansion. This provided an occasion for Spanish theologians to adapt the teleological frame of Thomas Aquinas' *Summa theologiae* to the massive geopolitical and commercial transformations under way. Although natural law remained immutable, much of it was formulated in general and open-ended terms that allowed contextual variation, including by universally valid conclusions about secular institutions "without which men cannot live together".[3] These included sovereignty and property, *dominium juridictionis* and *dominium proprietatis*. It is true, the Spaniards explained, God had created the world so that all humans were free and possessed things in common. After the fall, however, they no longer were able to live together without a firm central power; the need to work for living necessitated division of properties so that each could enjoy the fruits of his labour in tranquillity. If sovereignty and property were justified by the common secular good, its ultimate finality lay in the supernatural beatitude that was the point of all earthly endeavours.

This construction allowed the theologians to lay out the rules applicable to the "conquest of the Indies" and to the massive expansion of commercial relations across Europe and beyond. How to deal with the pagan communities in the Americas? What to do with the increasingly secular, profit-seeking behaviour spreading in renaissance Europe? *Jus gentium* enabled theologians to explain that even as the historical conditions of social life did not in all respects accord with natural law, the institutions of government, ownership and contract were vital for secular and spiritual happiness. Even as conquest and commerce did involve risks to one's soul—the theologians were by no means uncritical of the conquest or the practices of merchants—if conducted in accordance with the generally accepted rules of *jus gentium* they constituted acceptable aspects of political life. Through providence, God would assist human beings, as princes and subjects, soldiers and merchants, to develop Christian virtues and to attain happiness for their communities and personal encounter with God.

Much of this thinking was adapted by such Protestant jurists as Hugo Grotius and Samuel Pufendorf to the justification of the "modern" state

---

3 Aquinas, "Summa theologae, IaIIae 95", 135.

and the government of civil society. The *social theory* of natural law employed the hypothesis of the "state of nature" so as to justify the positive institutions that the lawyers saw around themselves. Either social contract or de facto occupation authorized the sovereign to govern so as to provide for the security and welfare of the subjects—the subjects were to comply as long as the sovereign respected their lives and properties. Balance of power would see to the tranquil operation of civil societies in Europe while expansion through commerce and the just war would frame the work of evangelization and "improvement" in the colonies. By distinguishing between "external" and "internal" rules as well as "perfect" and "imperfect" duties the jurists were able to fit their realistic focus on the institutions of trade and statecraft with an image of a future where Christian ideals of virtue and justice might one day become a reality. The separation of humankind into distinct territorial units did not necessarily lead to endless war and conquest. On the contrary, the search for happiness at home necessitated peaceful contacts with foreigners so as to purchase from them items that could not be produced at home. Absolutist rulers might not always see to what was needed by rational statecraft, late 17th and 18th century thinkers admitted, but there was no doubt that reason compelled peaceful labour at home and trade abroad.

The view that Christian Europe occupied a leading role in this process extended from scholasticism through to Immanuel Kant's influential teleology of peace and republicanism.[4] In mid-18th century natural law's obsessive concentration on the justification and operation of states began to give room to focus on spontaneous activities in civil society—activities that would be articulated within a theory of natural rights and human progress through division of labour. In the "four-stage theory" developed in the context of the Scottish Enlightenment, men such as Adam Smith canvassed a materialist teleology that measured progress everywhere by the development of techniques of production and exchange.[5] In the aftermath of the American and French revolutions, there was no longer any doubt that the future horizon was open, "progress" was Europe's destiny, to be realised by well-governed political states and enlisting the energies of civil society to productive labour and exchange. As for the outside world, law could always be used as an authoritarian imposition, though only in a

4 See Kant, Zum ewigen Frieden, Kommentar von Oliver Eberl und Peter Nielsen.

5 Smith, Lectures on Jurisprudence.

temporary way. In due course, the laws of secular sovereignty and commerce would ensure what Jeremy Bentham would call "the common and equal utility of all nations".[6]

The Rise of Professional International Law

At the beginning of the 19th century natural law's economic orientation pushed jurists on the sidelines. In France there was practically no interest at all in *Droit des gens* at this time while in Britain, John Austin did his best to prove that the whole idea was an oxymoron, at best a kind of positive morality that James Mill saw mostly evidenced in the many forms of public opinion.[7] Speculation about law in a world of nation-states was either left for philosophy faculties and pacifist organizations, or reformulated as descriptions of the forms and practices of European diplomacy. Perhaps it was because Napoleon's troops had twice run over his university that Georg Friedrich von Martens devoted the successive prefaces of his popular textbook to demonstrating that the principles of the French revolution had no constructive role to play in the world of state policy. "Modern international law" was not about realising contested futures but about coordinating state behaviour through diplomacy.[8]

In the last the decades of the 19th century international law re-emerged through the activities of liberal jurists across Europe as a platform to spread legal reform and to civilize the colonies.[9] The *social theory* of these men was profoundly influenced by the technological and socio-economic change they witnessed around themselves and the possibilities it seemed to offer for the spread of welfare, humanitarianism and liberal-democratic government. Their legal thinking focused on codification and comparative law that they hoped would distribute their preferred reforms of civil, commercial and criminal law across Europe. They also imagined the inherited rules of diplomacy as a legal system—a public international law—that would provide the frame for engaging European states in the work of

6 Bentham, "Principles of International Law".

7 Mill, "Law of Nations", 7–9.

8 See e.g. von Martens, Précis du droit des gens moderne de l'Europe, xv–xxix.

9 See Koskenniemi, The Gentle Civilizer of Nations. The Rise and Fall of International Law 1870–1960.

modernization and civilization. They felt their nationalism and their enthusiasm about colonization as perfectly compatible with their activism in the Red Cross (1864), the Berlin Congo conference (1884–85) and the Hague Peace Conferences (1899/1907). Their view of progress enabled them to distinguish between the civilized countries of Europe and the barbarian and backward nations of what they collectively termed the "Orient".

If the great institutional achievement of natural law had been the justification of the establishment of the "state", the international lawyers of the last decades of the 19th century focused on its desired structures of government. They understood the state as the embodiment and expression of the "nations" that they saw emerging everywhere. But they were also keenly aware of the dangers of "excessive" nationalism and focused on internal legal reform and the facilitation of external cooperation—free trade, technical coordination—to bind the states in a worldwide effort for shared liberal progress. However, a significant minority believed that absent legislation, adjudication and enforcement, international law remained "law" only in a metaphoric sense. The conservative nationalist Adolf Lasson spoke probably for a majority of intellectuals and politicians when he invoked the absence of any autonomous "social ideal" from international institutions.[10] International law, public lawyers across Europe believed, was predominantly a law of technical coordination, while future utopias would have to be worked out in the domestic contexts by reference to the histories and struggles of independent nations. In the first edition of his widely read treatise from 1905 Lassa Oppenheim held it a matter of definition that international law was a law "between, not above, the single states". It possessed no internal morality; it was a regulatory technique, available to nations at the appropriate level of civilization and accepted as part of the "family of nations" by existing family members.[11]

In 1870–1914 optimism about the inevitability of progress was only slightly shadowed by incidents of aggressive nationalism and the turn of the masses towards socialist ideas that the jurists little no sympathy with. This did not prevent the publication of the first works on multilateral treaties as instruments of federalism.[12] Free trade, arbitration, formal colonization and the unification of national laws were cited as instruments

10 Lasson, Princip und Zukunft des Völkerrechts.

11 Oppenheim, International Law. A Treatise, 4, 16–18, 32–34.

12 See Schücking, Der Staatenverband der Haager Konferenzen.

of a more united future world. Legal formalism accepted that international law arose from the will of states but also that this "will" was determined by an underlying progressive history pointing to an increasingly united world.

The Turn to Institutions 1919–1939

It was not to be so. The horrors of the Great War came as an incomprehensible shock. How could the most civilized part of humankind engage in such destructive violence for such a meaningless cause for such a long time? Almost 1.4 million Frenchmen and 1.7 million Germans lay dead on the battlefield. There was a sense that something about pre-war European culture and politics—including international law—had gone terribly wrong. One of the culprits of the catastrophe, it was widely assumed, had been the diplomatic system based on virtually unlimited right of states to go to war with only the weak and "political" principle of the balance of power to constrain them. The combination of nationalism and sovereignty had proven lethal. Increasing contracts between lawyers and diplomats across Europe, free trade, arbitration and technical cooperation had proven useless. Stronger mechanisms were needed to check the excesses of sovereignty.

If politicians and lawyers were united in rejecting the prewar diplomatic system they remained divided about the *social theory* that should underlie the reforms. Some rediscovered natural law and upheld the lofty ideal of a moral community of human beings, seeing perhaps that idea embedded in a historical teleology.[13] Others translated naturalism into a sociological language that gave institutional expression to a fundamental interdependence underlying human existence.[14] Yet others picked from Kant the view of a natural tendency in law towards cooperation and peace. Insights produced by Max Weber and Emile Durkheim suggested that peace and harmony were by no means an automatic consequence of what people learned to think of as complex modernity. Permanent institutions were necessary and appropriate institutional design was crucial for their success.

13 See e.g. Verdross, Die Verfassung der Völkerrechtsgemeinschaft.

14 Scelle, Précis de droit des gens. Principles et systématique.

There has never been more talk about international institutional change than in the years immediately following World War I. Although the League of Nations was established as part of the peace treaty—a solution that undermined its universalism from the outset—it was often interpreted as a functional equivalent to an international government. It did not take long for the first texts to appear suggesting that the Covenant was a kind of a world "constitution".[15] Institutions such as the *Deutsche Gesellschaft für Völkerrecht* in Berlin, the *Institut des hautes études internationales* in Paris and the *Grotius Society* in London as well as The Hague Academy of International Law (1923) tried their best to join liberal jurists in domestic societies and internationally but, inevitably, were attended only by a small number and did not always direct their activities in a cosmopolitan way. The settlement of 1919 was profoundly ambivalent. Even as its drafters were critical of sovereignty (especially the sovereignty of others), they simultaneously declared a right of national *self-determination* for everyone. They rejected war as an instrument of national policy but failed to limit the means of warfare or to develop a reliable system for addressing legitimate grievances. They gave up the pursuit of imperial expansion but set up a system of "mandates" that enabled the Western powers to consolidate and even expand their influence in non-European territories. They wanted a standing system of international organization to facilitate international co-operation but gave it no powers independent from the ambitions of members.

Interwar jurists used theories of functional interdependence to argue about technical co-operation as a means to strengthen international peace and security. This provided justification work on the 'improvement of conditions of human welfare' (Art. 23 of the Covenant) and for the integration of the international bureaus and organizations 'under the direction of the League' (Art. 24 of the Covenant). That Part XIII of the Versailles Treaty established the *International Labour Organization (ILO)* reflected the view that peace required conditions of social justice. Increasingly complex—"modernistic"—technical instruments were devised to tame what were assumed to be altogether atavistic sentiments of aggression and hostility among nations.

But despite all their meetings in Geneva and other international centres, international lawyers remained cantoned within their domestic academic-professional worlds and divided into more or less "traditionalist" and

15 See e.g. Lauterpacht, "The Covenant as 'Higher Law'", 54–65.

"modernist" camps, legal formalists and sociologically oriented directions, "right" and "left" factions. The future of the world could—and was—addressed only in terms that were so abstract that no definite institutional consequences could be deduced from them. Though many wrote in naturalist terms against sovereignty and about the coming international community, how that could be accessed from the weak institutions of the League in a period of conflict was anybody's guess. Such writings provoked skeptical reactions and gave vent to a political realism that sometimes returned to the antihistorical supposition of unending struggle for power, "rise and fall" or empires and the fundamental irreconcilability of national interests.[16] The perceived failures of the League in Manchuria, Ethiopia and with respect to German disarmament and the territorial settlements turned many away from an international law that had pinned its fate to the Geneva institutions.

Decolonization—UN in the Centre 1945–1975

Post World-War II lawyers no longer expected to work for an incipient word government. There was a widespread sense that the inter-war political system had failed at least partly owing to its "legalism", excessive faith in the power of legal rules and institutions, epitomised in the breakdown of its collective security system and in disappointments concerning the projects for disarmament, codification, peaceful settlement, and peaceful change. The formal equality of League members, reflected in the principle of unanimity in the Assembly and the Council had blocked effective action. World peace, both sides in the cold war agreed, necessitated that international institutions enlist the support of powerful nations.

In foreign ministries and universities, lawyers subscribed to a "realism" that emphasised the limits of legal ambition in a politically divided world. Law could not express any shared values of a future world. It was only to keep the peace and for that purpose needed the great powers. In one of the most incisive critiques, Hans Morgenthau pointed out that the League had failed in two ways: by not reflecting the sociological reality of the international world, but also by failing to enlist the moral sentiments of

16 E.g. Carr, The Twenty-Years' Crisis 1919–1939.

world peoples.[17] Morgenthau's Weberian existentialism did not allow much room for international law beyond the conventions of cold war diplomacy, however, and he never followed up his call for a new functionalist jurisprudence. But many American scholars did try to find a scientific or empirical basis for an international law of a new era. Perhaps it was inevitable that this scholarship ended up diluting international law's specificity as against debates about the desired direction of US foreign policy.[18] In Europe, lawyers turned inwards, discussing the transformation of treaties into domestic laws, and regional developments in the human rights and the economic fields. If lawyers played a key role in the setting up of the *Council of Europe* and the *European Economic Community* (EEC), it was not by applying old international law doctrines but integrationist techniques of peace-making. The adoption of the European Convention on Human Rights and Fundamental Freedoms in 1951, only three years after the Universal Declaration, signalled Europe's continued willingness to produce models for the rest of the world. A new jurisprudence focused on the operation of these institutions, interpreting their constitutive documents so as to contribute to reconstruction at home and to support the expansion of United Nations activities abroad. In a familiar reflex, Europe imagined international law's future as a larger version of itself.

The cold war prevented lawyers from being too clear about international law's *telos*. It was all right if it helped in containing conflict and assisting in "peaceful coexistence". Still, most subscribed to more or less well-developed theories about progressive modernization beyond the status quo. In Europe these ideas took the form of "integration" while "development" became the favoured vocabulary to address problems in in the Third World. In both regards, the role of the state remained predominant. The common market was a treaty-based arrangement and national liberation received a legal formulation in countless UN resolutions on decolonization and the many decisions, instruments and projects under the "New International Economic Order". The Non-Aligned movement adopted its "five principles of peaceful coexistence" at Bandung in 1955, coordinating Third World policies with Soviet pragmatism. Legal reform in the Third World took place by the transplantation of the model of the

17 Hans Morgenthau, "Positivism, Functionalism and International Law", 260–284.

18 See further my "Law, Teleology and International Relations: An Essay in Counter-disciplinarity", 14–18.

regulatory State with administrative modernisation and the creation of local industries through import substitution.[19]

The *legal thought* of progressive modernization was an eclectic combination of pragmatism and formalism under a strong "public international law"—an idea of limited international governance though global diplomacy animated by economic welfarism. The spirit of the period was reflected in Wolfgang Friedmann's *The Changing Structure of International Law* (1964) where the "international community" was assigned with a very large scope of tasks in the social, environmental, and humanitarian fields and which advocated a transformation from a "law of coordination" to one of "co-operation" in the resolution of global problems The word "interdependence" was not new (it came from the 19th century) but it expressed a new awareness about the global nature of economic and environmental problems. The image of "Spaceship Earth" produced an urgent version of the old ethic of international community.

As a result, lawyers began to argue about the lawmaking powers of General Assembly, the emergence of "new "subjects" such as individuals, transnational companies, national liberation movements as part of this change. Intervention in "domestic affairs" by the UN was no longer a taboo under article 2(7) of the Charter as UN agencies were imagined to lead an international legal "system" in which the law was constantly being produced and administered by analogy to the legislative processes of the domestic State. UNESCO, UNCTAD, the system of commodity agreements, the UN Conference on the Human Environment (Stockholm 1972) and Conference on the Law of the Sea (begun in 1974) were about managing "shared resources". The New International Economic Order (1974) supported state intervention and Keynesian policies while the Bretton Woods Institutions (World Bank, IMF) exported reconstruction techniques adapted from post-war Europe to the developing world.

The *ideal of future* was a public-law governed international community of states, collaborating to resolve common problems with the view of the just distribution of the fruits of progressive modernization across the world. That underneath diplomatic hubris there was no unanimity about this direction was visible in persistent conflicts regarding the uses of natural resources, surfacing for instance in the protracted negotiations in the Law

19 See e.g. Trubek/Santos, The New Law and Economic Development. A Critical Appraisal.

of the Sea conference, in the arbitrations regarding the right to nationalize foreign concession agreements and in UNESCO's effort to create a "new information order" that led to a temporary walk-out by leading Western states. The expectations were not met. Poverty and conflict persisted in the global south in part owing to externalization of cold war antagonism, in part due to indigenous problems and legacies of colonialism. By the eighties it began to seem impossible to carry out the needed reforms through the kinds of states and public administration that existed in the Third World. The future would not be brought about through international law but by liberating the spontaneous forces of civil societies everywhere. With the emergence of neo-liberal regimes in the West, donors and development institutions began to view the state as part of the problem of lack of development rather than its solution. The opening up of Eastern Europe further accelerated the sense that regulatory solutions and state-centrism had to give room to free markets as the instrument of change.

Washington Consensus

In the eighties international law's welfarism and public law orientation began to crumble. State-driven modernization was put to question. The New International Economic Order and its associated programs on commodity markets and technology transfer were set aside. The UN Convention on the Law of the Sea was concluded in 1982 but never set up the kind of International Seabed Authority (ISA) that had been planned to supervise the extraction of seabed minerals. Instead, Western companies were allowed "pioneer investors" status and privileged access to sites they had been prospecting. Official Development Assistance (ODA) was directed to restructuring state activities so as to enable domestic and foreign private actors more freedom to operate. Import substitution was replaced by integration in a global economic system. The policies of the IMF and the World Bank were now directed to combating inflation, supporting private investment and opening access to the markets. In the words of a World Bank Report from 1997, the State was to be "central to economic and social development, not as adirect provider of growth but as a partner, catalyst, and facilitator".[20] From its initial orientation to welfare policies in the fifties and sixties the GATT system was geared towards a neutral platform where governments would advance the interests of their exporters and fight "regulation" by non-tariff barriers and trade distortions. The US trade act of 1974 prompted aggressive uses of so-called Section 301 that enabled private exporters to push the US to take action against foreign states deemed to regulate in trade-distorting ways—with the result that much standard-setting deviating from US or EU standards was seen as distortion.[21]

While diplomacy oriented itself towards dismantling of institutions designed to advance global redistribution, novel optimism arose with respect to the security system. The termination of the Iran-Iraq war in 1988 through the good offices of the Secretary-General was a watershed. A chance to make the UN work more efficiently—"as it was intended by the drafters"—seemed confirmed by the Security Council's reaction to the Kuwait crisis in 1990 by a full-scale economic embargo and the authorizing the use of force (SCR 661 and 678, 1990). Its insufficient but nevertheless coordinated reactions to the Yugoslavian and Rwandan crises further reinforced the sense of an opportunity to make reality of rule-based security, as suggested by the Secretary-General' s *Agenda for Peace* of 1994. The rhetoric of the rule of law was present everywhere—most strikingly in the advances made by international criminal responsibility. The Yugoslavian and Rwandan war crimes tribunals were followed up by the adoption, in 1998, of the Rome Treaty, establishing the International Criminal Court (ICC). In the UN, "Peace-making, "peace-building" and "post-conflict governance" became new watchwords of an international public law that reimagined itself as a night-watchman securing the operation of civil societies everywhere.

The *preferred institutions* of this new sensibility were those of the market, courts and arbitral tribunals plus private-public relationships. The identifycation and application of technical standards and best practices became the order of international institutions with formal and legalized dispute settlement, geared towards enforcing contracts and creating predictability. Investor-state arbitration had been a possibility within the ICSID under

20 World Bank, World Development Report 1997: The State in a Changing World, 4; See further, Rittich, Recharacterizing Restructuring: Law, Distribution, and Gender in Market Reform.

21 Lang, World Trade Law after Neoliberalism, 221–271.

the World Bank since the seventies. With the failure of the Multilateral Agreement on Investment (MAI) in 1998, the growth of the number of bilateral investment treaties laid the foundations for limiting the regulatory powers of states vis-à-vis international investors. The World Trade Organization was set up in 1994, with a permanent, legally based mechanism for the settlement of disputes. The Appellate Body (AB) may have received its name and procedures from the reluctance of trade negotiators to establish a formal court. Nevertheless, it did not take long for commentators, or the members of the AB itself, to interpret its activity as that of a regular and in some respects even very advanced international tribunal whose jurisprudence was not to be "clinically isolated" from public international law.[22] In fact, the WTO dispute settlement system was seen as one of the most successful efforts to inject "rule of law" in the fluid process of globalization. The development of the climate change regime into bargaining about emission quotas between private polluters was paralleled by a little-noticed transformation of the vocabulary of environmental "liability" into "allocation of loss" that removed the regulatory burden and responsibility for large-scale activities from states to an insurance system linking private operators to the industry-wide resources backing them up.[23]

The *social theory* of the neo-liberal period was that of methodological individualism. Focus was on individuals—both "bad" and "good"—the latter manifested in the spread of institutional human rights activism. The Council of Europe expanded in Eastern and Central Europe and even Russia joined the European Convention on Human Rights. A new humanitarianism built on compassionate engagement. The Kosovo crisis of 1999 demonstrated the willingness of Western actors to undertake a military operation even against the UN Charter if only a conflict could be depicted as a humanitarian crisis or "state failure", a kind of systemic collapse that could be dealt with through regime change and transformative occupation.[24] The call for "democracy" received its most visible international form in groups of election observers traveling from country to country to check ballot boxes and interview opponents of local regimes.

22 See e.g Lindroos/Mehling, "Dispelling the Chimera of 'Self-Contained Regimes' International Law and the WTO", 857–877.

23 International law Commission, "Draft principles on the allocation of loss in the case of transboundary harm arising out of hazardous activities", United Nations 2006.

24 For useful analysis of the theory behind the novel practices, see Orford, International Authority and the Responsibility to Protect.

The Inter-American Court of Human Rights began its activity in 1979 and the African Charter of Human and Peoples' Rights was adopted in 1981 and a Commission began work in 1987. The number of treaties on human rights and non-discrimination, designed to protect specific groups together with the activity of the expert bodies set up under these treaties arose to create a real treaty congestion.

Lawyers began to learn the languages of global "governance" and "regulation".[25] While formal public international law continued to be practiced within the UN, specialized types of legal regime called for increasing specialization. "Diplomats' law" was not an effective governance instrument. Jurists were invited to learn from and cooperate with US-trained international relations experts so as to think in terms of strategic choices and optimal efficiency. European and US lawyers were seen travelling everywhere in Eastern Europe and the global south teaching the new elites about how to deal with corruption and to design political and legal institutions after the Western model.[26] For those worrying about the impact of change, human rights were proposed as a kind of super-normativity, valid everywhere to address the grievances of those who felt being treaded upon. As the process of re-defining the interests of special groups as the "rights" of the members of those groups had no end, it led to the redefinition of social conflict as rights-conflict. The result was an ubiquitous process of rights-balancing in authoritative institutions that, however, needed to apply rights-independent criteria that assist in building the necessary hierarchies. This led to contemplation on "indicators", standards, and criteria for benchmarking and assessment that would allow not only the measuring of rights but would present an ideal of decision-making as the calculation of commensurate values everywhere.[27] The technical aspects of legal work were stressed at the expense of openly normative ones. Not everyone was convinced that the "end of history" was here—but there was little alternative to a future where government and politics would become the administration of humans and things.[28]

---

25 See e.g. Braithwaite/Drahos, Global Business Regulation.

26 See Frankenberg, Order from Transfer. Comparative Constitutional law and Legal Culture.

27 See Davis/Fisher/Kingsbury/Merry (eds.), Governance by Indicators. Global Power through Classification and Rankings.

28 See further my "The Fate of International Law. Between Politics and Technique", 1–30.

By 2000 the Washington consensus had been dismantled. Restructuring had been wreaking havoc in developing countries and although there had been undoubted gains, they were very unequally distributed. Some spectacular successes—the Asian Tigers—were based on unabashed protectionism and State support. The result was a kind of "restructuring with a human face" in which the institutions of the state were enlisted to provide the rule of law so as to guarantee the security of private rights and the proper operation of the market and where democracy would operate as a channel to deal with political conflict.

Post-Neoliberal Futures

The great concern of the first years of the new millennium was that of international law's "fragmentation" which, though not a new theme, seemed to pose fundamental questions about international law's role in global governance. Specialized legal regimes in trade law, human rights law, humanitarian law, environmental law, security law and so on did not reflect any overarching objective, public ethos or vision of the future. The experts in each regime regarded their preferences overriding in regard to other preferences. Intra-regime problems were treated by deformalized law, reasonableness, proportionality, equitable apportionment and the informal search for efficiency. This meant a subtle move of power from legislators to law-appliers. Shared expertise meant shared political preferences and guaranteed trust and confidence among decision makers. Cross-regime problems were dealt with by hegemonic balancing where the competent institution's preferences would find their way to the top. Social protest was channelled to domestic institutions or took the form of regime-conflict: trade vs. environment, security vs. rights, criminal law vs. responsibility to protect. Lawyers learned to think strategically: was it possible to penetrate external regimes or integrate norms from an alien regime without destructive effects at home? Would rejection of extra-regime preferences lead to marginalization?

That institutions imagined their tasks in technical terms did not always leave room for anything distinctly legal. Law-making was geared to setting up procedures under framework conventions or within regional institutions where technical experts on trade, environment, development, security, human rights and so on would continue their struggles and negotiate compromises. But concern over "fragmentation" gradually dissipated. Although many stressed that "regime interaction" was more about policy-making than technical coordination, absent any meaningful reaction from formal political bodies (parliaments or general assemblies of international institutions), informal governance continued to consolidate itself.[29] The social theory of "fluid modernity" or of "complexity" fitted the situation well. Despite endless talk about the "constitutionalization" of this or that realm of international governance, no firm hierarchies were set up. The discordance between parliaments, parties and other representative institutions operating in a domestic setting, and the global character of expert governance ensured that while the former acted as buffer to popular discontent, the latter could carry out their business undisturbed.

As political priorities after 9/11 turned to "fight against terrorism", domestic security agencies were empowered and secret operations conducted in ways that few even attempted to justify under international law. The widely accepted "illegality" of the US-UK war against Iraq in 2003 led to no sanctions and the brutality of the occupation forces, epitomised in the debates on extraordinary renditions and the "closing" of Guantanamo made efforts to use law as the platform for imagining desired future seem simply out of step with the moment's needs. Curiously, the global human rights system and the global security system were able to create a *modus vivendi* that allowed each to operate as if the other did not exist. One offshoot of the ubiquitous turn to "exception" was that lawyers often saw fundamental distinctions between categories of war and peace, combatant and civilian, occupation and "regime change" vanish into thin air.[30] Reports of torture, secret operations, and of massive violations of privacy across the Western world were, after the first shocks, integrated into the new normality of a post-neoliberal age. The promises of the rule of law and democratization were still alive for a moment in events such as the "Arab Spring". Its brutal crushing and the expansion of civil war overtook the political agenda everywhere.

The *social theory* of the post-neoliberal period turned to traditions of political realism. There was talk about a resurgence of geopolitics and

29 See Young, Regime Interaction in International Law. Facing Fragmentation.

30 For a discussion, see Lorite Escorihuela, "Humanitarian law and Human Rights Law: The Politics of Distinction", 299–407.

scholars pursued interwar theories about "*Grossräume*" (large spaces) as stabilising factors.[31] The futility of pursuing desired futures through law seemed confirmed by the incommensurability of existential worlds across the globe. When antagonisms take on a religious tone, what possible role can law have? Nevertheless, complexity also had a distinct logic. The turn to informal institutional decision-making, strategic thinking and increasing recourse to secret or otherwise "exceptional" techniques highlights the role of the executive, not that of the law-maker. The same can be said of the replacement of formal top-down interventions by a softer "resilience approach" to engage local communities to adapt to liberal norms and processes. Giving up universalism for a more "pragmatic" kinds of intervenetion, whatever its results, at least ends up in absence of accountability.[32] In the neoliberal view of the international world as a market of competing projects and agendas, it was assumed that something like a "general equilibrium" would in due course emerge where good ideas would win and others would be balanced against each other in some procedurally acceptable way. But the fact that some—usually the same—interests continued to win while those who already were vulnerable, continued losing *whatever the procedure*, marked a shift from a neoliberal to an altogether more authoritarian future. Instead of a general equilibrium there was marginalization on the one hand, unabated grasp for resources on the other. The intensification of ideological antagonism contributed to the sense that the peaceful normality of law could not be trusted; stronger executive rule was needed. Because liberal lawyers had all these years been speaking against situating that rule within states, it had to be created internationally. Let domestic politicians speak about justice, equality or self-determination; this will have no significant consequences for the world of global governance. Instead, strengthen international institutions, expert regimes and technical procedures. Create at the international level the Hobbesian pact of protection/obedience broken at home.[33]

31 E.g. Salter/Yin, "International Law and Relations: The Shanghai Cooperation Organisation as a Grossraum?", 819–877.

32 See Chandler, "Resilience and the 'Everyday': Beyond the Paradox of 'Liberal Peace'", 27–48.

33 Orford, International Authority.

And the Future now?

Ceterum censeo…

One place from which to start examining present sensibilities might be the debates in Europe and the United States the "Transatlantic Partnership Treaty" (TTIP), especially booming interest in investor-state arbitration (ISDS). Examined in its context, the project is clearly is part of the process of globalization taking place outside multilateral public diplomacy aiming to liberate powerful actors in civil society against the "obstructions" of state policy. The objective of this kind of international law is the production of "wealth" through empowering private investors as against the agencies of the state. Yet, as a regime, investor protection both competes and conflicts with such other processes as those of environment, human rights, security etc. How are those conflicts to be settled? What about conflicting preferences in a global world with neither a centre nor a political process?

The *social theory* of investor protection makes no fundamental distinction between public and private interests, the position of the state and that of the foreign investor. Each is understood as an interest-holder in a world of *spontaneous acceleration* where the optimal realization of conflicting interests is allocated to the state understood as a "regulator" whose operations are checked and supervised by groups of impartial international "experts". This is an image there is little reason to share. For states are not just regulators, although that is how it may seem to outsiders. They are also constitutional compacts that allocate rights, powers and privileges, telling people what some may do, and others must suffer, in view of the images of future that are constantly debated in the political organs of the state. Citizens accept this because their relations are defined by the legislature that constitutes, redefines, adjusts and limits the rights and duties of everyone. We may disagree about how the public good has been defined in our laws or executive measures or the latest Supreme Court judgment. But we still have reason to defer to them because they are *our* institutions, set up and operating in accordance with *our* constitution, by virtue of the compact *we* have made.

It has long been accepted that commercial disputes may be directed to special arbitration tribunals. They have a better grasp of the details and customs of trading and a *Fingerspitzgefühl* about what merchants might regard as fair. But those are disputes between private parties, and private interests. If public interest is concerned—question of the conditions under which the market should operate for instance—public authorities must decide. It is sometimes argued that we need ISDS because arbitrators are experts, they know better. But the greatest number of cases have had to do with policing, financial regulation or taxation, environment, health care, and rules of competition. No tribunal has ever claimed they know better how to adjust such concerns. And if they did, nobody would believe them. Instead, they have suggested that the state measure has been in other ways inappropriate. In the case of *Inmaris v. the republic of the Ukraine* (1 March 2012), the tribunal opined that

> "[a] government act could be unfair or inequitable if it is in breach of specific commitments, if it is undertaken or political reasons or other improper motives, if the investor is not treated in an objective, even-handed, unbiased, and transparent way, or for other reasons".[34]

This is a banal statement. Tribunals often make such. And yet a constitutional order always allocates rights and duties in a political way. Political parties fight and ally in pursuit of political motives. This is what they are expected to do. The determination, limitation or balancing of a right does not take place by some scientific algorithm, an objective calculation about what might be optimal in view of some utilitarian standard. It involves a contestable decision in a field of action where strategic actors try as best they can to win over their opponents, the only limitation to this process being provided by the constitution and what the electorate thinks.

ISDS has many problems. Its standards are open-ended, obscure and amenable to the application of bias; its procedures are unbalanced and non-transparent, arbitrators are few and have vested interests. Mistakes are frequent and procedures costly. Many books now describe the "backslash" against the system, and it is no surprise to anyone—apart from the EU Commission—that the result of the recent consultation showed 90 per cent of the responses as utterly negative towards the system. The more we learn about the details of the cases, the more stunned the public is about the breadth of the powers of review handed to individuals with no accountability. But none of this is really vital. What is important is that ISDS is part of the re-definition, within the fluid process of "globalization", of political communities as no longer masters of their own lives,

34 Inmaris vs. The Republic of the Ukraine (ICSID Case No. ARB/08/8, Award 1 March 2012, para. 265.

but turned into localized "regulators" of global wealth extraction. In this system, as the Oxfam report of last week showed, the richest 1 per cent in the world owned 48 per cent of global wealth, leaving only 5,5 per cent to be shared by the poorest 80 per cent.[35] Is it a coincidence the curb showing the rise of ISDS cases is almost identical with the curb showing the rise of global inequality?

* * * * *

With the end of formal teleologies, Western thinking about the future turns easily to either of its two temporal homes. First is that of Polybian circles where everything endlessly repeats itself. Human nature does not change; nor that of human community. The search for maximal gratification continues from generation to generation, everyone seeking to maximise their utilities. Every preference is commensurate with every other preference, struggle continues and nothing really changes. All that can be done is to enjoy the cycle while one is part of it. In this narrative which Northrop Frye once labelled "ironic", the "forces of history" are beyond human understanding and individuals completely at the mercy of their unchanging natures.[36] The other one is that we can learn, and that the future will emerge from the choices human beings make on the basis of what we know. This "knowledge" is not objective or uncontested and much of our political debate is focused on how we should understand it. Of course, the danger of illusion is real; perhaps there is no choice after all. But nobody can live with such an assumption, and it unlikely to be supported by what we otherwise believe to be true. Perhaps Kant was after all onto something when he supposed that the fact that we cannot objectively "know" the future and that the past is not available as an impartial verification, has no bearing onto our duty to work in order to make the future better than the present, and not just for ourselves, but for all. This would be to think not of a future "then" (to which intermediate generations would be sacrificed), but "now".

35 Hardoon, Oxfam, Having it All and Wanting More, Report on Inequality 2015, http://policy-practice.oxfam.org.uk/publications/wealth-having-it-all-and-wanting-more-338125?cid=rdt_havingitall (accessed 16.02.2015).

36 Frye, The Anatomy of Criticism. Four Essays.

Works Cited

Aquinas, St. Thomas (2002): "Summa theologae, IaIIae 95", in: R.W. Dyson (ed.), *Aquinas Political Writings,* Cambridge, 135.

Bentham, Jeremy (1838–43): "Principles of International Law", in: J. Bowring (ed,), *The Works of Jeremy Bentham*, 11 vols, Edinburgh, vol 2, reproduced in http://oll.libertyfund. org/title/1921/114295 (13.02.2015).

Braithwaite, John/Drahos, Peter (2000): *Global Business Regulation,* Cambridge.

Chandler, David (2015): "Resilience and the 'Everyday': Beyond the Paradox of 'Liberal Peace'", in: 41 *Rev. of Int'l Stud.*, 27–48.

Carr, E.H. (1946): *The Twenty-Years' Crisis 1919–1939,* 2nd edn., London.

Cassese, Antonio (2012): "Introduction", in: id (ed.), *Realizing Utopia. The Future of International Law,* Oxford, xx.

Davis, Kevin/Fisher, Angelina/Kingsbury Benedict/Engle Merry, Sally (eds) (2013): *Governance by Indicators. Global Power through Classification and Rankings,* Oxford.

Frankenberg, Günter (2013): *Order from Transfer. Comparative Constitutional law and Legal Culture,* London.

Frye, Northrop (1957): *The Anatomy of Criticism. Four Essays,* Princeton.

Hardoon, Deborah (2015): Oxfam, Having it All and Wanting More, Report on Inequality, http://policy-practice.oxfam.org.uk/publications/wealth-having-it-all-and-wanting-more-338125?cid=rdt_havingitall (accessed 16.02.2015).

Kant, Immanuel (2011): *Zum ewigen Frieden, Kommentar von Oliver Eberl und Peter Nielsen,* Berlin.

Koskenniemi, Martti (2002): *The Gentle Civilizer of Nations: the Rise and Fall of International Law 1870–1960*, Cambridge.

Koskenniemi, Martti (2007): "The Fate of International Law. Between Politics and Technique", in: *Modern Law Review*, 1–30.

Koskenniemi, Martti (2012): "Law, Teleology and International Relations: An Essay in Counter-disciplinarity", in: 26 *International Relations*, 14–18.

Lang, Andrew (2013): *World Trade Law after Neoliberalism,* Oxford.

Lasson, Adolf (1871*): Princip und Zukunft des Völkerrechts,* Berlin.

Lauterpacht, Hersch (1936): "The Covenant as 'Higher Law", in: *British Year Book of International Law* (BYIL) 17, 54–65.

Lindroos, Anja/Mehling, Michael (2006): "Dispelling the Chimera of 'Self-Contained Regimes' International Law and the WTO", EJIL 16, 857–877.

Lorite Escorihuela, Alejandro (2011): "Humanitarian law and Human Rights Law: The Politics of Distinction", in: 19 *Michigan State Journal of International Law*, 299–407.

Mill, James (1825): "Law of Nations", in: id (ed.), *The Supplement to the Encyclopaedia Britannica*, London, 7–9.

Morgenthau, Hans (1940): "Positivism, Functionalism and International Law", in: *American Journal of International Law* (AJIL) 34, 260–284.

Oppenheim, Lassa (1905): *International Law. A Treatise,* Vol I, London, 4, 16–18, 32–34.

Orford, Anne (2011): *International Authority and the Responsibility to Protect,* Cambridge.

Rittich Kerry (2002): *Recharacterizing Restructuring: Law, Distribution, and Gender in Market Reform,* The Hague.

Salter, Michael/ Yin, Yina (2014): "International Law and Relations: The Shanghai Cooperation Organisation as a Grossraum?", in: 13 *Chinese Journal of IL*, 819–877.

Scelle, Georges (1984 [1933]): *Précis de droit des gens. Principles et systématique,* Paris.

Schücking, Walther (1912): *Der Staatenverband der Haager Konferenzen*, Leipzig.

Smith, Adam (1978): *Lectures on Jurisprudence,* Oxford.

Trubek, Dave/Santos, Alvaro (2006): *The New Law and Economic Development. A Critical Appraisal,* Cambridge.

Verdross, Alfred (1926): *Die Verfassung der Völkerrechtsgemeinschaft,* Wien.

von Martens, Georg Friedrich (1821): *Précis du droit des gens moderne de l'Europe*, xv-xxix.

World Bank (1997): *World Development Report 1997: The State in a Changing World,* Washington D.C.

Young, Margaret (2012): *Regime Interaction in International Law. Facing Fragmentation,* Cambridge.

Taking (Europe's) Values Seriously

*Joseph H.H. Weiler**

You certainly do not expect, and rightly so, a disquisition or some kind of historical account of the evolution of positive European Union law.

Our minds turn, thus, to policy. Habitually, when we think of law in policy terms we proceed in one of two directions. Either law is seen as part of the transmission chain between the policy objective (political, economic, social or all of the above) i.e the law being an *instrument* for achieving an exogenous goal the effectiveness or utility of which can be judged. Or we may think of legal policy itself—the policy of the law and the legal system itself where endogenous goals are identified—certainty, efficiency, effectiveness.

But I am not interested in policy either. My essay—which will certainly problematize certain aspects of the Union and its law—does not call for policy responses, and in my view has no policy response; indeed, the habitual reflex "if there is a problem, what is the solution," which is a conditioned reflex of Modernity, is part of the problem. In some deep sense, I hope, we will be dealing with the human condition.

I am interested in the spiritual condition of Europe and the role law plays in shaping it. It is part of my growing interest in, and research of, three related themes: The way in which legal norms and practices reflect and shape political culture; a more general interest in 'non-instrumental' and non functionalist dimensions of law; and the spiritual dimensions of legal regimes generally and the European legal order more specifically.

* Thanks to Isabel Feichtner and Bosko Tripkovic for their wise interlockership and research assistance.

Values—History and Historiography

I.

It is still quite common, even today, to tell a history of European integration according to which it was originally an economic project which slowly transformed into a political project.[1] The very preamble of the Treaty of Paris[2] establishing the European Coal and Steel Community in the early fifties gives the lie to this proposition. It lifts its language directly from the Schuman Declaration[3] and attests that from its inception European Integration was a project with deep political ends, which used economic instruments as means to achieve those political ends. Those political ends were not simply a new way of vindicating the national interest of its partners (though it was, naturally, also that[4]), but were predicated on a set of values which have been part of its foundations from inception.

If we consider Monnet's famous aphorism—*Nous ne coalisons pas des Etats, nous unissons des hommes*[5]—we realize that in its meta-objetives the project went even beyond politics. It had a spiritual dimension: Redefining

---

1 "C'est de cette dynamique que procède le passage d'une Communauté économique à une Communauté de citoyens. C'est-à-dire d'une Communauté qui repose sur la réalisation d'un Marché commun, dans lequel la libre circulation des personnes (en tant qu'agents économiques), des marchandises, des services et des capitaux est garantie à une Communauté de citoyens, c'est-à-dire une Communauté d'individus appartenant à une Union politique fondée sur les principes—ou pour reprendre la terminologie retenue par le Traité de Lisbonne—de valeurs de liberté, de démocratie, du respect des droits de l'Homme et des libertés fondamentales, ainsi que l'Etat de droit. Autrement dit, c'est de cette dynamique que procède le passage d'une intégration négative à une intégration positive." Jaibi/Landolsi, "L'Union européenne: d'une Communauté Economique à une Communauté de Citoyens", 250.

2 Traité instituant la Communauté Européenne du Charbon et de l'Acier, Préambule, 18 avril 1951, non publié au journal officiel, available at http://europa.eu.int/eur-lex/lex/fr/treaties/dat/11951K/tif/11951K.html; Preamble to 1951 Treaty of Paris, reprinted in European Community Information Service, Treaties Establishing the European Communities (1987).

3 Déclaration Schuman, Discours prononcé le 9 mai 1950 par Robert Schuman, ministre français des Affaires étrangères, available at http://europa.eu/abc/symbols/9-may/decl_fr.htm. Schuman Declaration of May 9, 1950, reprinted in Bulletin of European Communities, 1980, vol. 13, 14–15.

4 Milward, The European Rescue of the Nation-State.

5 Monnet, Mémoires. Nous ne Coalisons pas des Etats, Nous Unissons des Hommes.

human relations, the very way individuals relate to each other and to their community.[6]

That it should have had this spiritual dimension is not surprising if we remember the historical context—the horror of World War II—against which the project of European integration was conceived and the deep religious commitment of its founding fathers.[7] Make no mistake: The project and the process were also *realpolitik* of the highest order.[8] But that, too, should not surprise us for those very same reasons—the historical moment and the political biography of those same men: One should

---

6 Cf. Schuman, Pour l'Europe, Écrits politiques, 38, "Nous ne sommes, nous ne serons jamais des négateurs de la patrie, oublieux des devoirs que nous avons envers elle. Mais au-dessus de chaque patrie nous reconnaissons de plus en plus distinctement l'existence d'un bien commun, supérieur à l'intérêt national, ce bien commun dans lequel se fondent et se confondent les intérêts individuels de nos pays. La loi de la solidarité des peuples s'impose à la conscience contemporaine. Nous nous sentons solidaires les uns des autres dans la préservation de la paix, dans la défense contre l'agression, dans la lutte contre la misère, dans le respect des traités, dans la sauvegarde de la justice et de la dignité humaine."; ibid, 46, "Que cette idée d'une Europe réconciliée, unie et forte soit désormais le mot d'ordre pour les jeunes générations désireuses de servir une humanité enfin affranchie de la haine et de la peur, et qui réapprend, après de trop longs déchirements, la fraternité chrétienne."; ibid, 47, "Il faut préparer les esprits à accepter les solutions européennes en combattant partout non seulement les prétentions à l'hégémonie et la croyance à la supériorité, mais les étroitesses du nationalisme politique, du protectionnisme autarcique et de l'isolationnisme culturel. A toutes ces tendances qui nous sont léguées par le passé il faudra substituer la notion de la solidarité, c'est à dire la conviction que le véritable intérêt de chacun consiste à reconnaître et à accepter dans la pratique l'interdépendance de tous. L'égoïsme ne paie plus".

7 "Schuman was an ardent Roman Catholic, and his views about the desirability of political unity in Western Europe owed much to the idea that it was above all the continent's Christian heritage which gave consistence and meaning to the identity of European civilisation. And the Europe he knew and loved best was the Carolingian Europe that accorded with his religious faith and his experience of French and German cultures." Sutton, France and the Construction of Europe, 1944–2007: The Geopolitical Imperative, 34. "It is with deep faith in our cause that I speak to you, and I am confident that through the will of our free peoples, with your support and with God's help, a new era for Europe will soon begin." Extracts from a speech by Alcide De Gasperi at the Consultative Assembly of the Council of Europe in Strasbourg on 16 September 1952 – volume 3/1952 of the Official Reports of Debates of the Consultative Assembly of the Council of Europe. De Gaspari & Adenauer had similar sensibilities.

8 Moravcsik, The Choice for Europe: Social Purpose and State Power from Messina to Maastricht.

eschew monolithic motivations and explanations when attending to the affairs of all men and women, not least men and women in public service.

The narrative of European Integration has, thus, since its inception, combined two notable strands—the functional and the idealist—pragmatism and values, combined. Thus, one of the European construct's claims for originality had been the proposition that what it put in place was not simply useful, but also an expression of deep values and transformative of human relations: *Nous ne coalisons pas des Etats, nous unissons des hommes.*

II.

In addressing values, rather than articulating a normative theory of European integration,[9] I propose to be empirical: Identifying the content of value discourse as a matter of fact, situating it conceptually and then examining it critically.[10]

9 Cf. Richardson, "The European Union in the World—A Community of Values", 14; Boniface, Quelles valeurs pour l'Union européenne?; Dony, "Les Valeurs, objectifs et principes de l'Union", 33; Benoît-Rhomer, "Valeurs et droits fondamentaux dans la Constitution"; Éditorial, "L'Union, une communauté de valeurs?"; Euzéby, "La Constitution—Constitution de l'Union Européenne: des valeurs à défendre!".

10 In this section of the essay I have no interest in "unmasking". I am interested instead in a distillation of the most common value laden vocabulary gleaned from speeches of Heads of State and Government and from official texts. It is a story of how we want to appear in the mirror. The following is a selection of such statements by authorities of several of the Member States. Austria: "It [the discussion about the European Constitution] is also about the European way of life. I have never understood why the USA can boast about the American way of life, while we Europeans never have the confidence to refer to our own way of life with pride: peace, democracy and solidarity are not self-evident and come at a price." Speech by the President of the European Council, Federal Chancellor Wolfgang Schüssel (Austria), to the European Parliament, 18.1.2006, available at http://www.eu2006.at/en/News/Speeches_Interviews/1801schuesselredeep.html 18.01.2006. "The Memorandum of Understanding [between the EU and the Council of Europe] should deepen and extend the co-operation and political dialogue between the two organisations, building on existing agreements of 1987 and 2001. We should build on and around, the attachment of both organisations to the same values, our common commitments to the promotion of a pluralistic democracy, respect for and protection of human rights, fundamental freedoms and the rule of law." Speech by Bundeskanzler Wolfgang Schüssel before the Parliamentary Assembly of the Council of Europe, 11.04.2006, available at http://www.eu2006.at/de/News/Speeches_Intervie

ws/1104 schuesseleuroparat.html. Czech Republic: "In my view, the main European values, as shaped by the turbulent spiritual and political history of Europe, and as adopted by other parts of the world, or at least some parts of the world, are obvious. Respect for the individual and for his freedoms, his rights and his dignity, the principle of solidarity, equality before the law and the rule of law, protection of all ethnic minorities, democratic institutions, separation of the legislative, executive and judicial estates, political pluralism, respect for private property and free enterprise, a market economy and the development of the civil society. The form which these values currently assume naturally reflects countless modern European experiences, including the fact that our continent is becoming a main multicultural crossroads." Speech by Mr Vaclav Havel, President of the Czech Republic, to the European Parliament, 16.2.2000, available at http://www.europarl.europa.eu/sides/getDoc.do?pubRef=-//EP//TEXT +CRE+20000216+ITEM012+DOC+XML+V0//EN&language=EN&query=INTER V&detail= 3-228. Denmark: "The Copenhagen Summit also marked the beginning of a new era for the European Union. In Copenhagen, the EU carried out the greatest task in the history of the Community. Following the Copenhagen Summit, the European Union stands as the overall framework around the Europe of the future: cooperation based on the shared values of freedom and the market economy, community spirit and social responsibility, democracy and human rights; effective cooperation that respects the national characteristics of our peoples and states (...)." Speech by Fogh Rasmussen, Prime Minister of Denmark, to the European Parliament,18.12.2002, available at http://www.europarl.europa.eu/sides/getDoc.do?pubRef=-//EP//TEXT+CRE+200 21218+ITEM-003+DOC+XML+V0//EN&language=EN&query=INTERV&detail= 3-010. Finland: "The importance of European cooperation and integration to promote peace, stability and prosperity in our continent is obvious, and the results are striking. Our efforts are based on a common set of values. They are freedom, democracy, a respect for human rights and fundamental freedoms and a commitment to the principles of the rule of law (...)." Speech by Tarja Halonen, President of the Republic of Finland, to the European Parliament, 5.9.2006, available at http://www.europarl.europa.eu/sides /getDoc.do?type=CRE&reference=20060905&secondRef=ITEM-008&format=XML &language=EN. France: "As a result of this Charter [of Fundamental Rights], our Union will be stronger and have greater guarantees of the values of dignity, freedom and solidarity that are its cornerstones. We shall now echo this as widely as possible and very shortly consider its status. I realise how much importance your Parliament attaches to this Charter." Speech by Jacques Chirac, President of the French Republic, to the European Parliament, 12.12.2000, available at http://www.europarl.europa.eu/sides/get Doc.do?type=CRE&reference=20001212&secondRef=ITEM-004&format=XML& language=EN. Germany: "I am very glad—and I think the majority of us here are agreed on this—that we succeeded in finding a solution regarding the Charter of Fundamental Rights. The Charter strengthens the citizens' rights vis-à-vis the institutions. The Charter of Fundamental Rights will be legally binding, which in my view is entirely fitting for a value-conscious Europe. Ladies and Gentlemen, all institutional

progress and the reorientation of the European Union are in the end only possible if we Europeans are conscious of our values, indeed if we make these values the guiding principles for all our actions. I believe these guiding principles can also help to convince the citizens about Europe, if we make it clear that we are acting together in the world on the basis of our values. Europe does not mean "anything goes". Europe is an obligation to help ensure that our Earth remains a habitable planet, that fewer and fewer people are forced to leave their homes because of war or violence, that diseases such as Aids, malaria and tuberculosis can be fought successfully." Speech by Federal Chancellor Angela Merkel to the European Parliament, 27/6/2007, available at http://www.eu2007.de/en/News/Speeches_Interviews/Juni/0628BKinEP.html. "When we look at the Berlin Declaration, we see that highlighting our common values forms an important part. It also very ambitiously states that we have an ideal of European society and that we will work together to preserve this ideal. This ideal of European society consists of a canon of values close to our hearts: freedom, solidarity, equity." Speech by Federal Chancellor Angela Merkel to the European Parliament, 28.03.2007, available at http://www.eu2007.de/en/News/Speeches_Interviews/March/0328BK.html. Ireland: "Through our European neighbourhood initiative, we will enhance relations with those countries to the east and south on the basis of the values of democracy, respect for human rights and the rule of law." Speech by Prime Minister of Ireland Bertie Ahern to the European Parliament, 14.1.2004, available at http://www.europarl.europa.eu/sides/getDoc.do?pubRef=-//EP//TEXT+CRE+20040114+ITEM-001+DOC+XML+V0//EN&language=EN&query=INTERV&detail=3-005. Italy: "(…) establishing conditions for international security is now a key task for the countries which share a set of universal values based on freedom, democracy and peace." Speech by Prime Minister of Italy Silvio Berlusconi to the European Parliament, 2.7.2003., available at http://www.europarl.europa.eu/sides/getDoc.do?pubRef=//EP//TEXT+CRE+20030702+ITEM 001+DOC+XML+V0//EN&language=EN&query=INTERV&detail=3-005.
Netherlands: "Europe is a respected world player, and an example to the world. What makes it that is our unique form of cooperation, our focus on solidarity, and our capacity for commitment, united by values and dialogue rather than by battle." Speech by Prime Minister of the Netherlands Jan Peter Balkenende to the European Parliament, 23.5.2007, available at http://www.europarl.europa.eu/sides/getDoc.do?pubRef=//EP//TEXT+CRE+20070523+ITEM-009+DOC+XML+V0//EN&language=EN&query=INTERV&detail=3-241. Poland: "Freedom and democracy know no borders. A united Europe is not just about a common market, funds and subsidies. It is a community of values. A society cannot be about just a bit of freedom, a bit of democracy and a few rights. A Europe without the Berlin Wall cannot be a Europe with just a bit of freedom, a bit of cooperation and a bit of solidarity." Address by Mr Aleksander Kwasniewski, President of the Republic of Poland, to the European Parliament, 14.5.2003, available at http://www.europarl.europa.eu/sides/getDoc.do?pu bRef=-//EP//TEXT+CRE+20030514+ITEM-016+DOC+XML+V0//EN&language=EN&query=INTERV&detail=3-237, Portugal: "(…) On taking the presi-dency of the

The substantive discourse of values in European Union discourse typically involves two trilogies.

The first trilogy was a direct manifestation of the European circumstances *circa* 1951. For the generation which experienced the horrors of war, the depredations of want (triple digit inflation, lifetime savings wiped out, hunger) and witnessed the murderous—genocidal—excesses of nationalism, Peace-Prosperity- and, for want of a better word, Supranation-

---

Union's Council of Ministers for the third time, I want to reassert before you all the Portuguese government's determination and commitment to defend and further the values of peace, freedom, solidarity and prosperity that inspired the founding fathers in 1957. The now twenty seven member states, with almost 500 million citizens, all reaffirmed these values together in Berlin last March." Presentation of the Programme of the Portuguese Presidency, Speech by Prime Minister José Sócrates to the European Parliament, 11.7.2007, available at http://www.ue2007.pt/NR/rdonlyres/ 4DBF3C34-31C4-483F-8CAC-6753B9EBFDB5/0/70712ENParlamentoEuropeufinal.pdf. Sweden: "(...) Firstly, foreign policy action is increasingly a matter of values, democracy and human rights. Secondly, foreign policy action is also increasingly linked to economic relations, not least trade. Thirdly, foreign policy action is increasingly tied—and where we are concerned will continue to be tied—to a progressive and just development assistance policy. This last aspect is a point to which we devote too little time and attention. It is an underestimated factor in foreign relations. These three factors in combination indicate that developments are going the EU's way. Given this situation, if we are able to act on the basis of our values we will also be in a position to make an impact." Speech by Prime Minister of Sweden Göran Persson to the European Parliament, 3.7.2001, available at http://eu2001.se/eu2001/news/news_read.asp?iInformationID=16429. United Kingdom: "This week's European Council in Brussels takes place at the end of a tumultuous year for the European Union. It has been a year in which the voters of France and the Netherlands rejected the draft Constitutional Treaty; a year in which the need for Europe to face the realities of a globalised economy has become ever clearer; and most tragically, a year in which terrorism has once again struck in the streets and trains of a European capital. But Europe has responded. We have developed a clearer sense of our common response to globalisation. We have shown a sheer determination, which Mr Schulz has been generous enough to acknowledge in previous debates in this chamber, in the face of terrorism which has reaffirmed the strength of our solidarity, our democratic values and our common resolve to see those values triumph. We have asserted Europe's truly global role and responsibility, whether it is in New York, in Montreal last week, the Gaza Strip, or in Aceh, Indonesia." Speech by Douglas Alexander, UK Minister of State for Europe, to the European Parliament, 14.12.2005, available at http://www.eu2005.gov.uk/servlet/Front?pagename=OpenMarket/Xcelerate/ShowPage&c=Page&cid=1115146994906&a=KArticle&aid=1134649715170&date=2005-12-14.

alism (as a proxy for those arrangements designed to combat the excesses of the nation-state) expressed their noble vision, their 'holy trinity,' for the project.

That generation is disappearing. The majority of Europe's populations, including the present *classe politique*, have grown up in a Europe which is radically different from that of their parents. Maybe an apt appellation for this generation would be the Schengen generation—for whom traveling from Strasbourg to Karlsruhe or from Paris to Brussels is no different than traveling from Mannheim to Karlsruhe or from Paris to Lille. Already 20 years ago or so, there was something comic, endearing and uplifting to see the aging Helmut Kohl and Francois Mitterrand campaigning for the Maastricht Treaty and speaking about the historic reconciliation between France and Germany to an audience which, to put it bluntly, simply did not understand, experientially, what they were talking about. On all three counts, peace, prosperity and supranationality, Europe has been remarkably successful, the present crisis notwithstanding, in realizing what, a mere sixty years ago, seemed a dream.

Peace, prosperity, supranationalism have become, to the Schengen generation, part of a European *acquis*. They have lost their mobilizing force.

And yet values, as a political artifact, have remained central to the European construct. They are at the core—as a means of constructing community—an indispensable foundational block of democracy. Europe continues to shy away from an earlier generation's self-understanding of communal bonds rooted in organic, territorial communities—let alone ethnic. In Germany, for example, that has the odor of blood and soil. The word patriotism, *simpliciter*, is still largely banished from our vocabulary unless qualified as 'Constitutional Patriotism,' the only Kosher variant. Values, thus, are not a side game. They go to the core of Europe's self-understanding, its self-understanding as a Community of Values.

The second trilogy of values which is habitually trotted out and which has gradually come to dominate political rhetoric is the new trinity of Democracy, Human Rights and Rule of Law with a nod to solidarity (once a code for the European Welfare State—Ah, what happened to that) and environmentalism.[11]

The content and sequence of the two trilogies of values is revealing. Even a moment of reflection should provoke surprise that democracy and human rights become part of European value speak only in the second trilogy. The first trilogy emerged at the moment of founding when self-doubt and moral soul searching (provoked by the enormities of WWII) were at their most acute. On the one hand it led to a remarkably audacious construct of inter-nation and inter-state relations encapsulated by the word supranationalism and by the innovative Institutions of the new European Community, notably the High Authority—the antecedent of the present day Commission. But no less remarkable in both the vision and institutional set up was a seeming indifference and lack of concern for democracy and human rights—two words and concepts conspicuous in their absence. It may appear surprising given that at the Member State level this was the moment in which constitutional democracy was entrenched and protection of fundamental human rights, even at the transnational level, was dramatically articulated. The traditional explanation, which I myself offered in earlier work,[12] tried to explain this paradox on functionalist grounds, namely that in its early phases the European Community was not perceived as capable of threatening democracy or violating human rights. This may be part of the explanation. But another part may be rooted in a deep distrust of popular democracy and popular politics—national socialism and fascism emerged, after all, democratically and were wildly popular in their home societies and embarrassingly admired elsewhere. Further, the overwhelming existential social craving emanated from a profound and deep fatigue with war which had engulfed Europe of the mid 20th Century in every single generation in the previous two hundred years and from an all too natural yearning for economic stability and security—it is, thus, not at all surprising that Peace and Prosperity featured prominently in contemporary value speak and it is equally not altogether surprising that the discourse of values was primarily an ends

11 I privilege the first three and the Trinity allusion is deliberate. They are, I would contend, to be understood as interdependent—democracy having no validity without human rights and the Rule of Law etc.

12 Weiler, "Eurocracy and Distrust: Some Questions Concerning the Role of the European Court of Justice in the Protection of Fundamental Human Rights within the Legal Order of the European Communities".

related discourse rather than a means related one. It is equally not altogether surprising that in setting up the means for ensuring peace and security, the supranational community, legitimacy was to be gained by result rather than by process.

If there is any merit at all in this historiography it leads at a deeper level still to a further surprising conclusion. The European construct is usually thought of as representing the clearest break from its recent past, an antidote to the worldviews which preceded it, rooted in excessive nationalism, intolerance towards the other and violent statecraft. And, of course, in many ways it is just that. But paradoxically, the deep structure of the value speak of the new construct, of the European Community, represents also continuity. As noted, its legitimacy is rooted in results, in ends (what it promises and what it will achieve) rather than in process, in means (how things are to be achieved).

The community it creates is a classic community of destiny and in the early years—the years of the Coal and Steel Community before the establishment of the Common Market—hugely *dirigiste*, very much predicated on the 'leader' principle. The content—pacific and civilian—is of course a radical break with its predecessors. But the underlying political structure represents a surprising degree of continuity. The advent of the European Economic Community and the Common Market—the core of the European construct—till this day represents a major displacement by (German inspired) ordo-liberalism of (French inspired) *Dirigisme.*[13] The liberal market becomes thus legally entrenched in the constituent Treaties. But this is precisely the point, since this may be thought of as illiberal liberalism. The difference in specificity between the American Commerce Clause and the European Market provisions is very sizable.[14] What in most Western polities is left to the messiness of democratic politics and voter preferences becomes, here, the content of the Rule of Law. When, the

---

13 Gerber, Law and Competition in Twentieth-Century Europe: Protecting Prometheus, ch. 7; Gerber, "Constitutionalizing the Economy: German Neo-Liberalism, Competition Law and the 'New' Europe"; Gerber, "Competition Law and International Trade: The European Union and the Neo-Liberal Factor"; Maier, "The Politics of Productivity: Foundations of American International Economic Policy after World War II"; Moravcsik, The Choice for Europe: Social Purpose and State Power from Messina to Maastricht.

14 Kommers/Waelbroeck, "Legal Integration and the Free Movement of Goods: The American and European Experience".

Treaties become 'constitutionalized' in the hands of the European judicature (in an interesting coalition of the European Court of Justice and national judges[15]) these socio-political market choices become the content of the Rule of Constitutional Law.

This historiography is, I believe, of more than historical interest. It helps explain deep-seated habits and practices which characterize the European Union till this day.

First, and most profoundly, it helps explain why 'Europe' is till this day perceived as a 'project' of things to be done and achieved, and hence understandably contested politically and socially, as any project may be, rather than a 'way of doing things,' embedded in the European democratic institutional matrix and thus, like democracy itself, largely outside politics except at the margins of this or that rule. Europe is part of the 'primary rules' of the European polity rather than part of its secondary rules. Let me illustrate: To contest one of the market disciplines—say liberalization of services or the weight one should give to the principle of competition—is not just that, i.e. part of a banal debate between right and left on some market discipline, but is to contest Europe itself.

Second, it helps explain why the grafting in the second cycle, of values such as Democracy (and human rights) has been so difficult. Part of the reason is, of course, structural. The Union, as a system of governance without government, and as a political polity without a demos as understood in its Member States, does not and cannot adapt easily to the artifacts of democracy which are predicated on, and designed for, State, demos and government. But another part of the reason is to realize that the second generation of values do not simply complement the first as one would assume, but in some way stand in tension with them. Democracy in some way threatens the Commission and its unique position. I am not suggesting, of course, that the Commission is some kind of nefarious antidemocratic cabal. The tension and threat is structural and is manifest in at least two interrelated ways. First, democracy comes with politics. Democracy means politics. A political deficit means a democracy deficit and vice versa. And, yet, the uniqueness of the Commission, a major source of its authority, is the fact that it is meant to be, and to be seen to be, above (partisan) politics. Its power and legitimacy are rooted in its expertise, in its

15 Alter, Establishing the Supremacy of European Law: The Making of an International Rule of Law in Europe.

competence, and in its ability to realize the integration project and accomplish its socio-political objectives. It is 'political' body which, however, is meant to be above politics. This classical role sits perfectly well within the first cycle of values as articulated above, but far less well within the second cycle. Second, democracy cannot but affect the much hallowed 'Institutional Balance.' Only the wishful thinkers or feeble minded could imagine that one could, for example, have meaningful democratic empowerment of the European Parliament (through direct elections and close equation of its legislative function and power to that of the Council) and meaningful political empowerment of the Council (through majority voting in the Council of Ministers and institutionalization of the European Council) without irreversibly affecting the institutional balance to the detriment of the Commission. Direct democratic legitimation pushes the Commission willy-nilly in the direction of a Secretariat rather than an independent political actor. More than ever the legitimacy of the Commission in its historical role will depend on results, rather than on the process underscoring the deep tension reflected in the two trilogies of values, the Commission being an organic creature of the first but structurally at odds with the second.

Protection of fundamental human rights has been, and remains, a discourse high on rhetoric and far less impressive in realization. Its conspicuous absence from the Union constituent documents in its first three decades and the torturous road to, say, the Charter, cannot be explained simply by the thesis that it was not felt to be needed. A competing explanation might well be a deep seated fear of human rights at the Union level—both because of their *etatique* patina, but also because of, for want of a more delicate way to put it, their nuisance potential for the European agenda. Even as regards the Court, which introduced judicial protection of human rights in the late sixties and early seventies, there is a well founded suspicion that at least part of its motivation was to consolidate its supremacy project rather than a concern for the individual.

Be all this as it may, the centrality of value speak as part of general European Union discourse has not abated. Riding on the success of the process, the value discourse has often evolved into an important identity marker (even if at times containing an element of smug self-satisfaction).[16]

16 Von Bogdandy, "The European Constitution and European Identity: Text and Subtext of the Treaty Establishing a Constitution for Europe".

It is most noticeable in the self-distancing from the US with, for example, its enthrallment with the death penalty or its deficient health system. 'Third Way', Civilian Power, Global Warming, these are some of the key words in that comfortable self-understanding affirming a form of European exceptionalism.[17]

III.

I want to introduce law now. European Union law has had, too, a remarkably express and explicit value discourse—which in its content is, I would suggest, a synthesis of the two value trilogies. In three successive legal waves European Union law transformed classical international law:

---

17 Nowhere does this self-satisfaction—with one's self and with the instrumentality of the Union find better expression than in the original Preamble to Europe's defunct Constitution as produced by the Convention. From the unintended ironical reference to Thucydides (quoting that 'democrat' Pericles for whom, if only the drafters of the preamble had actually taken the trouble to read the original and not lift something out of a dictionary of quotations, Thucydides had contempt)

Our Constitution ... is called a democracy because power is in the hands not of a minority but of the greatest number.

to a text which in the eyes of some outshines even characteristic American bombast in its triumphalist self-congratulation and self-serving evasions. Consider the following selection:

Conscious that Europe is a continent that has brought forth civilisation; that its inhabitants, arriving in successive waves from earliest times, have gradually developed the values underlying humanism: equality of persons, freedom, respect for reason...Drawing inspiration from the cultural, religious and humanist inheritance of Europe, the values of which, still present in its heritage, have embedded within the life of society the central role of the human person and his or her inviolable and inalienable rights, and respect for law...Believing that reunited Europe intends to continue along the path of civilisation, progress and prosperity, for the good of all its inhabitants, including the weakest and most deprived; that it wishes to remain a continent open to culture, learning and social progress; and that it wishes to deepen the democratic and transparent nature of its public life, and to strive for peace, justice and solidarity throughout the world,...Convinced that, thus "united in its diversity", Europe offers them the best chance of pursuing, with due regard for the rights of each individual and in awareness of their responsibilities towards future generations and the Earth, the great venture which makes of it a special area of human hope.

In Wave 1 State obligations were converted into enforceable individual Community Rights—turning, in the language of the European Court of Justice, the individual from Object to Subject.[18]

In Wave 2 Human Rights opposable against the Community and Union Institutions (and in some cases against the Member States directly) were articulated *ex nihili* injecting a human centered core into the market instrumentalities.[19]

In Wave 3, through which we are living now, Citizen rights are being fleshed out, destined in the rhetoric of the European Court to constitute the fundamental status of Individuals in the Union.[20]

The common thread of all three waves is the Individual. In Union law it is claimed with considerable justification, even at the core of market law, stands the individual—as nowhere else in a non-domestic legal regimes.

Both in the rhetoric of the European Court of Justice itself and in endless commentary, legal Europe is celebrated as a polity in which the *individual* is in the Center—a very efficient way of summarizing the two trilogies of values the underlying ethos of which is, indeed, a deep humanist commitment.

Beyond History and Historiography: Values and Virtues—the Conceptual Apparatus

IV.

I now will introduce the central conceptual and theoretical foundation of my thesis in this essay. It is simple enough and rests on the resurrection of the concept of virtue—as distinct from values—which was central until not long ago to the moral discourse of Western Civilization in both its

18 Case C-26/62 Van Gend and Loos [1963] ECR 1; Weiler, "Van Gend en Loos: The individual as subject and object and the dilemma of European legitimacy".

19 Case C-29/69 Stauder v City of Ulm [1969] ECR 419; Case C-11/70 Internationale Handelsgesellschaft [1970] ECR 1125; Case C-4/73 Nold [1974] ECR 491; Case C-44/79 Hauer v Land Rheinland-Pfalz [1979] ECR 3727.

20 Case C-184/99 Grzelczyk [2001] ECR I-6193; Case C-413/99 Baumbast [2002] ECR I-7091; Case C-148/02 Garcia Avello [2003] ECR I-11613; Case C-147/03 Commission v Austria [2005] ECR I-5969.

secular and religious facets—Athens and Rome—a perfect illustration of which may be found in, for example, Aristotle, Maimonides and Aquinas, and more recently in MacIntyre.[21]

Values and virtues have a complicated relationship. The two do not necessarily correspond. A value is a moral or ethical proposition: An abstraction, an ideal which we may believe in. Virtues relate to personal traits, an 'operative habit' in the language of Aquinas. A 'disposition to act' in the language of Aristotle.

Do you believe in honesty—we may ask? Sure—would be our response—honesty is part of our matrix of societal values. Are you honest? That may be a very different question. Evidently, we do not, often enough, possess the necessary virtues which would enable us to honor our values. This, somewhat simplistically, illustrates the distinction between the two concepts.[22]

But there is, too, an inevitable nexus. If there is too big a distance between the discourse of professed collective values, and the practices of individuals, the values encapsulated in those collective mores become compromised, even a sham. (Note, I am not talking of hypocrisy i.e. someone who pretends to accept certain values whilst not believing in them in his or her heart. A true patriot, might simply not have the virtue of courage necessary to defend the patria. But his love of country should not be put into doubt. He may be a coward but not necessarily a hypocrite.)

In contemporary moral discourse to a considerable extent and in political theory of polities almost entirely, the notion of virtue, has largely

21 Aristotle, The Nicomachean Ethics; Aquinas, Summa Theologica, Vol. 2, Part II, 1st Section; Maimonides, "Eight Chapters"; MacIntyre, After Virtue: A Study in Moral Theory.

22 Here, I have to bracket the general discussion on the distinction between values and virtues. While there is much disagreement on what exactly values and virtues denote, I believe that the distinction I am making is an important one regardless of the terms used, and even if it does not correspond to some inherited understandings of values and virtues that one can find in the literature. I shall thus continue using terms values and virtues in the sense I already explained. For a general discussion on the concept of virtue and its relationship with values, see Chappell, Values and Virtues: Aristotelianism in Contemporary Ethics, and Hurka, Virtue, Vice, and Value. On virtue ethics as an alternative or an addition to more usual ethical traditions see: Foot, Virtues and Vices; Hursthouse, On Virtue Ethics; McDowell, "Virtue and Reason"; Slote, Morals from Motives.

vanished. There can be many reasons for this.[23] One reason is that involves a certain type of judgmentalism which is far more invasive and far more discomfiting to ourselves. To profess values requires much less than to practice them. The other reason is the loss of naiveté about moral objecttivity: Aristotle's virtue ethics was firmly grounded in his account of *eudaimonia*, and involved teleological speculations about human nature that we—children of Modernity—may find hard to digest.[24] But as we renounced the view that our life goals can float free from the cultural context, we also repudiated virtues; this, of course, was a mistake, not only because virtue ethics does not commit us to robust moral objectivity (at least not more than any other ethical tradition),[25] but also because—as we focus solely on values—we deprive ourselves of the opportunity to understand our ethical experience in its full complexity.

In this essay, a central part of my thesis will be the argument that upholding or believing in a value, has replaced virtue or rather has become the virtue. Put differently that believing, say, in the importance of honesty as a value, counts as practicing the virtue of being honest. In bringing the distinction of values and virtues to European Integration I follow Aristotle, Maimonides and Aquinas in two respects, but not in a third.

First, all three explain what may seem as obvious that virtue is a personal characteristic, a habit, a disposition. It is not purely or merely cognitive. That proposition is indispensable to my thesis.

Second, it is a habit or disposition that is acquired, perfected through practice, impacted by what today we would call the environment, reflective (and constitutive) of the prevailing political culture. That proposition, too, is indispensable to my thesis.

---

23 The often-repeated explanation, which draws on G.E.M. Anscombe's diagnosis of the state of moral philosophy, credits Judeo-Christian ethics for the expulsion of virtues from our moral vocabulary. I have serious reservations about this view, because it does not sit well with the work of Maimonides and Aquinas, who put virtues at the very center of their ethical universe. See Anscombe, "Modern Moral Philosophy".

24 Williams, Ethics and the Limits of Philosophy, ch. 3.

25 Solomon, "Internal Objections to Virtue Ethics". There are a number of ways in which virtue ethicists answer this objection, but they all reject the view that the foundation of moral objectivity, if there is one, can be found outside of our ethical beliefs. For a variety of responses, see: Swanton, Virtue Ethics: A Pluralistic View; Foot, Natural Goodness, ch. 6; MacIntyre, After Virtue: A Study in Moral Theory.

Law is part of the environment and culture which shape and impact the virtues of those operating within its sphere. Aquinas is particularly explicit on that: "Virtue, which is an operative habit, is a good habit productive of good works."[26] Aquinas considers whether the goodness of men and women is an effect of law. His position is that the goodness or virtue of citizens is an effect of good laws. "Law is given for the purpose of directing human acts, and insofar as human acts conduce to virtue, to that extent does law make man good."[27] The law is there not simply to ensure certain outcomes but to affect our virtuous dispositions.

This goes to the core of my intellectual endeavor in this essay. What impact does the political culture of the Union, expressed and shaped through its structures and processes and, notably, through its legal structures and processes, have on the virtues of its citizens and residents? It is an obvious and urgent question and yet one that, to my knowledge, has never been asked before in our reflection on the European integration.

However, in one crucial respect my project is infinitely less ambitious than that of Aristotle and Aquinas: As part of the search for what Aristotle calls 'happiness'—living well (not in the material sense which these words are used today) both were seeking '*The* Virtues'—general, essential, universal. My objective is in one sense far more modest (and doable…!)—I am concerned with a more limited set of virtues, those which are important for the vindication of the values of European Integration. If, say, citizens do not have certain civic virtues—for example caring enough to go and vote, to stand for election, democracy will fail. It will remain a formal and empty structure. Belief alone in the value of democracy is not enough. It has to be practiced. And that practice requires certain personal habits, dispositions, characteristics—certain virtues.

In another sense my approach is far more ambitious: To put it bluntly, I think the ancients and medievals were simply wrong: For they collapsed into their notion of virtue implicit values. They, too, failed to distinguish between virtues and values. The virtues of Aquinas and Maimonides were predicated on Christian and Jewish ideals. To be a good Christian, to be a good Jew, you needed certain virtues (of strength of character, integrity, and above all the willingness to make sacrifices for your beliefs —all virtues which they borrowed from Aristotle (and Plato)). The turn away

26 Aquinas, Summa Theologica, Vol. 2, Part II, 1st Section, Question 55, Article 4, 821.

27 Aquinas, Summa Theologica, Vol. 2, Part II, 1st Section, Question 92, Article 1, 1001.

from virtue theory was in part because what was presented as a general universal virtues simply masked their embedded religions in the case of Aquinas and Maimonides, and in the case of Aristotle the danger was even worse—his virtues (honor, strength, above all the willing to sacrifice) could serve any set of values. Aristotelian virtue theory allow us to say 'He was a virtuous Nazi: true and loyal to his (abhorrent) values and willing to sacrifice for them.'

I believe that a resurrection of virtue theory requires an understanding that virtues cannot stand alone from values and that values cannot stand alone from virtues—but nonetheless, the two are distinct. To make a comprehensive moral evaluation requires an enquiry into both values and virtues.

A clarification is needed also in relation to our use of the concept of 'Value' or 'Ideal'. A simple desirable state of affairs—an idyllic state: 'If I were a rich man'—does not in and of itself qualify as a value in the sense we are discussing here. I am interested in values as ideals. What prevents us from making all our fantasies of desired—idyllic—states values, is that so often they are selfish, self-serving. We perceive these desiderata, in fact, as an expression of desire, greed, jealousy, of our Hobbesian side. Value discourse involves not simply putting forward a desired state of affairs—material or spiritual—but a recognition of our selfish tendencies. Values will oft represent a challenge to the ego, a call to our better half. And the virtues necessary to vindicate them share in that same sense—they typically require us to overcome selfishness, personal comfort and personal interest. Values, as discussed here, and this is a central part of their allure, contain an altruistic component. Virtues involve exertion. Things that demand sacrifice are cherished more than things that come easily. Sacrifice in and of itself does not invest things with value but it does seem to be a regular cohabitor of virtue.

VI.

I may now outline my thesis. I do not contest the values of European Integration as such—with all the difficulties outlined in the historiographical section, they are noble. I do not even contest their *bona fides*. Instead, my claim is that the habits and practices of European integration, and some of its foundational legal structures and processes, militate against those very values.

They do this in one of two ways and sometimes in both. First they corrupt the meaning of the value itself. Second, these habits and practices play a role in cultivating personal dispositions inimical to those values; they contribute to the erosion of the virtues necessary for the vindication of the values of European Integration.

The focus on Law gave us a unifying, synthetic concept for the value discourse of European integration: The individual at the center! The habits and practices of European integration generally and European legal structure and process more specifically are, according to my thesis, instrumental in cultivating self-centered individuals. The 'Self-Centered Individual' stands in this contention in defiant contrast with Europe's deepest spiritual meta-objectives of redefining human relations of creating community—'*Nous Unisson des Hommes.*' When values are compromised, these practices and habits have the effect of displacing and at times even eradicating the sense of personal and collective responsibility for these undesirable states of affairs. Both passive responsibility for the state of affairs and active responsibility to correct it are typically shifted. Thus not only are the virtues compromised, but their realization is masked since if responsibility for compromised values (e.g. violation of human rights) is never mine, how will I ever realize that I lack the virtues necessary to vindicate the values I hold dear?

The manner in which this corrupting effect takes place should also be outlined. It is often the case that practice can shape or reshape the concrete meaning an abstract value may have or affect what we may consider virtuous or non-virtuous behavior. It often relates to the distinc-tion between a cognitive and experiential epistemology: The different type of knowledge I may have by, say, reading about friendship and actually having a friend.

Let me illustrate this by an example: We may present, say, the ideal of marriage. Imagine, then, a social situation in which domestic violence is accepted and normalized. For those growing up in such a society, the very ideal of marriage may be defined, or redefined, to include domestic violence. The very value is thus corrupted. The political and social culture become modified.

In the alternative, if the articulation of the ideal of marriage posits harmony as one of its values, the normalization of the domestic violence will instill vices, corrupt the personal virtues such as a disposition to, say, respect and self-control, which are needed for such harmony. If the law, either in its structure or its process, excluded domestic violence from its criminal purview, the impact would be similar. The central socio-psychological instrument is, indeed, normalization of praxis. The effect of praxis can be direct or indirect. It may affect directly specific actors which are involved directly in the praxis. It will affect more slowly society as a whole to the extent that it becomes a part of public mores.

I will now try to illustrate my thesis—the corrupting tendency of European practices on both values and virtues which are central to the realization of the deepest objectives of European Integration.

The Praxis of Value and Virtue—Prosperity, Democracy et. al

VII.

It is, I believe, easy enough to illustrate this mechanism in relation to the value and ideal of prosperity and solidarity.

Prosperity was one of the grand ideals in the formative years of the Founding Fathers. It still remains a very important part of European value discourse. This is captured in, among other places, Article 2 of the original Treaty of Rome.

The Community shall have as its task ... to promote throughout the Community a harmonious development of economic activities, a continuous and balanced expansion, an increase in stability, an accelerated raising of the standard of living ...

The focus on prosperity at the inception of the Union should not come as a surprise. After all, the economic reconstruction of the devastated Continent was intimately connected with the notion of peace. Each was the means for the other. The collapse of European prosperity in the current circumstance is perceived as a failure of the very value of European integration.

At first blush it is hard to capture the altruistic, non-hedonistic dimension of the quest for prosperity. Are we not here in the presence of pure self-interest, something to be almost ashamed of —the very antithesis of altruism, challenge, sacrifice which are essential parts of idealistic narrative? Where is the value?

There was an idealistic dimension, nuanced to be sure, to the quest for prosperity which mediated its utilitarian aspects. Its virtue appears when set against a backdrop of destruction and poverty. In these conditions (individual and social) prosperity assumed an altogether different meaning: Dignity—both personal and collective. In an Enlightenment bound vision of the individual, poverty resonates with the embarrassment of dependence on others, with the humiliation bred by helplessness, with the degradation of lack of autonomy. There is, thus, nothing shameful in aspiring for prosperity when it comes to mean dignity.

More importantly, linking prosperity to a cooperative enterprise inevitably blunted the sharp edges of avidity. The Community in its reconstructive effort was about collective responsibility: It was a regime which attempted to constrain unchecked search for economic prosperity by one Member State at the expense of others. And the Member States share a basic commitment to solidarity with the weakest elements in society through the networks of the welfare state.

Put in this way—we also detect here the deeper roots of the Community notion of Prosperity as a basic ethical value; It links up with, and is evocative of, a different but no less central strand of European idealism since the mid 19th century: Be it Socialism, Fabianism, Communism, Welfare Statism, all sharing an underlying ethos of collective societal responsibility for the welfare of individuals and the community as a whole. It is not surprising, it is very typical of Europe at that time—that it could reach into its self-understanding with perfect equanimity both to its Christian and Enlightenment, even social heritage.

It is when we come to the means to achieve these objectives that the picture becomes complex. For let us look at the very structure of the Treaty, in a methodology which combines both positive law but also symbolic meaning. The organization of the market revolves around negative and positive integration. Let us look at each in turn.

At the core of the Union enterprise, its 'Pillar One,' its original EEC, is the Common Market Place—the Market.[28] The principal motor towards

28 Article 2 of the Treaty of Rome of 1957 determined the goals of the European Economic Community as follows: "The Community shall have as its task, by estab-lishing a common market and progressively approximating the economic policies of Member States, to promote throughout the Community a harmonious development of economic activities, a continuous and balanced expansion, an increase in stability, an accelerated raising of the standard of living and closer relations between the States belonging to it".

prosperity is based on ordo-liberalism of the Freiburg school.[29] Competition, level playing field and strict regime on State Aids are the superstructural mechanisms which Pillar One represents. And at the deeper human level, market models appeal to, are driven by the very notion of self-interest and competition, of winners and losers. Losers are necessary for this model. That is their premise. And they work. They do generate prosperity.

But note now the internal structure of Pillar one, represented for example in the most central provisions, of the Pre Lisbon Treaty, Articles 28–30. Article 28 is materially about Open Markets and spiritually about self-interest. About the efficient displacing the inefficient, thus resulting in higher productivity and wealth creation. It does not, however, represent a monolithical free market commitment. Article 30 represents the competing values—public morality, public order, ecological concerns, health and safety etc.

But several things are noticeable in this structure (which is replicated in relation to all factors of production, services, labor etc.).

a. Europe represents the Market. The Member States represent the competing values.
b. The norm, the "default" position, the legal "presumption" is Free Market. Competing values have to be defended, proven, justified.
c. We apply to this construct one of the great hermeneutic principles of Treaty interpretation in general and European Union interpretation more specifically: Derogations to a general norm must be interpreted strictly. Derogations to a Fundamental Freedom must be interpreted even more strictly. The fundamental freedom here is not freedom of expression, or of association etc. It is Market Freedoms: Free movement of the factors of production. The market we interpret expansively; the competing values, restrictively.

This is the dogma you will find in most expositions of positive Union law.

---

29 Cf. Eucken, Die Grundlagen der Nationalökonomie; Eucken, Grundsätze der Wirtschaftspolitik; Peacock/Willgrodt, Germany's Social Market Economy: Origins and Ecolution; Friedrich, "The Political Thought of Neo-Liberalism"; Böhm, Freiheit und Ordnung in der Marktwirtschaft; Grossekettler, "On Designing an Economic Order: The Contributions of the Freiburg School"; Kasper/Streit, Lessons from the Freiburg School: The Institutional Foundations of Freedom and Prosperity; Razeen, "Ordoliberalism and the Social Market: Classical Political Economy from Germany".

Vis-à-vis the external world, the matter is even more problematic. As Europe attained untold and unprecedented prosperity, we continue to utter the notion of solidarity. But do we live it globally at the level of the Union? Is it internalized—in our policies of agricultural trade? In the social attitudes and legal regimes vis-à-vis migrants from the new Member States? I spend a great part of my time researching, teaching and trying to understand frameworks such as the WTO and the discontents of Globalization. I have learned caution. Very often (not always to be sure) the 'value speak' against social dumping, about linking trade to labour conditions is a comfortable moral shield for the protection of the privileges of the already prosperous. Can we put our hand on our heart and claim that there are not strong shades of that in our internal European discourse about market, solidarity and the future of the welfare state?

If we turn now to positive integration, we must examine the Union's own legislative program to counterbalance the social and spiritual rigors of the market, and explore the notion of subsidiarity.[30] Subsidiarity is meant to determine when the Union should legislate or leave such action to the Member States or sub units within the Member States. Though borrowed from Catholic social doctrine, it really inverts the Catholic tradition.[31] We normally think of Subsidiarity as a principle which may limit the reach of the Union since it requires that the Union act only when its action can be shown to be more efficient than that of other levels of government. But note how implicitly it is always about finding the most apt level of *government.* It is reflective and constitutive of a pervasive dimension of our political culture—responsibility through Agency. Thus, even our social solidarity is almost entirely through agency—agency of the State, of the Union, of the Region, of the City, but always of some public authority.

30 See generally, Lenaerts/Ypersele, "Le principe de subsidiarité et son contexte: étude de l'article 3 B du Traité de l'Union Européenne"; Mattera, "Le principe de subsidiarité au service d'une Communauté á la dimension des problèmes de notre temps"; Strozzi, "Le principe de subsidiarité dans la perspective de l'intégration européenne. Une énigme et beaucoup d'attentes"; Cass, "The word that saves Maastricht? The Principle of Subsidiarity and the Division of Powers within the European Community"; Inman, "Subsidiarity and the European Union"; Peterson, "Subsidiarity: A Definition to Suit Any Vision?"; Constantinesco, "Les clauses de coopération renforcée, Le protocole sur l'application des principes de subsidiarité et de proportionalité"; Bribosia, "Subsidiarité et répartition des compétences entre la Communauté et ses États membres".

31 Barber, "The Limited Modesty of Subsidiarity".

Make no mistake, one would not wish to live in a society which did not provide a social safety net to the less fortunate. Those are important values. But they risk the impoverishment of private virtue. These are values which responsibilize others, and deresponsibilize the self. There is a telltale sign in the level of charitable giving and voluntary organization in Europe—which leaves food for thought.[32]

And thus, even at that core value of prosperity and solidarity we find the inadvertent and surprising tendency towards corruption of private virtue. Individual self-interest (Article 28) will produce the prosperity. Public Agency (Article 30) at national and infranational level will take care of the less fortunate. As we strive for prosperity, we forget about the virtues of compassion, generosity and responsibility.

VIII.

Democracy, too, may provide a similar illustration. Historically, Europe had been powerfully instrumental in democratizing trends in Greece, in Spain and Portugal and later in the new Member States. More generally, Europe has been hugely successful not simply in the attainment of many of its specific market goals but also in the continued effectiveness, despite many doomsayers, of its classical governance structures and processes. Even today, with twenty-eight Member States and without the necessary institutional changes Europe has not imploded, even if it is under stress.

Success is risky because of a simple fact—it has a powerful legitimating effect. The best way to legitimate a war is to win it. This has always been such in human affairs: Good outcomes legitimate, in the social empirical sense, questionable means.

What are the questionable means in this context? There is no subject which is more likely to bring a yawn to the face of academics and a groan to the faces of politicians than the democracy deficit of the European Union.[33] It is a matter which should be dealt with without shrill notes. But

32 According to the World Giving Index 2014, only one EU Member State—the United Kingdom—is among the top ten most charitable countries in the world. The report is available at https://www.cafonline.org/docs/default-source/about-us-publications/caf_wgi2014_report_1555awebfinal.pdf.

33 In this note I track some of the signal contributions chronologically from the seventies through the present. Sommer, "The Community is Working", 747; Weiler, "Eurocracy

it will not go away. How to describe and explain the structure and process of European governance is contentious.

In essence it is the inability of the Community and Union to develop structures and processes which adequately replicate at the Union level even the imperfect habits of governmental control, parliamentary accountability and administrative responsibility which are practiced with different modalities in the various Member States. Even the basic condition of Representative Democracy that at election time the citizens '...can throw the scoundrels out'—that is, replace the Government—does not operate in Europe. The form of European Governance is—and will remain for considerable time, perhaps forever—such that there is no 'Government' to throw out.

---

and Distrust: Some Questions Concerning the Role of the European Court of Justice in the Protection of Fundamental Human Rights within the Legal Order of the European Communities"; Laprat, "Réforme des Traités: le risque du double déficit démocratique. Les Parlements nationaux et l'élaboration de la norme communautaire"; Reich, "Qu'est-ce que … le déficit démocratique"; Scoffoni, "Les relations entre le Parlement européen et les parlements nationaux et le renforcement de la légitimité démocratique de la Communauté"; Boyce, "The Democratic Deficit of the European Community"; Featherstone, "Jean Monnet and the 'Democratic Deficit' in the European Community"; Piris, "Après Maastricht, les institutions communautaires sont-elles plus efficaces, plus démocratiques et plus transparentes?"; Neunreither, "The Democratic Deficit of the European Union: Towards Closer Cooperation between the European Parliament and the National Parliaments"; Obradovic, "Policy Legitimacy and the European Union"; Viciano Pastor, "El futuro de la Unión Europea ¿déficit democrático o déficit constitucional?"; Norris, "Representation and the Democratic Deficit"; Craig, "Democracy and Rulemaking within the EC: An Empirical and Normative Assessment"; Majone, "Europe's Democratic Deficit: The Question of Standards"; Matlary, "Democratic Legitimacy and the Role of the Commission"; Lindseth, "Democratic Legitimacy and the Administrative Character of Supranationalism: the Example of the European Community"; Quermonne, L'Union européenne en quête d'institutions légitimes et efficaces; Höreth, "No Way Out for the Beast? The Unsolved Legitimacy Problem of European Governance"; Moussis, "La Construction Européenne et le Citoyen: Déficit Démocratique ou Déficit d'Information?"; Decker, "Mehr Demokratie wagen: Die Europäische Union braucht einen institutionellen Sprung nach vorn"; Moravcsik, "Reassessing Legitimacy in the European Union"; Mény, "De la Démocratie en Europe: Old Concepts and New Challenges"; Majone, "Deficit democratico, istituzioni non-maggioritarie e il paradosso dell'integrazione europea", 3; Giuliani, "Il deficit democratico dell'Unione"; Petit, "Dispelling a Myth? The Fathers of Europe and the Construction of a Euro-Identity"; Kohler-Koch/Rittberger, Debating the Democratic Legitimacy of the European Union, 34.

Dismissing the Commission by Parliament (or approving the appointment of the Commission President) is not the equivalent of throwing the Government out.

Likewise, there is no civic act of the European citizen where he or she can influence directly the outcome of any policy choice facing the Community and Union as citizens can when choosing between parties which offer sharply distinct programmes.

Thus the two most primordial norms of democracy, the principle of accountability and the principle of representation are compromised in the actual practices of the Union.

Further, as more and more functions move to Brussels, the democratic balances within the Member States have been disrupted by a strengthening of the Ministerial and Executive branches of government. Certain groups are privileged and others underprivileged. The value of each individual in the political process has inevitably declined including the ability to play a meaningful civic role in European governance.

Added to that is the ever increasing remoteness, opaqueness, and inaccessibility of European governance. An apocryphal statement—usually attributed to Jacques Delors—predicted that by the end of the century, 80 percent of social regulation would issue from Brussels. Even if it turns out that it was only 50 percent, the drama lies in the fact that no accountable public authority has a handle on these regulatory processes. Not the European Parliament, not the Commission, not even the Governments. The press and other media, a vital Estate in our democracies, are equally hampered. Consider that it is even impossible to get from any of the Community Institutions an authoritative and mutually agreed statement of the mere number of committees which inhabit that world of Comitology.[34] A

34 The Select Committee on European Communities of the House of Lords in the third report of 2 February 1999 ('Delegation of Powers to the Commission: Reforming Comitology'), observed that 'The fact that these committees [that participate in the comitology procedure] exist is fairly well-known. But who sits on them, when they meet, how they work and what they decide is something of a mystery, except to insiders, assiduous Brussels watchers and a few academics and students', and that 'There is no definitive list of comitology committees, their functions, activities and membership.' The report is available at http://www.parliament.the-stationery-office.co.uk/pa/ld199899/ldselect/ldeucom/23/2302.htm. To counter these kinds of criticisms, the Commission has established the 'Comitology Register' which contains all the documents related to the work of the committees (available at http://ec.europa.eu/transparency/regcomitology/index.cfm?CLX=en).

complex network of middle level national administrators, Community administrators and an array of private bodies with unequal and unfair access to a process with huge social and economic consequences to everyday life—in matters of public safety, health, and all other dimensions of socio-economic regulation. And now one can add the institutions of Economic and Monetary Union and the constitutional framework within which they work which, while being very vigilant against all manners of financial, fiscal and monetary deficit, contribute appreciably to the existing political and democratic 'deficit' of the Union.[35]

Despite this litany of democratic woes, we must take note of the fact that the European construct, democratic deficit notwithstanding, has been approved *democratically* again and again. The Treaties have been subjected to the constitutional and democratic disciplines prescribed in each Member States with the ratification of the SEA, of Maastricht, of Amsterdam and of each Enlargement. I do not expect this to change. These regular ratifications—despite their 'fast track' take-it-or-leave-it nature—are an authentic expression of the Member States' democratic institutions and, in some countries, of the European electorate. They are a regular 'referendum' on the success of the European construct.

Here we are witness to that paradox of success. Let us not mince words: These successful 'referenda' which give a valid democratic patina to the European Union, represent, too, the corrupting effect of the European success on the civic virtues of the European peoples and on the very meaning of what it means to be a democracy. The fact that so regularly the European construct is approved without a serious challenge to its questionable democratic quotidian praxis represents the invasion of a market mentality into the sphere of politics whereby citizens becomes consumers of political outcomes rather than active participants in the political process. It represents the process whereby we come to cherish the closeted deliberations of civil servants because of the quality of their dialogue and the merit of their outcomes, but in which citizens or their representatives are at best partially informed consumers of such deliberative paradise.[36] In this respect Europe seems to produce a negative moral 'spillover' effect. Even in our Member States we are moving to result legitimacy rather than

35 Verdun, "The Institutional Design of EMU: A Democratic Deficit?"; Bellamy/Staiger, "The Eurozone Crisis and the Democratic Deficit".

36 Streeck, "Citizens as Customers: Considerations on the New Politics of Consumption".

process legitimacy—at best to a Schumpeterian style of elite democracy, or more ironically, to a Pericles type of Democracy which the Convention so extolled.

It would be, of course, absurd to hang all the ills of our polities at the door of the European Union. It is not only Europe that suffers from democratic deficiencies. The degradation of political culture is part of the story of democracy in many of the Member States. Its signs are obvious enough and we need list only a few. These include the prominence of image and electronic media in political discourse with the consequent blurring (or Blairing) of the lines between politics and entertainment as part of a culture of celebrityship. It includes the trumping of ideology by pragmatism and the ascendance of technocracy and technical competence as supreme criteria of legitimacy. All these things would be with us with or without the European Union. But Europe helps accentuate them, aggravate them and, most insidiously, render them normal and, thus, acceptable.

The external impact of the EC on the political culture of democracy mirrors its internal ethos. Legitimization though successful technocratic accomplishment rather than through the messy processes of democracy has become, too, a central feature of the internal Commission culture. On the one hand a central feature of the self-understanding of the Commission is the notion that it is an autonomous, policy-making political Institution and not simply the secretariat of, say, the Council.[37] This self-understanding compels the Commission to be acutely aware of the need to have political legitimacy—both internally to sustain institutional morale and cohesion and externally to sustain support, essential for its power given its lack of a popular political constituency. Legitimation through accomplishment, professionalism and results instead of through process becomes thus, the surrogate for democratic process and democratic legitimation.

Additionally, the Commission celeberates its 'non-ideological' identity. It was Renaud Dehousse who coined the term Political Deficit[38]—as inimical to political culture as Democracy Deficit. It is not simply the self-

37 See more on this issue in Kassim/Peterson/Bauer/Connolly/Dehousse/Hooghe/Thompson, The European Commission of the Twenty-First Century, and Hooghe, The European Commission and the Integration of Europe: Images of Governance.

38 Dehousse, "Constitutional reform in the European community: Are there alternatives to the Majoritarian avenue?".

delusion or deceit: How can anyone really be non-ideological?[39] One can only mask one's ideology. But "Politics without politics" (the essence of

39 In this footnote I have tried to assemble the most important literature that tracks the debate on the character of the Commission as technocratic v political. Wessels, "Reassessing the Legitimacy Debate: A Comment on Moravcsik". The technocracy argument is also taken up—though in a specific variation—by a school of thought that stresses the technical nature of the legal output. The EU is portrayed as 'Zweckverband' (an association for limited purposes) (Ipsen, Europäisches Gemein-schaftsrecht, 66–67), as a functional agency (Mitrany, A Working Peace System, 145), or as a purely regulatory state (Majone, Regulating Europe; Majone, "Europe's Democratic Deficit: The Question of Standards"). Such machinery does not need to pass the conventional litmus test of democratic standards, since its legitimacy rests on its contribution to problem-solving. The apolitical nature of the decisions to be taken by technocratic bodies simply does not demand traditional input procedures as applied in states. Fischer, "European Governance Still Technocratic? New Modes of Governance for Food Safety Regulation in the European Union", 3: "The democratic deficit of Commission decisions is not the only reason why the Commission is deemed to be a technocratic institution. Due to limited human and financial resources of the Commission and the mainly regulatory character of European policy-making, the Commission is heavily dependent on expert advice. Some scholars argue that the deliberative style of this technocratic system leads to efficient and effective decision-making in the European Union and will increase the output legitimation. Others point out that politicians merely pretend to solve purely technical problems, and that the European Commission in particular has an interest in presenting its policy proposals as depoliticised technical solutions. However, both agree that the European decision making is done by experts in a technocratic way." (citations omitted). Harcourt/Claudio, "Limits to EU technocratic regulation?", 107: "In public discussions on technocracy, the European Union (and particularly the European Commission) almost invariably takes the lead when notorious examples of technocracy are brought up. Nothing better illustrates the idea of a Moloch alienated from the ordinary citizen, yet endowed with extraordinary powers to change our daily lives, than the European Commission"; ibid, 110: "The point to stress is that the whole institutional set-up of the European Community was designed in order to support the growth of the European regulatory state. Copinage technocratique, regulatory policy, incrementalism, and de-politicised technocratic debate among experts (or epistemic communities, see Haas 1992) represent the genetic code of European institutions. H. Wallace (1996: 22) has even asserted that the debate on the role of epistemic communities 'in some senses is a reprise of the Monnet approach to European integration'. W. Wallace (1996: 442), consistent with this argument, points out that 'the institutions were designed to stress administration and regulation, to minimise the visibility of the political choices at stake, and to operate on the basis of a permissive popular consensus'." Citing: Haas, "Introduction: Epistemic Communities and International Policy Coordination"; Wallace, "Politics and Policy in the EU: The

Challenge of Governance"; Wallace, "Government Without Statehood: The Unstable Equilibrium". But see contra, 119: "If the EU is becoming a polity, political conflict cannot be avoided. Of course, experts, bureaucrats, pressure groups and highly technical policy issues are bound to remain central features of the EU policy process, but the smooth making of regulatory policies has been substituted by political conflict. […] The arguments raised in section three above suggest that technocracy can continue to operate in certain regulatory policies, but not in others. How can this trend toward politicisation be assessed, in conclusion? We argue that the trend illustrates a shift along the trade-off between efficiency and democracy. Technocratic regulation is undoubtedly more efficient: regulation is produced among experts in a highly consensual style. By contrast, regulating for media pluralism engenders contestation and even periods of policy stalemate, so much so that we are still waiting for a formal proposal of the Commission for a directive to be adopted by the Council. But what is lost in terms of efficiency is gained in terms of democratic policy-making. Nobody has ever argued that democracy is the most efficient device for producing public policy: indeed, the democratic choice is advocated for very different reasons (Dahl 1989). In this sense, inefficiency and prolonged conflict may be the price that the EU is forced to pay in its progress toward a more democratic polity." Citing: Dahl, Democracy and Its Critics. Bracq, "La Commission Européenne entre Fonctions d'Arbitrage et Rôle Politique"; Wonka, The European Commission: Technocratic Bureaucracy or Fully-Fledged EU Executive?; Bach, "Vom Zweckverband zum technokratischen Regime: Politische Legitimation und institutionelle Verselbständigung in der Europäischen Gemeinschaft"; Haas, "Technocracy, Pluralism and the New Europe"; Dubois/Dulong, "Introduction générale"; Radaelli, Technocracy in the European Union. Contra: Christiansen, "Tensions of European Governance: Politicized Bureaucracy and Multiple Accountability in the European Commission", 76: "It is a common reflex to view the Commission as a bureaucracy. In many ways, of course, the Commission does fulfil functions and appropriates roles comparable to bureaucracies in domestic systems. Regularly, the Commission acts as the extension of national bureaucracies. Indeed, the Commission has for many in Europe become synonymous with the very concept of 'bureaucracy'. But to treat the Commission as just another bureaucracy either disregards its exceptional circumstances or else implies a departure from established definitions of 'bureaucracy';" ibid, 77: "What detracts from the bureaucratic element in the Commission's activity—what makes the Commission 'less bureaucratic' than other bureaux—is the nature of continuous bargaining in the Union. The major fields of Commission activity—proposing legislation and supervising the implementation of decisions—are highly politicized tasks. In the EU systems, policies are not only subject to the extensive deliberations in the legislative phase, but are also bound to be renegotiated when it comes to their implementation in different national contexts. In this system the Commission is a 'politicized bureaucracy', faced with a dilemma between its duty to develop and apply common rules and continuous political pressure for deviation. This dilemma is with any bureaucracy, national or international. But the nature of much of the political deficit) has in and of itself a corrupting effect, since it takes the citizen who is reduced to a consumer of political results (rather than a meaningful participant in political process) and subtly encourages him or her to make choices based on non-ideological grounds i.e. often a proxy for material self-interest. The Council, too, inadvertently plays a powerful

---

the Commission's work—the overarching regulatory function it fulfils for the European Union, the large degree of symbolism that is often involved in EU decision-making, the continuing process of expansion of the EU's institutional framework, the ongoing process of 'constitutional reform'—has meant that numerous political forces take exceptional interest in the internal proceedings of the Commission." Quermonne, "La question du gouvernement européen", 23: "Mais en agrégeant, dans un souci de cohésion, la pluralité des intérêts nationaux afin de dégager un intérêt général européen, la Commission dite de Bruxelles a donné au processus de décision une plus-value que la négociation intergouvernementale à elle seule aurait été incapable d'apporter. D'ailleurs, il ne faut rien exagérer, l'apolitisme de la Commission a toujours été relatif. Car sa composition a mêlé, dès l'origine, des hommes politiques expérimentés (tel son premier président Walter Hallstein) à des personnalités choisies en raison de leur compétence, pour ne pas dire des 'technocrates'." (citations omitted); Majone, "Europe's Democratic Deficit: The Question of Standards", 23: "Also, the Commission's right of legislative initiative—which, as we saw in the first part of the paper, is regarded by many as the root cause of the democratic deficit—is best understood as a way of ensuring that EC policies are directed towards the advancement of the general interests of the Community (as defined by the Treaties) as opposed to national or sectoral self-interests. Like any bureaucracy, the Commission has interests of its own, and is not free from pressures from special interests when making decisions. It is, however, better placed than the other political institutions to take into account the general interests of the Community in its legislative proposals. The members of the Council are often swayed by short-term considerations relating to the needs of their own constituencies, while the European Parliament is not yet institutionally suited to develop a coherent legislative strategy to achieve the objectives laid down in the Treaties. On the other hand, the fundamental interests of the Commission are aligned with those of the Community as a whole. Indeed, the Commission has never subscribed to the view that there is no conception of the Community public interest which is independent of the competition between individual state preferences. On the contrary, it has always seen itself as the guardian of that interest. This commitment is credible not only because it is sustained by institutional self-interest, but also because the Treaties are considerably more explicit than national constitutional documents in identifying the public good: the four economic freedoms, a system of undistorted competition, prohibition of discrimination on the basis of nationality or gender and, since the Single European Act, the protection of non-commodity values like environmental quality." (emphasis added, footnotes omitted).

role in this. In their respective Member States, Presidents and Prime Ministers are, of course the embodiment of a political and ideological choice—socialist, Gaullist, Christian Democrat etc. But when they arrive in Brussels and are situated in the Union Institution such as the Council, an interesting political neutering takes place. First, from the perspective of their Member State, they are meant to represent the whole Nation, not the political preference of their party. And from a European perspective, by definition the Council is a non-ideological body, after all, its political /ideological color is totally haphazard, depending on the accident of national elections. It is distinctly not Bon Ton to play "party politics" (vis. Ideological and political preferences) in the European Council process.

We have thus a bi-directional or circular process whereby the degradation of politics in the Member States enables the Community to claim its legitimation on the basis of its achievement and receive its regular constitutional pound of flesh from the Member States after each IGC: a legitimization which in-turn contributes to that very degradation of what democracy is meant to be about. Needless to say, when 'output legitimacy' collapses—as it has in the recent circumstances—the result is not simply a collapse in European Union legitimacy, but a collapse of faith in democratic institutions and processes themselves.

One will also note that the tendency of Citizen-as-Consumer (of political outcomes), and a consumer who is subtly conditioned to make his choices not on the basis of principle, but self-interest, provides another building block to my parallel thesis about a legal system which places the individual in the center but renders him a self-centered individual—in strong tension with the spiritual ideal of human integration. European democratic deficit cannot be understood unless we also understand how civic virtues—character traits that are necessary for attaining and maintaining democratic values—gradually declined.

IX.

I turn now to peace. It is a delicate value. It can be noble, worthy, human. But like all values and ideals it is such when it requires courage and sacrifice. For Rabin and Arafat it was called, *a titre juste*, the Peace of the Brave.

Peace can also be the negation of values—a "leave me in peace", an "I don't care—so long as I am left in peace." The "Peace in our Time" of

Chamberlin, that piece of paper he came back with from Munich, appeasing the unappeasable, remains a badge of dishonor and illustrates well the Janus aspect of Peace as a value and a vice.

In the immediate wake of World War II, peace was the most explicit objective of the new construct, an objective for the attainment of which the would-be-polity was to be an instrument. This is a hard-nosed desideratum of all contemporary diplomacy to which the functionalist European methodology was to be employed to the full.

Nowhere is this captured better than in the oft repeated phraseology of the Schuman Declaration of May 9, 1950.

World peace cannot be safeguarded without the making of constructive efforts proportionate to the dangers which threaten it....

The gathering of the nations of Europe requires the elimination of the age-old opposition of France and the Federal Republic of Germany; The first concern in any action undertaken must be these two countries....

[This] solidarity ... will make it plain that any war between France and the Federal Republic of Germany becomes, not merely unthinkable, but materially impossible....

It is readily apparent that in the historical context in which the Schuman Plan was put forward the notion of peace—as articulated in the European construct—probed a far deeper stratum than simple cessation of hostilities, co-existence, the kind of stuff one saw at the end of World War I.

These were, after all, the early fifties with the horrors of War still fresh in the mind and, in particular, the memory of the unspeakable savagery of German occupation. It would take many years for the hatred in countries such as the Netherlands, Denmark or France to fully subside. The idea, then, in 1950, of a Community of Equals as providing the structural underpinning for long-term peace among yesteryears enemies, represented more than the wise counsel of experienced statesmen. It was also a call for forgiveness, a deep spiritual challenge to overcome an understandable hatred. In that particular historical context the Schumanian notion of Peace resonates with, and is evocative of, the distinct discourse, imagery and values of Christian Love, even of Grace—not, I think, a particularly astonishing evocation given the personal backgrounds of the Founding Fathers—Adenauer, De Gaspari, Schuman, Monnet himself.[40]

40 See the references in note 7.

That context, which allowed peace to touch the depths of human dignity, of humanity, no longer exists. The peace which Europe thankfully gained from that age old opposition of France and Germany, shows signs of ossifying, and imploding on itself, betraying the commitment to the very values of which that peace was meant to be foundation. Today we want peace in the Leave-me-in-peace mode. In some respects the very success of Europe has sapped our commitment to the values for which peace seemed so important.

Europe has eschewed the responsibility for peace. It hides behind slogans like 'Civilian Power'—a small fig leaf to cover up its concession that ultimately it will be the USA to whom it always has to turn. That fatal choice, made with the rejection of the European Defense Community in the mid fifties, was emblematic of a Europe, recoiling from the use of force, relying for decades on American guns to enable it to produce European butter and has conditioned a pervasive public ethos that nothing is so important that it is worth fighting for. A 'peace at all costs' mentality.

Bosnia (and Kosovo) are traumatic events about which Europe has developed almost instant amnesia. In the heart of Europe horrible persecution of a religious minority was taking place, leading eventually to genocidal acts.[41] Europe prevaricated, talked and talked, and eventually, far too late, when it decided to take action, it was clear that it did not have the means to assert its alleged values. Once again American forces from across the Atlantic had to be called in. It was a moment of shame.

Even at a micro level one cannot rid the mind of the images of those Dutch soldiers who stood by as some of the worst massacres took place. They were not fascists, they believed in human rights. Still, they did not

41 Prosecutor v. Radislav Krstic (ICTY, Trial Chamber I Judgment of 2 August 2001, IT-98–33), paras. 539–599, confirmed in Prosecutor v. Radislav Krstic (ICTY, Appeals Chamber Judgment of 9 April 2004, IT–98–33):

"598. The Chamber concludes that the intent to kill all the Bosnian Muslim men of military age in Srebrenica constitutes an intent to destroy in part the Bosnian Muslim group within the meaning of Article 4 and therefore must be qualified as a genocide.

599. The Trial Chamber has thus concluded that the Prosecution has proven beyond all reasonable doubt that genocide, crimes against humanity and violations of the laws or customs of war were perpetrated against the Bosnian Muslims, at Srebrenica, in July 1995."

move.[42] In some respects they too are emblematic of one thesis of this essay—the growing gap between social mores and personal virtue.

42 'Report of the Secretary General pursuant to General Assembly Resolution 53/35: The Fall of Srebrenica', United Nations doc. A/54/549, 15 November 1999:

"Para. 252: during the early afternoon, the Dutchbat Commander appears to have spoken to the UNPROFOR Chief of Staff in Sarajevo, again requesting close air support in response to the attack on OP Foxtrot. As before, the Chief of Staff discouraged the request, favouring instead the option to withdraw the personnel from that post. His immediate superiors at UNPF headquarters in Zagreb appear to have concurred with the decision. (…)

Para. 253: (…) Accordingly, the Company Commander, with the concurrence of the Dutchbat Commander, ordered the personnel in OP Foxtrot not to return fire but to withdraw instead.

Para. 304: (…) Srebrenica had fallen. Until that point, at least three (but possibly up to five) requests for air support by Dutchbat had been turned down at various levels in the chain of command. Dutchbat had also not fired a single shot directly at the advancing Serb forces. (emphasis added)

Para.312: Upon the Force Commander's request, the acting UNPROFOR Commander then issued instructions to Dutchbat, ordering them to enter into negotiations with the BSA to secure an immediate ceasefire. He added that 'giving up any weapons and military equipment [was] not authorized and [was] not a point of discussion'. He ordered Dutchbat to concentrate their forces in the Potocari compound and to withdraw from the remaining observation posts. He ordered them to 'take all reasonable measures to protect refugees and civilians in [their] care'. He added that they should 'continue with all possible means to defend [their] forces and installation from attack'. This was 'to include the use of close air support if necessary'. While noting the clarity of the instructions, the Dutchbat commanders assessed that they were simply no longer in a position to carry them out. (emphasis added)

Para. 315: Returning to the battalion compound at Potocari, the Dutchbat Commander sent a report to Zagreb, Sarajevo and Tuzia, as well as to the crisis staff in the Hague, describing the two meetings that he had had with Mladic. He concluded his report by stating 'there are now more than 15,000 people within one square kilometer, including the battalion, in an extremely vulnerable position: the sitting duck position, not able to defend these people at all'. (sic) He went on describe precisely the location of BSA artillery and tanks within direct sight of the compound. He ended his message with a plea:

'I am responsible for these people [yet] I am not able to: defend these people; defend my own battalion; (…)'

Para. 371: (…) However, the Dutchbat debriefing report reveals that two Dutchbat soldiers, on their way back from Nova Kasaba to Bratunac on 14 July, had seen between 500 and 700 corpses on the roadside. However, the same report indicated that two other members of Dutchbat traveling in the same vehicle saw only a few corpses. No written

The peace of Schuman was an act of strength, of self-control, of collective magnanimity of spirit. Bosnia was the degradation of all of that. Peace here, was about comfort, about turning, not the other cheek, but turning the eyes away form that which one did not want to face.

It was Samuel Johnson who famously suggested that patriotism was the last refuge of a scoundrel. Dr Johnson was, of course, only partly right. Patriotism can also be noble. But Europe's response or rather non response to Bosnia and Kosovo are a reminder that Constitutional Patriotism can provide equal refuge.

It is here that one may add a delicate note on Supranationalism. Nationalism and patriotism, as European history demonstrates, can be easily abused leading to unspeakable degradation of the human spirit. It is only right that the European construct sought to tame them. But part and parcel of the patriotic package was the spirit of public service, of commitment to the community, of loyalty to one's co-national even when he or she were not family or even tribe. Patriotism at its best is a discipline of love. It is, perhaps, an unintended victory of the fascist regimes. One has to wonder whether in relation to these altogether positive virtues, the European construct has not thrown out the baby with the bath water?

X.

As we turn to the rule of law—we shift our focus to the Court.

It is quite common when assessing the jurisprudence to cast the European Court, virtuously, in a dialectical relationship with (a typically stalling) political process. The following has been told in many, many variants over the years:[43]

In the face of political stagnation and stasis in the late sixties and a lack of 'political will' (favorite, meaningless phrase) the Court steps in and compensates by its remarkable constitutionalizing jurisprudence, virtually salvaging European integration.

record has been located indicating that Dutchbat made either account available to the UNPROFOR chain of command on 14 July, or in the days immediately thereafter. (…)." (emphasis added).

43 For an overview of this literature, see Craig, "Institutions, Power, and Institutional Balance".

In the face of a growing democratic legitimacy, the Court develops its human rights jurisprudence. Community (and Union) norms might suffer from democratic deficiencies, but at least they will be protected against violation of fundamental human rights.

In the face of the failure of the harmonization process in constructing the common market place, the Court steps in with its highly innovative doctrine of functional parallelism (Mutual Recognition) in Cassis providing a jurisprudential breakthrough to move ahead.

There is more than a grain of truth in all the variants, more and less sophisticated, of this narrative. But, grant me, they are also very self-serving and partial. In all of them, the political problem is extraneous to the Court, which, within the limits of its powers, steps in, Knight in Shining Armor, to correct that which politics and politicians are unable to do. According to this view—the Court cannot (and should not) solve all the problems but it is always cast as part of the solution rather than part of the problem. It is tempting, particularly in the present circumstance, to view the Court as such, after all, it was not the Court that advocated for the new formal constitution etc.

Be that as it may, I want to argue now that the Court is part of the problem. That the very jurisprudence, inescapably and inextricably, implicates the Court in the very issues of democratic and social legitimacy which are at least partially at the root of current discontent. I want to argue further that the Court has responsibilities all of its own which do not even fit under the rubric of "implicated".

But before I explain this thesis I want to state clearly what I am not arguing:

My critique is not part of 'the Court has no legitimacy,' *gouvernement des juges* and all that.[44] Nor is it an attack on the "activism" of the Court or its hermeneutics i.e. it is not part of more contemporary trends, notable in the USA, which have (re)discovered Bickel's silent virtues and normatively embrace restraint and a reduced role for courts and all that. I do not think Europe has a *gouvernement des juges* (whatever that means) nor do I find fundamental fault with the hermeneutics of its essential jurisprudence. Importantly, this critique does not have as its purpose to argue that the constitutional jurisprudence was a normative mistake, a road which should

44 Adams/de Waele/Meeusen/Straetmans, Judging Europe's Judges: The Legitimacy of the Case Law of the European Court of Justice; De Witte/Muir/Dawson, Judicial Activism at the European Court of Justice.

not have been taken. As a matter of its underlying values I believe it was not simply expedient but, in post WWII Europe, no less than noble. The critique is, thus, not methodological but substantive.

My approach rests on two propositions. First, it highlights a certain irony in the constitutional jurisprudence. As noted above it was often perceived (and there are indications in the cases that it was so perceived by the Court itself) as being a response to, and part of, a broader political discourse of integration, as a reaction to non-functioning dimensions of the political process. But there has been, both by the Court itself and its observers a myopic view which failed to explore deeper some of the consequences and ramifications of the constitutional jurisprudence. There has been a refusal to see the way in which the essential [legal order] constitutional jurisprudence is part and parcel of the political democratic legitimacy crisis; how the essential market integration case law is part of the social legitimacy crisis, how certain elements in the human rights jurisprudence mask and impede the most essential in the human rights agenda of the Union and, finally, how the brave new case law on citizenship feeds and aggravates some of the worst challenges facing Europe in the area of immigration. Very often one has the impression that though the political (in the sense of institutions) is well grasped in relation to the case law, the social (in the sense of human dimension and communities) has been far less understood.

How then is the Court implicated in the democratic deficit?

Our starting point can be, the fountainhead of this part of the constitutional jurisprudence, *Van Gend en Loos* itself. In arguing for the concept of a new legal order the Court reasoned in the following two famous passages as follows:

The conclusion to be drawn from this is that the Community constitutes a new legal order of international law for the benefit of which the states have limited their sovereign rights, albeit within limited fields, and the subjects of which comprise not only Member States but also their nationals. Independently of the legislation of Member States, Community law therefore not only imposes obligations on individuals but is also intended to confer upon them rights which become part of their legal heritage. These rights arise not only where they are expressly granted by the Treaty, but also by reason of obligations which the Treaty imposes in a clearly defined way upon individuals as well as upon the Member States and upon the institutions of the Community.

This view is confirmed by the preamble to the Treaty which refers not only to governments but to peoples. It is also confirmed more specifically by the establishment of institutions endowed with sovereign rights, the exercise of which affects Member States and also their citizens. Furthermore, it must be noted that the nationals of the states brought together in the Community are called upon to cooperate in the functioning of this Community through the intermediary of the European Parliament and the Economic and Social Committee.45 (Emphasis added)

The problem is that this 'cooperation' was extremely weak. This is, in truth, a serious 'dumbing down' of democracy and its meaning by the European Court. At the time, the European Parliament had the right to give its opinion—when asked, and it often was not asked. Even in areas where it was meant to be asked, it was well known that Commission and Council would tie up their bargains ahead of such advice which thus became *pro-forma.* But can that level of democratic representation and accountability, *seen through the lenses of normative political theory* truly justify the immense power of direct governance which the combined doctrines of direct effect and supremacy placed in the hands of the then Community institutions? Surely posing the question is to give the answer.

The implication of the Court of Justice in the democratic travails of the Union is easily stated even if usually uncomfortably discussed. The late Federico Mancini in his *Europe: The Case for Statehood*[46] forcefully articulated the democratic malaise of Europe. There were many, myself included, who shied away from Mancini's remedy, a European State and shied away from his contention that this remedy was the only one which was available. But few quibbled with his trenchant and often caustic denunciation of the democratic deficiencies of European governance.

But could the Court distance itself from this malaise so trenchantly and caustically denunciated?

It is precisely on these occasions, I argued[47], that I rejoice most that I am not a judge on the Court. What would I do if I felt, as Mancini did, that the European Community suffered from this deep democratic deficit which he described so unflinchingly and which according to him could only be cured by a European State? Would I want to give effect to a

45 Case C-26/62 Van Gend and Loos [1963] ECR 1.

46 Mancini, "Europe: The Case for Statehood".

47 Weiler, "Europe: The Case Against the Case for Statehood", 58–59.

principle which rendered the Community's undemocratic laws—adopted in his words by 'numberless, faceless and unaccountable committees of senior national experts'[48] and rubber-stamped by the Council—supreme over the very constitutional values of the Member States? If democracy is what one cared about most, could one unambiguously consider much of the Community edifice a major *advance?* Whatever the hermeneutic legiti-macy of reaching supremacy and direct effect, the interaction of these principles with the non-democratic decision making process was and is, highly problematic. Similar dilemmas would of course face national judges.

The paradox is thus that the legitimacy challenge to the Court's constitutional jurisprudence does not rest—as often has been assumed in its hermeneutics—on a thesis about a good outcome based on a questionable interpretation. But quite the opposite: An unassailable interpretation but an outcome which underpins, supports and legitimates a highly problematic decisional process. Substantively, then, the much vaunted Community rights which serve, almost invariably the economic interests of individuals were "bought" at least in some measure at the expense of democratic legitimation.

Procedurally we find a similar story. The secret of the Rule of Law in the legal order of the European Union is that genius process of Preliminary References and Preliminary Rulings. The Compliance Pull of law in liberal Western Democracies does not rest on the gun and coercion. It rests on a political culture which internalizes, especially public authorities, obedience to the law rather then to expediency. Not a perfect, but one good measure of the rule of law is the extent to which public authorities in a country obey the decisions, even uncomfortable, of their own courts.

It is by this very measure that international regimes are so often found wanting. Why we cannot quite in the same way speak about the Rule of International Law. All too frequently, when a State is faced with a discomfiting international norm or decision of an international tribunal, it finds ways to evade them.

Statistically, as we know, the Preliminary Reference in more than 80 percent of the cases, is a device for judicial review of Member State compliance with their obligations under the Treaties. It is ingenious for two

48 Mancini, "Europe: The Case for Statehood", 40; Mancini/Keeling, "Democracy and the European Court of Justice", 190 (also mentions 'faceless and unaccountable' committees of national experts).

reasons: First, it deploys individuals, vindicating their own rights as the monitors and enforcers of Community obligations vis-à-vis the Member States. It has been called the Private-Attorney-General Model. And second, it deploys national courts. The judgment is spoken through the mouths of Member State courts. The habit of obedience associated with national law is, thus, attached to European law. The gap between the rule of law and the rule of international law is narrowed, even closed.

However, it is precisely in this context that we can see the dark side of this moon. The situation implicated in Preliminary References always posits an individual vindicating a personal, private interest against the public good. That is why it works, that is part of its genius, but that is also why this wonderful value also constitutes another building block in that construct which places the individual in the center but turns him into a self-centered individual. Community rights, in some interesting way, become anti-community rights. If the social reality of the European construct were stronger, this could be seen as mitigating this effect. But the reality of the situation from a social perspective is that—for good legal reason—the principal artifact of the Rule of Law in the thin political space constituted by Union places the individual at odds with his or her thicker political space. This is how it should be legally. This is what creates the most effective compliance pull. But it has this collateral effect.

XI.

Protection of fundamental human rights has been a central feature of modern constitutions as well as much of the judicial review activity of supreme courts in Western Countries in the Post War era. Concepts such as individual dignity and privacy as well as more classical notions of liberty and equality before the law have been the standard repositories of constitutional interpretation by courts exercising judicial review of governmental legislation and administrative action. Both the concept and practice of judicial review have penetrated, albeit in a limited way, even legal cultures which for long have resisted, such as Britain and France. Indeed, judicial review in general and the protection of individual rights in particular are widely considered as a *conditio sine qua non* of constitutional democracy and the rule of law.

The Treaties establishing the European Community—the Constitution of the EC—neither contained a Bill of Rights nor, indeed, any reference at all to the need for, or the means of, protecting fundamental human rights against encroachment by Community and Union public authorities.

The absence of a reference to human rights in the Treaties was not unique. Many regulatory treaties do not contain human right protection clauses. Should a State in pursuance of its international treaty obligation seek to violate the rights of the individual, or should an international organization seek to do the same thing, the individual would, it could be thought, receive his or her protection from national courts applying national constitutions and from transnational bodies specifically set up for the protection of Human Rights. But the European Community developed in a way which rendered the absence of human right protection problematic. It was not after all a mere coordinatory treaty: It was a treaty of governance. Moreover, the European Court of Justice put in place starting in the early sixties a constitutional reading of the Founding Treaties which gave many of their provisions 'direct effect' meaning that they were to be considered part of the law of the land. What is more, these directly effective provisions were to be the 'supreme' law of the land—a higher law overriding conflicting national provisions. It became legally and politically imperative that a way be found to vindicate fundamental human rights at the Community level. How could one assert the direct effect and supremacy of European law—vesting huge constitutional power in the political organs of the Community—without postulating embedded legal and judicial guarantees on the exercise of such power? After all, the effect of direct effect and supremacy would be to efface the possibility of national legislative or judicial control of Community law. This imperative was all the more urgent given the notorious democratic deficiencies of European governance, in some respects more acute in the sixties than in the eighties and nineties. How could one expect the constitutional and other high courts of the Member States, especially of those Member States with national constitutional orders and judicial review such as, at the time, Germany and Italy, to accept the direct effect and supremacy of Community norms without an assurance that human rights would be protected within the Community legal order and, critically, that individuals would not lose any of the protections afforded under national constitutions? Protecting human rights became a joined legal and political imperative.

Among the human rights narratives in the European Union two themes seem to be of utmost importance. The first is structural, namely the ways in which the constitutional gap came to be fully or partially filled. The second relates more directly to the theme of this essay: The way in which the concept of human rights as a value enmeshes (or otherwise) with the specificity of European integration as distinct from normal constitutional orders.

The Standard Version of the Human Rights narrative reads something like this:[49] In the absence of a written Bill of Rights in the Treaties and an apparent freedom to the Community legislative and administrative branches to disregard individual rights in Community legislation and administrative action, the European Court of Justice, in an exercise of bold judicial interpretivism, and reversing an earlier case law, created an unwritten higher law of fundamental human rights, culled from the Constitutional traditions of the Member States and international agreements such as the European Convention on Human Rights, and against which legislative and administrative acts of the Community organs binding on or affecting individual citizens could be struck in the normal course of judicial review provided by the Treaty. In later years the Court extended the purview of this judicial power to certain limited classes of Member State acts, principally in cases where Member State authorities act as the executive arm of the Community. The content of this 'unwritten bill of rights' was rather traditional and represented an attempted synthesis of the constitutional traditions of the Member States. The Court has also stated that Community measures which violate the relevant substantive provisions of the European Convention on Human Rights are not acceptable in the Community.

Early attempts to codify such practices into a written 'bill of rights' entrenched in the Treaties—such as the April 1989 European Parliament Declaration of Human Rights—did not find favor in the several IGCs convened over the years to modify the Treaties. Likewise, several initiatives to push for the adhesion of the Communities to the European Convention on Human Rights—notably a Commission initiative in 1978—were rebuffed by both the Member States and the European Court of Justice. But

49 See, for example: Tizzano, "The Rule of the ECJ in the Protection of Fundamental Rights"; Lenaerts, "A 'Bill of Rights' for the European Union"; Jacobs, "Human Rights in the European Union: The Role of the Court of Justice"; Defeis, "Human Rights and the European Court of Justice: An Appraisal".

then, in a celebrated 'change of heart' as part of the 'Constitutional Process' of the first years of this decade, the Charter of Fundamental Human Rights was adopted and is now formally integrated into the legal order of the European Union through the Lisbon Treaty.

There is an undeniable celebratory tone to our human rights discourse and that celebratory tone is in part justified. We brandish human rights, with considerable justification, as one of the important achievements of our civilization. We hail our commitment to human rights and their embedment in our legal systems among the signal and mature proofs of Europe's response to, and overcoming of, its inglorious recent past in World War II. We consider human rights, alongside democracy, as a foundational value of our political order, something that is even worth fighting for. The 'adoption' of the EU Charter—through 'stealth'—in the Treaty of Lisbon is a final apotheosis of this discourse. Human rights have undoubtedly achieved an iconographical position in European culture. And though we distance ourselves, with disdain, from the more vulgar expressions of American end-of-history triumphalism which gushed forth with the fall of the Soviet empire, that very disdain cannot but conceal Europe's sense of its cultural superiority and hence its own brand of self-satisfaction and triumphalism. We raise the mirror of human rights, as evidenced by both national and transnational instruments before our collective face, and smile with satisfaction in at least three ways:

1. First, human rights are part of a broader discourse of, and commitment to, constitutions and constitutionalism, often to the thick, hard version of constitutions and constitutionalism found in, say, the German and Italian legal orders, which embody the notion of Constitution as a higher law. Such developments are noticeable even in countries such as Denmark, Belgium, France and others which had a softer version of constitutionalism and a long tradition of skepticism towards American style judicial empowerment. For its part, the EU already has a very robust version of constitutionalism and the EU Charter is, as noted, perceived by many as the first element in a would-be European Union formalization of that brand of constitutionalism.

Concomitantly, human rights also signify the ever increasing acceptance of (and resignation to) the central role of courts and judges in public discourse. Courts are most audacious in asserting their power when they garb themselves in the mantle of guardians of the human rights guaranteed by constitutional documents. They are, too, most successful in mobilizing support for and legitimating their power in the context of human rights. Europe adds an interesting nuance to this phenomenon too. Whilst there have always been and there is currently perhaps an even increasing specific critique of the so called "activism" of the European Court of Justice and it has even been couched, from time to time, in the language which objects to a *Gouvernance des Juges*, a more careful look at such criticism usually discovers that it issues from a nationalist sentiment worried more about the loss of national sovereignty to Europe than of popular or parliamentary power to judges. If the European Court were 'activist' in the opposite direction, namely slashing European Union power (and make no mistake, this too would be a form of judicial activism) you would find the same critics celebrating the European Court of Justice. In other words, most of the critique is not of the judicial empowerment as such, but of the content which it embraces. Significantly, when national courts, in acts of *national judicial empowerment,* claiming to protect *nationally defined human rights,* strike out at the European Court of Justice (and there have been quite a few such expressions) they are celebrated as protecting national values and identity and sovereignty. Few seem to protest that it is the judiciary, often in ways constitutionally shielded from parliamentary challenge, which is deciding fundamental issues which define the relationship of a Member State to the Union.

2. Second, beyond constitutionalism and its concomitant commitment to, or acceptance of, courts and judges as such, there is in the discourse of human rights a great faith in the *judicial protection* of human rights. We may call this the Habeas Corpus syndrome. The point I wish to make is simple enough: Increasingly, the measurement of the efficacy of these documents, of their very reality as meaningful legal instruments, is in their invocability by individuals and their enforcement, at the instance of individuals, against public authority by courts. It is the *Writ* of Habeas Corpus which solidified its position in legal history. In today's world, documents and declarations which do not have such a quality are oft derided as 'hortatory', aspirational, embryonic, all awaiting realization of their potential by arriving at the promised lands of individual invocability and judicial enforceability.

3. Finally, human rights have become an important part of European Integration and European identity discourse. This debate takes place at two

levels. The first is the bland affirmation of human rights as being part of a common patrimony et cetera et cetera, good stuff for politicians to drone on about, something akin to Beethoven's Fifth or the Blue Flag with the Golden Stars.[50] But there is a more serious dimension to this prattle. As the polity grows, as the ability of national mechanisms and instruments to provide democratic legitimacy to European norms is increasingly understood as partial and often formal rather than real, the necessity of democratizing decision making at the European level become ever more pressing. Such democratization requires, in its turn, the emergence of a polity with social commitments, allegiances and ties which is a *conditio sine qua non* for the discipline of majoritarian decision making. No demos, no democracy. Europe rightly shies away from an ethnic, religious or any other thick form of organic self-understanding and political identity. The only normatively acceptable construct is to conceive the polity as a Community of Values, much in the original spirit (though not practice) of Post-Revolution France and the United States. When one grasps for a content for such a community of values, the commitment to human rights becomes the most ready currency. Here are values around which, surely, Europeans can coalesce (and celebrate).

There is much truth and much value to our polities in our commitment to constitutional orders which celebrate democracy, human rights and the rule of law; in the seriousness with which we take this commitment as evidence by our willingness to make human rights a veritable legal instruments, often of superior normative value, opposable by individuals against public authorities and adjudicated and enforced by our courts; and in our placing human rights, alongside markets and economic prosperity as defining the values of our emerging European polity. But there are shades, nuances, warts and downright ugly aspects to this picture too, which are also worth bearing.

The celebration of the Charter is somewhat puzzling. European citizens and residents do not suffer from a deficit of judicial protection of Human Rights. Their human rights in most Member States are protected by their constitution and by their constitutional court or other courts. As an additional safety net they are protected by the European Convention on Human Rights and the Strasbourg organs. In the Union, they already

50 See for example, the Preamble to the European Constitution, cited in footnote 17, and speeches by European politicians, cited in footnote 10.

received judicial protection from the ECJ using as it source the same Convention and the Constitutional Traditions common to the Member States. So why a new Charter at all? One rejoices, it seems, in the symbol, in the value it represents, rather than in the results it may or may not achieve.

The real problem of the Community is the absence of a *human rights policy* with everything this entails: A Commissioner, a Directorate General, a budget and a horizontal action plan for making those rights—already granted by the Treaties and judicially protected by the various levels of European Courts—effective. Much of the human rights story, and its abuse, takes place far from the august halls of courts. Most of those whose rights are violated have neither knowledge nor means to seek judicial vindication. The Union does not need more rights on its lists, or more lists of rights. What is mostly needed are programs and agencies to make rights real, not simply negative interdictions which courts can enforce. It is still to be seen to what extent the Fundamental Rights Agency will constitute a first step to remedy this.

But I want to probe the question of human rights and European values even deeper. With the lessons of European history, our commitment to a political and social order in which fundamental rights are constitutionally protected should be without compromise. And, yet, the culture of human rights may produce unintended consequences on that very deep ideal of European integration, the one that places the individual at the center and calls for a redefinition of human relations.

I do not intend here to replicate a European version of the American critique of rights, but to try and articulate at least a variant that brings into sharp relief the manner in which it most affects virtues. In normal rights discourse the 'I', the subject, is the bearer of the rights. The ciritique is premised on this proposition. Notionally, this of course is true. But it does not correspond to the reality of how we actually experience rights discourse in action. That reality is 'triangular' with a violator (typically a public authority), the victim of the violation who, when it comes to fundamental human rights (as distinct, say, from consumer rights), is an outsider of sorts, and the 'I' or the 'We' are typically observers—reading about it in the press, or through some other media.

Against that reality it is easy to observe that the culture of human rights demands very little of all of us who believe in them. In fact for the most part it demands little more than that we should profess a belief in them.

The responsibility for their violation is typically not individuals, but public authority, and the responsibility for addressing such violation falls on other public authorities such as courts. Our role is typically to say 'Tz Tz' as we read about it during breakfast. What is a fundamental social more becomes a pretty cheap private virtue. The point made here is not one that inveighs against laziness and indifference. It *is* indeed the case that the violation of human rights is mostly at the hands of public authorities and there is, in fact, not much one can do than protest at different level of intensity and express our preferences through our voting (though commitment to human rights seems to be a common asset of all parties and thus of no electoral consequence.) The point is that there is something significant about the fact that the value placed higher than any other in the inventory of European integration, is precisely the one that is structured on the responsibilization of the other, of public authorities and one that demands so little of those who, in good faith, profess such. The way human rights play out in the broader matrix of political culture resembles the critique offered in relation to solidarity—it is constitutive of the culture of Agency which itself is not conducive to the virtues and sensibilities necessary for real community and solidarity.

Second, in the passage from social more to private virtue, frequently the vocabulary of human rights is lost-in-translation. The inviolability of human dignity becomes the inviolability of the I, of the ego. The culture of rights, want it or not, undermines somewhat the counter culture of responsibility and duty. We vastly underplay the language of responsibility and duty at the individual level compared to the language of rights and liberties. The individual has rights; society, public authorities have duties and responsibility. It is easy to see how not only the prosperity of the market but its very internal set of values and ethos of competition and material efficiency coupled with the culture of rights contribute to that matrix of personal materialism, self-centeredness, Sartre style ennui and narcissism in a society which genuinely and laudably values liberty and human rights.

XII.

It was only the Treaty of Maastricht—the Treaty of European Union of the early nineties—which introduced a Citizenship clause into the constitutional vocabulary of the Union.[51] Nationals of the Member States are henceforth, the Treaty proclaimed, European Citizens entitled to all rights and duties therein mentioned. European citizenship was meant, *inter alia,* to deepen the quality of human interpersonal relations among the nationals of the Member States. The articulation of Citizenship both in the legislative structure and the jurisprudence of the European Court might be producing the opposite effect.

It is, first, noticeable that in the Citizenship Chapter in the Treaty, duties are nowhere to be found. Citizenship thus clearly falls into the culture of rights. Even the list of rights remains mostly inane, not to say meaningless.[52] Noticeably, one right which actually had substance, i.e. the right of European Citizens to move and live anywhere throughout the Union, was drafted in such a way as to make it co-terminus with the pre-existing free movement of workers.

In a jurisprudential line coming up to the two decade mark, the Court has been hailed as giving robust substance to this anemic provision—i.e. taking citizenship seriously.[53] From its early jurisprudence, it proclaimed that European Citizenship was destined to become the fundamental status of individuals in Europe.[54] It gave the citizenship clause direct effect and tied it to the prohibition on discrimination on grounds of nationality. It

51 The Treaty on European Union, signed in Maastricht on 7 February 1992, expressed in the Preamble that the heads of states were 'resolved to establish a citizenship common to nationals of their countries', included as one of the objectives of the Union 'to strengthen the protection of the rights and interests of the nationals of its Member States through the introduction of a citizenship of the Union' (Title I, article B), and introduced a new part on 'Citizenship of the Union' (Part Two, articles 8a–8e).

52 The rights of the citizens, as defined by the Treaty of Maastricht, included: the right to move and reside within the territory of the Union (article 8a); the right to vote and stand as a candidate in municipal and EP elections in the Member State of residence (article 8b); the right to protection by the diplomatic or consular authorities of any other Member State, when residing in a third country in which his or her state is not represented (article 8c); and right to petition to the European Parliament and to apply to the European Ombudsman (article 8d).

53 Notably, the ECJ used the new citizenship provision to extend the scope of prohibition of discrimination. See for example: Case C-274/96 Bickel and Franz [1996] ECR I-7637; Case C-85/96 Martínez Sala [1998] ECR I-2691; Case C-184/99 Grzelczyk [2001] ECR I-6193.

54 See for example: Case C-184/99 Grzelczyk [2001] ECR I-6193; Case C-148/02 Garcia Avello [2003] ECR I-11613; Case C-147/03 Commission v Austria [2005] ECR I-5969.

reversed the presumption of 'right to residence', and as a consequence materially extended its scope—no longer a right the individual had to probe, but a presumption the curtailment of which the Member States had to justify.[55] On its face the free movement of persons was cut off from its market rationale and grafted on to the altogether more robust platform of citizenship.

And yet, a critical analysis of this jurisprudence would show that inadvertently the Court has not weaned itself from its market proclivities where deep down the individual is perceived as a factor of production, has failed to appreciate the rich and challenging nature of citizenship as a political concept, and is inadvertently shaping the immigration debate in an area fraught with delicate tension where the judicial contribution might undermine other positions.

The thrust of my thesis is as follows: The free movement case law has historically been driven by two principal objectives. First, the elimination—as far as possible—of any obstacles to the movement of workers (and self employed persons) within the Union. Second, once allowed in, a vigorous protection of the rights of such workers. The two objectives are connected of course: Only the vigorous protection of such rights would make the free movement a real right rather than a paper right. Importantly, the rights that needed protection, went beyond the basic prohibition on discrimination on grounds of nationality, i.e. the right of a worker to be treated as an equal with national workers. The jurisprudence was particularly adept at ensuring rights of the migrant worker's special status as such—with great attention to his social condition, his unique identity, his vulnerability in a manner which mixed culminating in the notion of Reverse Discrimination under which the Migrant enjoyed rights that even the local worker did not. Interestingly, and germane to this discussion is the fact that the comparable jurisprudence in classical international law—which gives non nationals a higher level of protection under the doctrine of minimal international standards—also comes under the appellation of Protection of Aliens. The new citizenship jurisprudence of the Court took that case law and gave it an even sharper edge in relation to both limbs—access and treatment.

55 Case C-413/99 Baumbast [2002] ECR I-7091; Case C-200/02 Zhu and Chen [2004] ECR I-9925.

The troubling aspect of this jurisprudence is that it precisely fails to make the conceptual transition from a market based free movement to a citizenship based concept. What it does, both in its positive law, but also in its rhetoric and in the conversation it creates, is to militate against the integration of migrants into their host communities. Materially, it often 'pays off' to remain a migrant rather, than, say to naturalize. But it is not the material consequences of the jurisprudence that are problematic. Conceptually, the jurisprudence 'ghettoizes' the Migrant. The ideal type "free movement" is not one in which a host country embraces the migrant and the migrant embraces the host country—leading to a slowly developing new cultural synthesis and ever changing national identities. Instead it puts in place a model in which the Migrant is forever to regard himself or herself, and even their children as such, as migrants, and for the host society to regard them as migrants albeit, with very special rights, at times exceeding that which citizens enjoy.

The problem, I think, is not necessarily with the European migrant. The problem is that the European discourse becomes normative across the board, spilling over into the general conversation about the appropriate normative models for dealing with new "citizens".

Against policy

XIV.

A curious phenomenon—noble values, dearly held: democracy, prosperity and solidarity, human rights, rule of law, European citizenship, no less. Yes, the European Union is a legal order which places the individual in the center. But in its modus operandi it curiously militates against the very virtues which are necessary to achieve, and are meant to be the byproduct of, these very values. What has become of Monnet's famous aphorism—*"Nous ne coalisons pas des Etats, nous unissons des hommes?"* Wonderfully successful in bringing our states together. Far more questionable in its deep spiritual pursuit.

It is at this point that the discussion usually turns to the necessary policy fixes: What should the Union do? How could we or should we reform in order to avoid or at least mitigate some of these unintended consequences?

In inveighing against the typical 'turn to policy' move, I am not only motivated by a conviction that many of the features described above are structural and either incapable of reform, or that any reform will create other intended or unintended pernicious consequences.

The 'turn to policy' move itself is part of the problem—of responsibilizing others, of addressing the issue in technocratic, governance terms. The redress, if any, may be found in greater attention to the spiritual dimensions to our lives and that of our children; the way we think of ours and educate, and cultivate theirs. Education to the necessary virtues of decency and true human solidarity, if achieved, can easily enough counteract the almost inevitable impact of the structure and process of governance. If achieved.

Works Cited

Adams, Maurice/de Waele, Henri/Meeusen Johan/Straetmans Gert (eds.) (2013): *Judging Europe's Judges: The Legitimacy of the Case Law of the European Court of Justice*, Oxford.

Alter, Karen J. (2003): *Establishing the Supremacy of European Law: The Making of an International Rule of Law in Europe*, Oxford.

Anscombe, G.E.M. (1958): "Modern Moral Philosophy", *Philosophy 33*, 1–19.

Aquinas, Thomas (2007): *Summa Theologica*, Vol. 2, Part II, 1st Section, New York.

Aristotle, *The Nicomachean Ethics*, in: L. Brown (ed.) (2009), Oxford.

Bach, Maurizio (1993): "Vom Zweckverband zum technokratischen Regime: Politische Legitimation und institutionelle Verselbständigung in der Europäischen Gemeinschaft", in: H. Winkler/H. Kaeble (eds.), *Nationalismus, Nationalitäten, Supranationalität: Europa nach 1945*, 288–308, Stuttgart.

Barber, Nicholas W. (2005): "The Limited Modesty of Subsidiarity", *European Law Journal 11*, 308–325.

Bellamy, Richard/ Staiger Uta (eds.) (2014): "The Eurozone Crisis and the Democratic Deficit", *UCL European Institute Working Papers*, 1/2014.

Benoît-Rhomer, Florence (2005): "Valeurs et droits fondamentaux dans la Constitution", *Revue Trimestrielle de Droit Européen 41*, 261–284.

Böhm, Franz (1980): *Freiheit und Ordnung in der Marktwirtschaft*, Baden-Baden.

Von Bogdandy, Armin (2005): "The European Constitution and European Identity: Text and Subtext of the Treaty Establishing a Constitution for Europe", *International Journal of Constitutional Law 3*, 295–315.

Boniface, Pascal (ed.) (2004): *Quelles valeurs pour l'Union européenne?*, Paris.

Boyce, Brigitte (1993): "The Democratic Deficit of the European Community", *Parliamentary Affairs 46*, 458–477.

Bracq, Stéphane (2004): "La Commission Européenne entre Fonctions d'Arbitrage et Rôle Politique", *Revue du Marché Commun et de l'Union Européenne 480*, 440–449.

Bribosia, Hervé (1992): "Subsidiarité et répartition des compétences entre la Communauté et ses États membres", *Revue du Marché Unique Européen*, 165–188.

Cass, Deborah Z. (1992): "The word that saves Maastricht? The Principle of Subsidiarity and the Division of Powers within the European Community", *Common Market Law Review 29*, 1107–1136.

Chappell, Timothy (ed.) (2006): *Values and Virtues: Aristotelianism in Contemporary Ethics*, Oxford.

Christiansen, Thomas (1997): "Tensions of European Governance: Politicized Bureaucracy and Multiple Accountability in the European Commission", *Journal of European Public Policy 4*, 73–90.

Constantinesco, Vlad (1997): "Les clauses de coopération renforcée, Le protocole sur l'application des principes de subsidiarité et de proportionalité", *Revue Trimestrielle de Droit Européen 33*, 751–767.

Craig, Paul (1997): "Democracy and Rulemaking within the EC: An Empirical and Normative Assessment", *European Law Journal 3*, 105–130.

Craig, Paul (2011): "Institutions, Power, and Institutional Balance", in: P. Craig/G. de Búrca (eds.), *The Evolution of EU Law*, 2. Auflage, 41–84, Oxford.

Dahl, Robert A. (1989): *Democracy and Its Critics*, New Haven.

Decker Frank (B5/2001): "*Mehr Demokratie wagen: Die Europäische Union braucht einen institutionellen Sprung nach vorn*", *Aus Politik und Zeitgeschichte*, 33–38.

Defeis, Elizabeth F. (2007): "Human Rights and the European Court of Justice: An Appraisal", *Fordham International Law Journal 31*, 1104–1117.

Dehousse, Renaud (1995): "Constitutional reform in the European community: Are there alternatives to the Majoritarian avenue?", *West European Politics 18*, 118–136.

Dony, Marianne (2005): "Les Valeurs, objectifs et principes de l'Union", in: Marianne Dony/ Emmanuelle Bribosia (eds.), *Commentaire de la Constitution de l'Union européenne*, 33–46, Bruxelles.

Dubois, Vincent/Dulong, Delphine (1999): "Introduction générale", in: Vincent Dubois/ Delphine Dulong (eds.), *La question technocratique. De l'invention d'une figure aux transformations de l'action publique*, 5–12, Strasbourg.

Éditorial (2008), "L'Union, une communauté de valeurs?", *Revue Trimestrielle de Droit Européen 44*, 1–4.

Eucken, Walter (1989): *Die Grundlagen der Nationalökonomie*, 9. Auflage, Berlin.

Eucken, Walter (1952): *Grundsätze der Wirtschaftspolitik*, Tübingen.

Euzéby, Alain (2004): "La Constitution – Constitution de l'Union Européenne: des valeurs à défendre!", *Revue du Marché Commun et de l'Union Européenne 482*, 566–568.

Featherstone, Kevin (1994): "Jean Monnet and the 'Democratic Deficit' in the European Community", *Journal of Common Market Studies 32*, 149–170.

Fischer, Robert (2008): "European Governance Still Technocratic? New Modes of Governance for Food Safety Regulation in the European Union", *European Integration Online Papers 12*, available at: http://eiop.or.at/eiop/texte/2008-006a.htm.

Foot, Philippa (2001): *Natural Goodness*, Oxford.

Foot, Philippa (1978): *Virtues and Vices*, Oxford.

Friedrich, Carl J. (1955): "The Political Thought of Neo-Liberalism", *American Political Science Review 49*, 509–525.

Gerber, David J. (1995): "Competition Law and International Trade: The European Union and the Neo-Liberal Factor", *Pacific Rim Law and Policy Journal 4*, 37–57.

Gerber, David J. (1994): "Constitutionalizing the Economy: German Neo-Liberalism, Competition Law and the 'New' Europe", *The American Journal of Comparative Law 42*, 25–84.

Gerber, David J. (1998): *Law and Competition in Twentieth-Century Europe: Protecting Prometheus*, Oxford.

Giuliani, Marco (2004): "Il deficit democratico dell'Unione", *Il Mulino 412*, 341–351.

Grossekettler, Heinz G. (1989): "On Designing an Economic Order: The Contributions of the Freiburg School", in: Donald A. Walker, (ed.) *Perspectives on the History of Economic Thought, Volume II*, Aldershot.

Haas, Ernst B. (1968): "Technocracy, Pluralism and the New Europe", in: Joseph S. Nye (ed.), *International Regionalism: A Reader*, Boston.

Haas, Peter M. (1992): "Introduction: Epistemic Communities and International Policy Coordination", *International Organization 46*, 1–35.

Harcourt, Alison/Claudio, Radaelli (1999): "Limits to EU technocratic regulation?", *European Journal of Political Research 35*, 107–122.

Höreth, Marcus (1999): "No Way Out for the Beast? The Unsolved Legitimacy Problem of European Governance", *Journal of European Public Policy 6*, 249–268.

Hooghe, Liesbet (2002): *The European Commission and the Integration of Europe: Images of Governance*, Cambridge.

Hurka, Thomas (2001): *Virtue, Vice, and Value*, Oxford.

Hursthouse, Rosalind (1999): *On Virtue Ethics*, Oxford.

Inman, Robert P. (1998): "Subsidiarity and the European Union", *National Bureau of Economic Research Working Paper No. W6556*.

Ipsen, Hans P. (1972): *Europäisches Gemeinschaftsrecht*, Tübingen.

Jacobs, Francis G. (2001): "Human Rights in the European Union: The Role of the Court of Justice", *European Law Review 26*, 331–341.

Jaibi, Neila Dorra/Landolsi, Wafa (2008): "L'Union européenne: d'une Communauté Economique à une Communauté de Citoyens", in: Rafâa Ben Achour/ Slim Laghmani (eds.): *Les droits de l'Homme: une nouvelle cohérence pour le droit international?*, Paris.

Kasper, Wolfgang/Streit, Manfred (1993): *Lessons from the Freiburg School: The Institutional Foundations of Freedom and Prosperity*, St Leonards.

Kassim, Hussein/Peterson, John/Bauer, Michael W./Connolly, Sara/Dehousse, Renaud/Hooghe, Liesbet/Thompson, Andrew (2013): *The European Commission of the Twenty-First Century*, Oxford.

Kohler-Koch, Beate/Rittberger, Berthold (2007): *Debating the Democratic Legitimacy of the European Union*, Lanham.

Kommers, Donald P./Waelbroeck, Michel (1985): "Legal Integration and the Free Movement of Goods: The American and European Experience", in: Mauro Cappelletti/Monica Seccombe/Joseph H. H. Weiler (eds.), *Integration Through Law: Europe and the American Federal Experience, Vol. 1*, 165–227, Berlin.

Laprat, Gérard (1991): "Réforme des Traités: le risque du double déficit démocratique. Les Parlements nationaux et l'élaboration de la norme communautaire", *Revue du Marché Commun et Unique, n. 351*, 710–721.

Lenaerts, Koen/De Smijter, Eddy (2001): "A 'Bill of Rights' for the European Union", *Common Market Law Review 38*, 273–300.

Lenaerts, Koen/Ypersele, Patrick van (1994): "Le principe de subsidiarité et son contexte: étude de l'article 3 B du Traité de l'Union Européenne", *Cahiers de Droit Européen, n. 1–2*, 3–83.

Lindseth, Peter L. (1999): "Democratic Legitimacy and the Administrative Character of Supranationalism: the Example of the European Community", *Columbia Law Review 99*, 628–738.

MacIntyre, Alasdair (1981): *After Virtue: A Study in Moral Theory*, Notre Dame.

Maier, Charles S. (1977): "The Politics of Productivity: Foundations of American International Economic Policy after World War II", *International Organization 31*, 607–633.

Maimonides, Moses (1975): "Eight Chapters", in: Raymond Weis/Charles Butterworth (eds.), *The Ethical Writings of Maimonides*, 59–104, New York.

Majone, Gindomenico (2003): "Deficit democratico, istituzioni non-maggioritarie e il paradosso dell'integrazione europea", *Stato e mercato 67*, 3–38.

Majone, Gindomenico (1998): "Europe's Democratic Deficit: The Question of Standards", *European Law Journal 4*, 5–28.

Majone, Gindomenico (1996): *Regulating Europe*, London.

Mancini, G. Federico (1998): "Europe: The Case for Statehood", *European Law Journal 4*, 29–42.

Mancini, G. Federico/Keeling, David T. (1994): "Democracy and the European Court of Justice", *The Modern Law Review 57*, 175–190.

Matlary, Janne Haaland (1998): "Democratic Legitimacy and the Role of the Commission", in: Andreas Føllesdal/Peter Koslowski (eds.), *Democracy and the European Union*, 65–80, Berlin, Heidelberg.

Mattera, Alfonso (1994): "Le principe de subsidiarité au service d'une Communauté á la dimension des problèmes de notre temps", *Revue du Marché Unique Européen, n. 2*, 189–192.

McDowell, John (1979): "Virtue and Reason", *Monist 62*, 331–350.

Mény, Yves (2002): "De la Démocratie en Europe: Old Concepts and New Challenges", *Journal of Common Market Studies 41*, 1–13.

Milward, Alan S. (1992): *The European Rescue of the Nation-State*, Berkeley.

Mitrany, David (1966): *A Working Peace System*, Chicago.

Monnet, Jean (1976): *Mémoires. Nous ne Coalisons pas des Etats, Nous Unissons des Hommes*, Paris.

Moravcsik, Andrew (2002): "Reassessing Legitimacy in the European Union", *Journal of Common Market Studies 40*, 603–624.

Moravcsik, Andrew (1998): *The Choice for Europe: Social Purpose and State Power from Messina to Maastricht*, Ithaca.

Moussis, Nicolas (2000): "La Construction Européenne et le Citoyen: Déficit Démocratique ou Déficit d'Information?", *Revue du Marché Commun, n. 436*, 153–159.

Neunreither, Karlheinz (1994): "The Democratic Deficit of the European Union: Towards Closer Cooperation between the European Parliament and the National Parliaments", *Government and Opposition 29*, 299–314.

Norris, Pippa (1997): "Representation and the Democratic Deficit", *European Journal of Political Research 32*, 273–282.

Obradovic, Daniela (1996): "Policy Legitimacy and the European Union", *Journal of Common Market Studies 34*, 191–221.

Peacock, Alan/Willgrodt, Hans (eds.) (1989): *Germany's Social Market Economy: Origins and Ecolutio*n, London.

Peterson, John (1994): "Subsidiarity: A Definition to Suit Any Vision?", *Parliamentary Affairs 47*, 117–132.

Petit, Isabelle (2006): "Dispelling a Myth? The Fathers of Europe and the Construction of a Euro-Identity", *European Law Journal 12*, 661–679.

Piris, Jean-Claude (1994): "Après Maastricht, les institutions communautaires sont-elles plus efficaces, plus démocratiques et plus transparentes?", *Revue Trimestrelle de Droit Européen 30*, 1–37.

Quermonne, Jean-Louis (2002): "La question du gouvernement européen", *Groupement d'études et de recherches, Notre Europe, Études et Recherches, n. 20*, available at: http://www.institutdelors.eu/media/etud20-fr.pdf?pdf=ok.

Quermonne Jean-Louis (ed.) (1999): *L'Union européenne en quête d'institutions légitimes et efficaces*, Paris.

Radaelli, Claudio M. (1999): *Technocracy in the European Union*, Harlow.

Razeen, Sally (1996): "Ordoliberalism and the Social Market: Classical Political Economy from Germany", *New Political Economy 1*, 233–257.

Reich, Charles (1991): "Qu'est-ce que … le déficit démocratique", *Revue du Marché Commun et de l'Union Européenne 343*, 14–18.

Richardson, John (2002): "The European Union in the World – A Community of Values", *Fordham Journal of International Law 26*, 12–35.

Schuman, Robert (2000): *Pour l'Europe, Écrits politiques*, 3. Auflage, Paris.

Scoffoni, Guy (1992): "Les relations entre le Parlement européen et les parlements nationaux et le renforcement de la légitimité démocratique de la Communauté", *Cahiers de Droit Européen 28*, 22–41.

Slote, Michael (2001): *Morals from Motives*, Oxford.

Solomon, David (1988): "Internal Objections to Virtue Ethics", *Midwest Studies in Philosophy 13*, 428–441.

Sommer, Theo (1973): "The Community is Working", *Foreign Affairs 51*, 747–760.

Streeck, Wolfgang (2012): "Citizens as Customers: Considerations on the New Politics of Consumption", *New Left Review, n. 76*, 27–47.

Strozzi, Girolamo (1994): "Le principe de subsidiarité dans la perspective de l'intégration européenne. Une énigme et beaucoup d'attentes", *Revue Trimestrielle de Droit Européen 30*, 373–390.

Sutton, Michael (2007): *France and the Construction of Europe, 1944–2007: The Geopolitical Imperative*, New York, Oxford.

Swanton, Christine (2003): *Virtue Ethics: A Pluralistic View*, Oxford.

Tizzano, Antonio: "The Rule of the ECJ in the Protection of Fundamental Rights", in: Anthony Arnull/ Piet Eeckhout/Takis Tridimas (eds.) (2008), *Continuity and Change in EU Law: Essays in Honour of Sir Francis Jacobs*, 126–138, Oxford.

Verdun, Amy. (1998): "The Institutional Design of EMU: A Democratic Deficit?", *Journal of Public Policy 18*, 107–132.

Viciano Pastor, Roberto (1997): "El futuro de la Unión Europea ¿déficit democrático o déficit constitucional?", in: E. Linde Paniagua (ed.), *Los retos de la Unión Europea ante el siglo XXI*, Madrid.

Wallace, Helen (1996): "Politics and Policy in the EU: The Challenge of Governance", in: Helen Wallace/ William Wallace (eds.), *Policy-making in the European Union*, 3–36, Oxford.

Wallace, William (1996): "Government Without Statehood: The Unstable Equilibrium", in: Helen Wallace/William Wallace (eds.), *Policy-making in the European Union*, 439–460, Oxford.

Weiler, Joseph H.H. (1986): "Eurocracy and Distrust: Some Questions Concerning the Role of the European Court of Justice in the Protection of Fundamental Human Rights within the Legal Order of the European Communities", *Washington Law Review 61*, 1103–1142.

Weiler, Joseph H.H. (1998): "Europe: The Case Against the Case for Statehood", *European Law Journal 4*, 43–62.

Weiler, Joseph H.H. (2014): "Van Gend en Loos: The individual as subject and object and the dilemma of European legitimacy", *International Journal of Constitutional Law 12*, 94–103.

Wessels, Wolfgang (2003): "Reassessing the Legitimacy Debate: A Comment on Moravcsik", in: Joseph H.H. Weiler/Iain Begg/John Peterson (eds.), *Integration in an Expanding European Union – Reassessing the Fundamentals*, 103–109, Oxford.

Williams, Bernard (1985): *Ethics and the Limits of Philosophy*, Cambridge.

De Witte, Bruno/Muir, Elise/Dawson, Mark (eds.) (2013): *Judicial Activism at the European Court of Justice*, Cheltenham.

Wonka Arndt (2004): *The European Commission: Technocratic Bureaucracy or Fully-Fledged EU Executive?*, Cambridge.

Global Constitutionalism and the Internet: Taking People Seriously

Ingolf Pernice

I. Introduction

Talking about global constitutionalism encounters serious scepticism in constitutional theory and international legal thinking. There are reasons, however, for accepting that the concept of constitution is not applicable to states only, but also helps understanding and describing processes of establishing, legitimizing and limiting public authority beyond the state.[1] The present contribution does not go into this debate. It rather strives to emphasise the role of the individual in constitutional thinking beyond the state; this approach, therefore, focuses on people as individuals, not *the* people as a political entity.

From the perspective of the individual, and on the backdrop of European experience, constitutionalism is proposed to be understood as encompassing several levels—sub-state, state, regional (like the EU), global—of legitimate public authority established for different purposes and serving the interest of people that have decided to define themselves respectively as the citizens of the local, national, regional (European) and, arguably, global communities. Contrary to what the term "multilevel" may imply, the system is understood as non-hierarchical, as a pluralistically integrated legal system composed of political shells around the individual, with a division of attributed powers according to the principle of subsidiarity.[2]

---

1 For the debate see Kumm, "The Cosmopolitan Turn in Constitutionalism: An Integrated Conception of Public Law", 606 et seq.; Peters, "The Merits of Global Constitutionalism", 399–402; Wiener/Lang/Tully/Maduro/Kumm, "Editorial - Global constitutionalism: Human Rights, democracy and the rule of law", 5–10.

2 First: Pernice, "Constitutional Law Implications for a State Participating in a Process of Regional Integration. German Constitution and 'Multilevel Constitutionalism'", 40–65; for a short summary of the debate see Pernice, "The EU—A Citizens' Joint Venture. Multilevel Constitutionalism and Open Democracy in Europe", 185 ff. For the

The concept of multilevel constitutionalism is driven by the basic understanding that what ultimately matters is the individual, not legal or political constructs like the states. States cannot be understood as an end in themselves and must always be considered instrumental to the individual, the human being or, as members of a political community, the citizens, for their purposes. All modern legal systems, as *Jürgen Habermas* states, are ultimately based upon the subjective rights of the citizens,[3] and so are states and any of the supranational or global institutions they may have established. Law serves the individuals and the protection of their rights, not less and not more.

The political community, be it a state, the EU or whatever may develop at the global level, has no other purpose.[4] This is what can be learned from the guarantee of human dignity, the mother of all other fundamental rights.[5] Contrary to a widespread approach on global constitutionalism,[6]

---

integrative approach see also Kumm (note 1), 612: "International law is neither derivative, nor is it autonomous. National and international law form an integrative whole." The consequence is that: "The standards of constitutional legitimacy are to be derived from an integrative conception of public law that spans the national-international divide" (ibid., 625). On the principle of subsidiarity in international law see also: Follesdal, "The principle of subsidiarity as a constitutional principle in international law", 55–62, with a convincing critique on „claims that a principle of subsidiarity may help justify several 'state-centric' features of international law, as a normative 'constitutional principle'."

3 Habermas, "Die Krise der Europäischen Union im Lichte einer Konstitutionalisierung des Völkerrechts – Ein Essay zur Verfassung Europas", 22.

4 See also Article 1 of the "Herrenchiemsee"-Draft for the German Grundgesetz (HChE): "Der Staat ist um des Menschen willen da, nicht der Mensch um des Staates willen"; see also Dreier, Grundgesetz Kommentar, Article 1 I, note 18.

5 See, for instance, Habermas, "The crisis of the European Union. Response", 76 f.: "...something that was inscribed in human rights implicitly from the outset, namely, the normative substance of the equal dignity of every human being that human rights only spell out". Crit. Dreier (note 5), Article 1 I, note 161.

6 See Müller, "Global constitutionalism in historical perspective: Towards refined tools for international constitutional histories", 73: "...constitutional structures as a set of fundamental and prioritized principles and rules that serves as a framework for the self-ordering of relations between polities" (not people!). See also Kumm (note 1), 607, who mentions the fact "the individual has long emerged as a subject of rights and obligations under international law", but this does not mean that the individual is understood as the source of legitimacy also of the law and institutions at the international level; the instruments he mentions—human rights, international criminal law—are still rule made

the perspective of the individuals—people—is key for constitutional thinking at the national level and beyond. This is what leads to the central ambition of the present paper: Global constitutionalism is about rethinking constitutional law from the perspective of global citizens. Despite the major challenges that democratic participation and activism are facing online[7] the internet has still certain potential of empowering people. To a new extend there is a chance to actively participate in political process and to legitimise regulation at all levels, including the global level.[8]

Obviously, the phrase: *taking people seriously* is borrowed from *Ronald Dworkin*: Taking rights seriously.[9] Among all that ought to be taken seriously people come first—because each of us bears his or her end in herself and deserves full recognition and respect as equal member of the human society, full respect of his or her individuality and otherness. What *Dworkin* develops as "the right of each individual to the equal respect and

and applicable among states.—With an individualistic approach, however, see: Peters (note 2), 399: "The ongoing process of humanizing sovereignty is the cornerstone of the current transformation of international law into a system centred on individuals." See also Petersmann, "Human Rights, Constitutionalism and the World Trade Organization: Challenges for World Trade Organization Jurisprudence and Civil Society", 641: "My publications define 'multilevel consti-tutionalism' from a citizen's perspective [...], thus proceeding from the value premise of normative individualism rather than state sovereignty" (original emphasis); Milewicz, "Emerging Patterns of Global Constitutionalization: Toward a Conceptual Framework", 422–3 and 427 ("[T]he recognition of human rights is synonymous with the recognition of the individual as the subject of international law. It implies that modern international law is no longer exclusively concerned with the regulation of state-to-state relations but also with relations between the individual and the state."); cf. Andreas L. Paulus, "The International Legal System as a Constitution", 72; Walker, "Reframing EU Constitutionalism", 156 ("[A]uthority rests upon a putative idea of the individual as the basic unit of society and as the (presumptively equal) source of moral agency, with the very idea of a political domain built upon and dedicated to that secular premise"); see further infra, III.1.

7 Sifry, The Big Disconnect: Why the Internet Hasn't Transformed Politics (Yet); Morozov, The Net Delusion: How Not to Liberate the World.

8 In this vein, e.g., Besson, "Whose Constitution(s)? International Law, Constitutionalism, and Democracy", 393 ff.; Follesdal, "When Common Interests Are Not Common: Why the Global Basic Structure Should be Democratic", 585.

9 Dworkin, Taking Rights Seriously, in particular 184 et seq.

concern of those who govern him",[10] seems to be closely connected to the concept of human dignity, the founding principle of how I understand "constitution". It is also a fundamental right of all citizens as members of a political community, at least according to the understanding known in German constitutional law and included in Article 1 of the European Charter of Fundamental Rights. It has been given a broader meaning, however, encompassing a social dimension, to serve as a basic theory of the state by *Hasso Hofmann* who defines the promise of individuals to mutually respect each other's dignity as the foundational concept of the state as a community of solidarity.[11]

If this proposition is correct, why should *Hofmann's* understanding of human dignity not apply *mutatis mutandis* for emerging political communities beyond the state?[12] What I am suggesting, thus, is to examine more deeply to what extent and under which conditions the approach of *dignity as mutual promise* among individuals (people) defining themselves as citizens of a political community can be beneficially harnessed not only with regard to the EU[13] but also to the global community emerging as a "constitutional community".[14]

---

10 Drawing from Rawls, Theory of Justice, ibid., xii, 149, 150–183, 205, 227 et al. But see his discussion of dignity as a primarily ethical principle in: Dworkin, Justice for Hedgehogs, 191 ff.

11 Hofmann, "Die versprochene Menschenwürde", 367 ff.

12 For a more general approach see only Habermas, Crisis (note 6), 81: "'Human dignity' performs the function of a seismograph that registers what is constitutive for a democratic legal order—namely, just those rights that the citizens of a political community must grant themselves if they are to be able to respect one another as members of a voluntary association of free and equal persons. The guarantee of these human rights first gives rise to the status of citizens who have a claim as subjects of equal rights to be respected in their human dignity". For the extension of the concept from a state-centered to a universal recognition of human dignity in a "constitutionalised world society" see ibid., 87 ff.

13 See my proposition in: Pernice, "Solidarität in Europa. Eine Ortsbestimmung im Verhältnis zwischen Bürger, Staat und Europäischer Union", 54 ff.

14 For the term see: Peters, "Membership in the Global Constitutional Community", 153 ff., observing a "dialectical process": "the emergence and extension of a global constitutional community is both a manifestation and a driver of global constitutionalism, while the constitutionalization of international law is at the same time an explanation and a promoter of this communitarization" (ibid., 157).

The Internet, it is submitted, could play a crucial role in catering to this mutual promise.

The subject "Global constitutionalism and the internet", thus, invites us to reflect upon the question, whether and, if so, under what conditions, driven by the need to meet the global challenges, globally available information and communication through the internet and, in particular, emerging social networks across borders amalgamate people of the existing local, regional, national communities progressively to constitute a global community "on top" of a multilevel global constitutional system. What I have developed as a theoretical approach under the heading of "the global dimension of multilevel constitutionalism"[15] would so gain a practical perspective.

While many questions regarding our daily life can be dealt with effectively at local, regional, national levels, there is an increasing list of problems—like international peace and security, terrorism, climate change, global trade, financial markets and the internet—that can not. Ruling these matters effectively is outside the reach of national democratically decided policies. In addition, it becomes more and more visible that policies "democratically" decided by one country may have (external) effects on other countries to an extent that is not acceptable to their peoples.[16] This is why the European Union, with the tasks and powers conferred upon it, does not take away, but adds to the sovereignty of her Member States. Thus, the EU is not a challenge to democracy but can be depicted as a remedy to democratic deficits at the national level.[17] The European constitution can therefore be conceived as establishing a complementary level of legitimate ruling and policies, it compensates for deficits of self determination at the national level.[18]

15 Pernice, "The Global Dimension of Multilevel Constitutionalism: A Legal response to the Challenges of Globalisation", 973–1005.

16 See also Kumm (note 2), 612 et seq., talking about "justice-relevant negative externalities". See also below II.1.

17 See for the European Union Neyer, The Justification of Europe. A Political Theory of Supranational Integration, 4; following this line: Pernice (note 3), 187 ff.

18 For the compensatory function, accordingly, of global constitutionalism see: Peters, "Compensatory Constitutionalism: The Function and Potential of Fundamental International Norms and Structures", 591. See also: Viellechner, "Constitutionalism as a Cipher: On the Convergence of Constitutionalist and Pluralist Approaches to the Globalization of Law", 605–6: "concept of compensation".

But also beyond Europe—due to trade, tourism, migration and new information technologies—modern societies are more and more interconnected, interdependent and embedded in a dense web of global relationships, to an extent that common ruling on the basis of mutual respect and understanding among people worldwide is required. Common rules and mutual respect among people, yet, exist only in part. People are first of all citizens of their respective countries. There is some sign, however, of people being conceived as global citizens too,[19] and international law is said by some observers to be transforming into a "World (Internal) Law" in a "multilevel system".[20] Legal instruments at this level, however, such as the Charter of the United Nations or international conventions on the protection of human rights can hardly be described as expressing sufficient commonality, and even less so as elements of a global constitution.[21] People do not consider themselves as origin and owners of these instruments, which indeed are laws or institutions among states, not among citizens.

Does the internet has the potential to change anything in this analysis? The answer is probably yes: It offers the potential as a tool for establishing a global public sphere allowing for a political discourse among people across borders and continents.[22] This discourse could become constitutional in the meaning outlined above. As *James Bohman* puts it:

19 Peters, "Dual Democracy", 296 ff., in particular 307 ff.: "the globalization of citizenship". Habermas, Crisis (note 6), 58 f., 62, 65, uses the term "world citizen". A number of civil society organisations use the term global citizen, e.g. http://www.global citizen.org/, or http://www.newglobalcitizens.org/.

20 Delbrück, "Prospects for a 'World (Internal) Law?': Legal Developments in a Changing International System", 401 f., 429 f., using the term "multilevel system", however, in a vague and unspecified sense.

21 For the UN Charter, see however the proposal of Fassbender, The United Nations Charter as the Constitution of the International Community.

22 See, e.g., Brunkhorst, Solidarity—From Civic Friendship to a Global Legal Community, 158–9: "It appears as if a worldwide people, made up of the addressees of law, is beginning to express itself for the first time as a globally 'active' and 'legitimating people' (represented by freely associated organizations): 'the vanguard of a slowly developing transnational 'people'".

"In public spheres there is a demand for the inclusion of all those who participate and recognize each other as participants; this inclusion is not merely a matter of literal size and or scope but of mutually granted equal standing".[23]

The internet could develop as the medium for achieving this at a global scale. Mutual recognition among people as equals or, with the words of Dworkin, the acceptance of a right to equal concern and respect, is close to what human dignity implies and requires. The Internet, thus, could emerge as an instrument through which the mutual promise of dignity mentioned above might reach a global dimension.

Some basic terms in this discussion need clarification. Four perhaps provocative definitions or theses shall serve as a point of departure:

- "Constitutionalism" means theoretical thinking about the idea and basic elements or values of a constitution[24] as well as the political and legal processes it implies and drives ahead; but it can also encompass the practice of political movements striving to make this idea a reality.
- "Constitution" is the political process and, finally, the legal instrument establishing, organising and limiting legitimate public authority within a political community, based upon the rule of law, democratic principles, separation of powers, and fundamental rights reflecting a mutual promise of human dignity.[25]
- "Global constitutionalism" is an extension of constitutionalism beyond the state and includes the instruments and processes for establishing, organising and limiting legitimate public authority at the global level as a matter of people so giving themselves the legal status of global citizenship.[26]

23 Bohman, "The Transformation of the Public Sphere. Political Authority, Communicative Freedom, and Internet Publics", 75.

24 For these values see Article 2 TEU; with regard to global constitutionalism see also: Wiener/Lang/Tully/Maduro/Kumm, "Editorial—Global constitutionalism: Human Rights, democracy and the rule of law", 1–2: rule of law, human rights protection, separation/limitation of powers of government, democratic self-determination of a polity.

25 Human dignity, though, is not regarded as a basic fundamental right in all constitutions, at least not expressly. For surveys see Mahlmann, "Human Dignity in Modern Constitutional Orders", 370 ff.; McCrudden, "Human Dignity and Judicial Interpretation of Human Rights", 664 ff.

26 This definition extends somewhat the general approach regarding the term of global constitutionalism (see Wiener et al. (note 2), 5 ff.), with the perspective of the individual—though critical views are mentioned, ibid., 7, stating "that a constitution without a

- The "internet" is one of the great global challenges requiring itself a global regulatory framework for which the constitutional bases are yet to be developed, but it is likewise an instrument that may enable the processes needed of establishing and legitimising rule-making at the global level.

The internet provides us with two closely linked aspects relevant to how global constitutionalism is understood here: The experience with internet governance can teach us about new forms of non-governmental norm-building processes. It also provides us with the public sphere needed for effectively setting up a framework and legitimating processes for constituting a global political community.

Some evidence for my assumption that there is an increasing democratic deficit and a need for new forms of democratically legitimate and binding regulation at the global level (infra II.) will be followed by examples for arrangements established to meet these challenges allowing to identify some principles guiding the constitutional foundations of such regulation (infra III.). Current concepts for the construction of legitimacy rooted in the individual as discussed under the heading of global constitutionalism (infra IV.) can, on this basis, be further developed to discuss some critical elements for a global constitutional arrangement sustaining democratically legitimate regulation at the global level (infra V.).

---

state as the context of the people as the constituent power of any constitution is neither desirable nor possible (Grimm 1995; Loughlin 2010)". Some hint for an individualistic perspective is given, however, by Peters, Merits (note 2), 399. For this self-referential approach of citizenship see Pernice, "Der Europäische Verfassungsverbund auf dem Wege der Konsolidierung Verfassungsrechtliche Aus-gangslage und Vorschläge für die institutionelle Reform der Europäischen Union vor der Osterweiterung", 211. Citizenship, thus, is not conceived here as "a status granted to citizens by a state or international legal regime and a set of private and public institutions in which its two main types of rights and duties can be exercised", as Tully, A Dilemma of Democratic Citizenship, 19, qualifies as "modern citizenship", as opposed to what he develops as "cooperative citizenship", available at: http://www.hivos.net/Hivos-Knowledge-Programme/Themes/Civic-Explorations/News/A-Dilemma-of-Democratic-Citizenship (last visit January 2, 2015); see also below, IV.1.

II. Democratic deficits and global regulation

The increasing interconnectedness of states and people around the globe gave David Held already in 1995 reason to reject, in his seminal book on "Democracy and the Global Order", the traditional concepts of democracy that assume "a 'symmetric' and 'congruent' relationship between political decision-makers and the recipients of political decisions". The problem, in his view,

> "for defenders and critics alike of modern democratic systems, is that regional and global interconnectedness contests the traditional national resolutions of the key questions of democratic theory and practice. The very process of governance can escape the reach of the nation-state. National communities by no means exclusively make and determine decisions and policies for themselves, and governments by no means determine what is appropriate exclusively for their own citizens".[27]

Two different phenomena allow us to explain in more detail the insight that—as Jürgen Neyer recently put it—the establishment of supra-national public authority like the EU should be understood not as a threat to democracy but as a solution to the democratic deficit of the Member States.[28] The first group of phenomena are the "external effects" of national policies (infra 1.); the second group are global challenges that individual states acting by themselves cannot sufficiently cope with (infra 2.). The remedy for the problems of democratic self-ruling of peoples in the actual system based upon nation states could be modes and methods of global regulation supported by the internet (infra 3.).

1. Externalities of national policies

Held does not primarily look at decisions made by supra- or international organisations like the EU, NATO or the IMF, which in one way or another limit the (regulatory) autonomy of states. As topical examples he rather refers to phenomena such as isolated monetary policy decisions, like the increase of interest rates, the permission for 'harvesting' of rain forests

27 Held, Democracy and the Global Order. From the Modern State to Cosmopolitan Governance, 16.

28 Neyer (note 17), 4.

and the construction of nuclear plants near the frontiers. Many other examples for "external effects" of national policies affecting neighbours or people worldwide can be identified.[29] Let me name but four areas of concern:

- Reckless and solipsistic energy policies disregarding the adverse effects on the global climate may cause droughts in other states or even make them disappear, in part (e.g. Netherlands, Bangladesh) or completely (e.g. low lying countries in the south pacific) and generate waves of refugees across continents.
- Likely, totalitarian government, inhuman treatment and human rights violations, or even corruption and selfish economic behaviour of public authorities in one country may cause such migration of political or economic refugees and result in unbearable pressures on neighbouring or other states.
- The establishment of tax havens threaten, in a globally interlinked financial market, the effectiveness of national tax and monetary policies of most states, built on solidarity and differing ideas of social justice, and, thus, could put at risk these policies as well as the functioning of the financial system altogether.
- Failures to provide for effective regulation on data protection and privacy, or on intellectual property rights—as well as policies of systematic mass surveillance—in one country are about to destroy the internet as a means of worldwide information and communication with all its benefits for other states and people.

Politics here, therefore, can be of great concern for people there, not only economically but also politically, as a matter of security or under a social or humanitarian perspective.[30] There is not only a need for respect and cooperation, but also a responsibility of each state for adverse effects of its policies abroad. European food aid may destroy economic structures in developing countries; western values and patterns undermine traditional cultures and civilisations. To avoid domination, Matthias Kumm, therefore, sees international law in demand:

---

29 For the problem see also Bogdandy, "Demokratie, Globalisierung, Zukunft des Völkerrechts – eine Bestandsaufnahme", 870; Kumm (note 1), 612 et seq.

30 See also the account of three types of "justice-sensitive externalities" made by Kumm (note 1), 617–624.

"It is the point and purpose of international law to authoritatively resolve these concerns by way of a procedure that involves the fair participation of relevantly effected stakeholders, and it is the duty of states to support and sustain the development of an international law that is able to effectively fulfil such a function."[31]

Beyond national self-determination, he pursues, States have a "duty of justice" to act as "trustees of humanity", and "adequately take into account the legitimate interests of effected outsiders".[32] This "duty of justice" seems to have much to do with the mutual respect of the other, as an aspect of human dignity. But there are questions: How can international law ensure this "fair participation"? How can "outsiders" practically be given a relevant voice in internal politics of a state? Is the "duty of states to support and sustain the development" of such an international law actually existing law, or is it a vision to be worked on?

2. Global Challenges

There are other issues and, in some way, there is another perspective on the issues just mentioned, indicating that there exists a democratic deficit in our societies. As mentioned, there are global challenges that individual states are not able to cope with: Impede climate-change, regulate the global financial markets, fight against organised crime and international terrorism or protect human rights as well as the security of the internet—to name but a few.[33] If we want to preserve suitable conditions of life for future generations, if we do not want to leave our future in the hands of some self-empowered private actors but continue to believe in the beneficial role of individual and collective self-determination through democratically elected and controlled public authorities, each accountable to those who

31 Kumm (note 1), 613 f.

32 Kumm (note 1), 614.

33 See also Tully (note 26), 2, who counts "four major local and global problems of public goods today: (1) the problem of environmental destruction and climate change; (2) the problem of the horrendous inequality, exploitation and poverty of the Global South and the growing inequalities within the Global north and south; (3) the problem of global wars and the militarization; and (4) the problem of distrust and disrespect for different civilizations and peoples", and states that "when global citizens try to exercise their civic response-abilities in response to these four problems they find the official modes of citizenship available to them are not very effective" (ibid., 3).

are affected, the establishment of new institutions capable to act efficiently and democratically beyond the reach of the state seems to be needed. This is a requirement of democracy that so far has been neglected. Jürgen Habermas rightly states:

> "In view of a politically unregulated growth in the complexity of world society which is placing increasingly narrow systemic restrictions on the scope for addition of nation states, the requirement to extend political decision-making capabilities beyond national borders follows from the normative meaning of democracy itself."[34]

Cooperation among sovereign states through international agreements and organisations are the traditional instruments of states for dealing with common problems since the Peace of Westphalia in 1648. Yet, history shows that they do not always serve the purpose, in particular with regard to the preservation of peace. The limited scope and reach of national policies in a state-centred system of global governance also shields the global challenges from public engagement or even give rise to these problems. I understand Tully in this regard to conclude from the existing "limits on official channels of citizenship", that in addition to the "four global problems" he as identified[35] that there is

> "a fifth problem, the limitation or *incapacitation* of responsible citizenship. This limitation on and ineffectiveness of the exercise of civic capacities or capabilities is what we can call a democratic deficit of local and global citizenship".[36]

3. The Remedy: Global regulation

The traditional answer to transnational questions among sovereign states was cooperation among sovereign states through international conventional law—if war was not an option. History shows that the effecttiveness of this system is limited. If meaningful international agreements on common issues can be reached at all, not all countries involved may participate and violations of the obligations laid down in the agreement cannot efficiently be sanctioned. And national citizens engaged in finding

34 Habermas, crisis (note 4), 15; see also ibid., 55, on the "global need for regulation".

35 See supra, note 33.

36 Tully (note 26), 3.

solutions have little impact in the development of inter-national cooperation even to address the problems.

Externalities of national policies and global challenges often require regulatory solutions at a supranational or even global level, because citizens of even states on their own are unable to handle them. Climate change is an example insofar as excessive greenhouse gas emissions in some industrial countries threaten future generations everywhere, and, in particular, threaten the conditions of life in other countries, or even the very existence of some low-lying states. Taking measures against climate change, thus, is a global common interest, but it is of a particular interest of states that are not responsible for climate change.

Data protection and privacy on the Internet is another example: EU legislation requires far-reaching protection standards for users without regard where in the world data are stored or processed. This is a particular interest of Europeans. Given that not only most of the technology but also a great deal of services, including cloud services are offered by American undertakings, however, this legislation either remains ineffective or has external effects in requiring these undertakings to apply European standards. As the global reach of the Internet does not easily allow for selectivity without threatening the idea of a globally free Internet, European standards need to be applied also in other regions of the world, where other rights or principles would prevail. Thus, if a globally open Internet were considered in the common global interest, only a global regulatory framework on privacy—and for other issues alike—would effectively protect the fundamental rights of the individual users.[37]

III. Models of governance beyond the state

Diverse attempts have been made to give an answer to the question how to set up appropriate structures and procedures for ensuring effective legitimate government and regulation regarding common issues at the appropriate levels of political action. Let me shortly discuss some examples

37 For the efforts made in this regard at the UN-level see Pernice, "Das Völkerrecht des Netzes. Konstitutionelle Elemente eines globalen Rechtsrahmens für das Internet".

in search of democratic or, at least, participatory or judicial effectiveness: The EU, the UN, the Rio process the WTO and Internet governance.

1. The European Union: Supranational legitimacy as a model?

The first and perhaps the most developed model for legitimate political action at a supranational level in the interest of the people concerned is the European Union. Historically, it has been established for—and indeed did achieve—preserving peace, freedom and prosperity for the European people(s). Despite of allegedly conceptual shortcomings and of recent failures to "deliver" the common goods of prosperity and general welfare its success is evidenced, for instance, by the number of people and states that are still eager to accede the EU. Faced with the pressing challenges of globalisation, however, the EU has its own limits of reach. For effectively participating in the shaping of a new world order—as sketched out in Article 21 TEU—it may serve as a vehicle as well as a model, but it is limited to one region of the world, it is the result of specific historical conditions and its founding treaties, therefore, may not serve as an institutional template for other regions in the world and less so for the development of a global constitution.[38]

2. United Nations: Usurped sovereignty at the global level

With the same purpose, but more limited both in scope and in effectiveness, the United Nations can be understood as the most important institution and building block of global governance. Nearly all nations are contracting parties of the UN system. The problem, however, is that its structures do not reflect the principles and values it is bound to. It has no express legislative powers, there is no adequate system of equal representtation of people and hence it lacks democratic accountability. What is more important, the architecture of the UN is not about to guarantee that its primary mission, to preserve international peace, is effectively implemented under changing conditions of the international system.

38 For attempts to further develop his approach, however, see Habermas, crisis (note 5), x–xii, 11–12, 57–70.

Nor can we find an effective protection of human rights insofar as the Security Council is acting as a quasi-legislator in the fight against terrorism, a fact that has given rise to the Kadi-jurisprudence of the European Court of Justice (ECJ)[39] and to the jurisprudence of "equivalent protection test" of the European Court of Human Rights.[40] Jean L. Cohen understands the resolutions of the UN Security Council on smart sanctions as a "usurpation of global constituent power" the legitimacy of which is questionable.[41] Although some authors already give the UN Charter a constitutional quality,[42] the typical characteristics of constitutionalism—a direct relationship between the authorities and the individuals concerned (elections, legislative competence, direct effect), a meaningful separation of powers or checks and balances, the protection of fundamental rights and general observance of the rue of law—are still absent. Without a substantial reform, thus, the UN-system would not be an appropriate model for a "constitution" of global governance and regulation.

3. The WTO System: Towards judicial dispute settlement

Since the establishment of the WTO the world trade system has a new face: What was started as a pure international agreement, the GATT, now developed towards a multifaceted system of agreements on trade of goods and services including issues of intellectual property and based upon an effective dispute settlement arrangement, all within the legal frame of the WTO. The Dispute Settlement Body and the Appellate Body of the WTO

39 ECJ Case C-402/05 P and C-415/05, Kadi and Al Barakaat International Foundation v. Council and Commission [2008] ECR I-6351; see on this Peters (note 15), 153, 164; Kokott/Sobotta, "The Kadi Case—Constitutional Core Values and International Law—Finding the Balance?", 1015–24; de Búrca, "The European Court of Justice and the International Legal order After Kadi", 44 ff., Cohen, Globalization and Sovereignty. Rethinking Legality, Legitimacy, and Constitutionalism, 278, 280, 282 et seq.

40 See recently Platon, "The 'Equivalent Protection Test'. From European Union to United Nations, from Solange II to Solange I" with reference to the Al-Dulimi and Montana Management inc. V. Switzerland Judgment of the European Court of Human Rights, 226–262.

41 Cohen, Globalization and Sovereignty, 278, 280, 282 et seq.

42 Fassbender, The United Nations Charter as the Constitution of the International Community.

seem to give the international agreement more bite, as the contracting parties can enforce their rights to a considerable extent, so coming close to judicial powers. This is, indeed, a big step towards effectiveness. It does not, however, allow talking about a constitutionalisation of the WTO[43] or even about the constitution of the WTO.[44] It remains a treaty among states that does not confer any direct rights upon individuals. Nor is there any provision for legislative powers and democratic participation in the procedures of decision-making.

4. The Rio Process —Towards Multi-stakeholder participation

More adequate as a conceptual approach could be the Rio-Process: Sustainable development is a common concern worldwide. Accordingly, a "global compact" was negotiated in 1992 and designated to inform and give guidance to the policies of all states. Both, the principles laid down in the Rio Declaration and the policies agreed to in the Agenda 21 initiate and stimulate a process of awareness-rising and action at all levels through international conventions and national policies monitored and discussed at the UN level by the "Commission for Sustainable Development" (CSD). With a view to establish a more effective system, the Rio+20 Conference in 2012 has replaced the CSD by the "High-Level Political Forum of Sustainable Development".[45] One of the innovations in this Forum is the idea that, to make the outcome of the reporting and review process on the implementation of the Rio Agenda in the Forum "relevant and impactful",

> "[...] it is important to engage fully non-state actors (UN system, major groups including business and industry and other relevant stakeholders) in the forum. This was seen as an important way to improve transparency and implementation at all

43 Critical for more reasons also Cass, The Constitutionalization of the World Trade Organization. Legitimacy, Democracy, and Community in the International Trading System; for a more theoretically grounded critique see Lawrence, "Contesting constitutionalism: Constitutional discourse at the WTO", 63–90.

44 See Petersmann (ed.), Reforming the World Trading System: Legitimacy, Efficiency and Democratic Governance.

45 See http://sustainabledevelopment.un.org/csd.html.

levels. Non-governmental stakeholders are an important part of shaping the forum and its work in the future".[46]

To set up the Forum, an Expert Group "on the role of the high-level political forum on sustainable development in post-2015 development framework" was established and met on April 30th and May 1st 2014. In one of its "key messages", the Experts highlight the "hybrid" structure of the Forum, "where major groups and other stakeholders can engage through solid modalities". It was qualified as "a great achievement for the UN". Another key message goes even one step further: "The UN is a 'norm-setting" institution; how best can the forum and international community help to translate agreed norms into policies at the national level?"[47]

At least the ambitions of the Expert Group seem to indicate that the new High-Level Political Forum of Sustainable Development will take the form of a multi-stakeholder body. Their architects intend so to give its work a relevant impact upon national politics in matters of common global concern: Such "norms" issued in a multi-stakeholder process may not be binding law, but they are intended to impact national policies and be transposed, as appropriate, into binding law.

The mechanism reminds the "open method of coordination" (OMC) invented by the EU for intergovernmental processes complementary to the exercise of EU competences.[48] It differs from the OMC, however, in that the OMC does not involve the civil society and other stakeholders. If multistakeholerism is open to their participation and even includes individuals, the question may be asked whether participatory multi-stakeholder processes—at the European or global level—can be regarded as more effective, and as more legitimate than coordination, cooperation and treaties among states or their governments.

In the ongoing process of defining and developing this new form of governance not only its strengths but also its limits gain visibility: Even though "multistakeholer governance has dramatically shifted traditional

46 UN Sustainable Development Knowledge Platform, Announcement for the Expert Group Meeting on the role of the high-level political forum on sustainable development in post-2015 development framework, 30 April – 1 May 2014, available at: http://sustainabledevelopment.un.org/index.php?page=view&nr=667&type=13&menu=1556.

47 See http://sustainabledevelopment.un.org/index.php?page=view&nr=998&type=12&menu =1556.

48 See for details: Braams, Koordinierung als Kompetenzkategorie, 215 f.

procedures of inter-governmental politics towards the inclusion of non-state actors", Stefania Milan and Arne Hintz suggest that „multi-stakeholderism risks becoming a smokescreen that involves civil society in—and thereby legitimizes—substantial transformations that may not necessarily be in the interest of users and citizens".[49] This does, however, not deny the potential of the approach for an openness and transparency of processes that were so far regarded as a matter of governments and their diplomats acting in secrecy. The question remains how multi-stakeholderism ought to be organised and structured so to produce legitimate outcomes.

5. Internet governance: Exploring Private-Public Ordering

Internet governance[50] is an example for regulation at the global scale where neither national legislation nor international agreements are the method for ensuring the proper functioning of the system. Though the initiative originates from the American military,[51] relevant rules were made originnally—and continue to be made—by private actors, academics, engineers and business-people. Those who invented and developed the Internet understood it to constitute a virtual second world characterised by openness and freedom: The "cyber-space" where governments and regulators had no say. What Jon Perry Barlow proclaimed in his "Declaration of the independence of Cyberspace" in February 1996,[52] however, could

49 Milan/Hintz, In Multistakeholderism We Trust: On the Limits of the Multistakeholder Debate.

50 For a comprehensive overview see: "Hofmann, Internet Governance: Zwischen staatlicher Autorität und privater Koordination", 10; Kleinwächter, "From Self-Governance to Public-Private Partnership: The Changing Role of Governments in the Management of the Internet's Core Resources", 1103–1126; for a new attempt to define the term "Internet Governance" see: Hofmann/Katzenbach/Gollatz, Between Coordination and Regulation: Conceptualizing Governance in Internet Governance.

51 Lessig, Code Version 2.0, 2, refers to a research project in the Defence Department; see also: Hülsbömer, Vom Arpanet zum WWW. Zeitreise: So entstand das Internet; Tietje/Nowrot, "Das Internet im Fokus des transnationalen Wirtschaftsrechts: Normative Ordnungsstrukturen für den E-Commerce", 328–331.

52 Jon Perry Barlow, A Declaration of the Independence of Cyberspace, 8 February 1996.

not develop without rules and institutions.[53] Today, nobody contests that there cannot be an exemption from the application of general law also in the cyberspace.[54] Yet, the global reach of the Internet implies that internet-law cannot be a matter of singular national legislators. Both, the infrastructure and the operation of the Internet need common global regulation.[55] Classical international law—for the difficulties to reach consensus on the critical points[56]—can only give partial solutions.[57] It is true that new initiatives are taken to explore the potential of an "international law of the net" more deeply i.e. with a view to ensure the respect of human rights also in the internet.[58] Yet, from the beginning, the legal setting of Internet governance differs profoundly from any national, supra- or international public law arrangement.

Technical norms or codes, indispensable for the functioning of the Internet and the interoperability of the network infrastructures, emerge from an open process based upon "requests for comments" that may get normative value through a "rough consensus" within the framework of the Internet Engineering Task Force (IETF).[59] For one of the key regulatory tasks of the internet, the distribution of the domain names, a private non-profit organisation incorporated in Californian law was formed in 1998,

53 For a short account on the development and debate, with some conclusions see also Lessig (note 51), 2–8.

54 On the debate and development see Viellechner, Transnationalisierung des Rechts, 111–114.

55 Ibid., 115 ff.

56 Ibid., 117–120, referring also to the difficulties of a hybrid regulation (Henry Perritt).

57 For an account, nevertheless, of international economic law, in particular WTO-law, setting important rules on e-commerce, intellectual property rights etc., see Tietje/ Nowrot (note 51), 335–359.

58 Initiative on „Völkerrecht des Netzes" in the coalition-agreement of the three German parties in government of November 27, 2013, available at: http://www.cdu.de/artikel/der-koalitionsvertrag-von-cdu-csu-und-spd, 149: "Um die Grund- und Freiheitsrechte der Bürgerinnen und der Bürger auch in der digitalen Welt zu wahren und die Chancen für die demokratischen Teilhabe der Bevölkerung am weltweiten Kommunikationsnetz zu fördern, setzen wir uns für ein Völkerrecht des Netzes ein, damit die Grundrechte auch in der digitalen Welt gelten. Das Recht auf Privatsphäre, das im Internationalen Pakt für bürgerliche und politische Rechte garantiert ist, ist an die Bedürfnisse des digitalen Zeitalters anzupassen." See already Mayer, "The Internet and Public International Law—Worlds Apart?", 617–622, and Pernice, Völkerrecht (note 37).

59 See Kleinwächter, "Editorial", in: id. (ed.), Internet und Demokratie, 7, 9.

named ICANN.[60] It is based on a number of agreements, including a memorandum of understanding with the US Department of Commerce, under which ICANN is entrusted with the management of the domain name system, notwithstanding some supervisory function of the Department of Commerce.[61] For the making of its policies ICANN follows a multi-stakeholder-model of decentralized governance placing "individuals, industry, non-commercial interests and government on an equal level".[62] Governments are represented in the Governments Advisory Committee (GAC) only, they have no direct control on the ICANN policies. It is a construction of private actors under private law, in addition, that ICANN has developed with a view to give a solution to the "cyber-squatting" problem: The Uniform Domain Name Dispute Resolution Policy (UDRP). The rules of procedure of the UDRP are made part of every single registration of a domain name, so, thanks to the access ICANN has on the register, it also can directly execute decisions made by the competent arbitration panels.[63]

The elaboration of specific standards of web-technologies, such as html5, is among the tasks of the World Wide Web Consortium (W3C). These standards too are proposed, discussed and adopted by the diverse stakeholders, members of the W3C, through a consensus-based process including also the public.[64]

The multi-stakeholder approach is applied, in particular, for the discourses organised at the Internet Governance Forum (IGF), and it has

60 ICANN Website: https://www.icann.org/resources/pages/what-2012-02-25-en. For the development and structure see: Viellechner, Transnationalisierung (note 55), 128–141; in short: id., "Constitutionalism as a Cipher: On the Convergence of Constitutionalist and Pluralist Approaches to the Globalization of Law", 613–4.

61 Memorandum of Understanding between the U.S. Department of Commerce and Internet Corporation for Assigned Names and Numbers. For the background see Uerpmann-Wittzack, "Multilevel Internet Governance Involving the European Union, Nation States and NGOs", 145, 150 et seq.

62 See ICANN, "Beginner's Guide to Participating in ICANN, 2013", 2.

63 For details see Viellechner, Transnationalisierung (note 54), 141–143. Generally on non-state actors as standard setters in the international arena see Peters/Förster/Koechlin, "Towards non-state actors as effective, legitimate, and accountable standard setters", 492 ff.

64 For details see Facts about W3C on the W3C website, available at: http://www.w3.org/Consortium/facts#public.

proven very effective at the NETmundial of April 23 and 24, 2014.[65] The IGF was initiated by the 2003/05 World Summit on the Information Society (WSIS) in Geneva/Tunis that was organised by the International Telecommunications Union (ITU) according to the Resolution 56/183 of the UN General Assembly.[66] One of the outcomes of this Summit is the "Tunis Agenda", that states on Internet governance in its paras. 29–31 as follows:

"29. We reaffirm the principles enunciated in the Geneva phase of the WSIS, in December 2003, that the Internet has evolved into a global facility available to the public and its governance should constitute a core issue of the Information Society agenda. The international management of the Internet should be multilateral, transparent and democratic, with the full involvement of governments, the private sector, civil society and international organizations. It should ensure an equitable distribution of resources, facilitate access for all and ensure a stable and secure functioning of the Internet, taking into account multilingualism.

30. We acknowledge that the Internet, a central element of the infrastructure of the Information Society, has evolved from a research and academic facility into a global facility available to the public.

31. We recognize that Internet governance, carried out according to the Geneva principles, is an essential element for a people-centred, inclusive, development-oriented and non-discriminatory Information Society. Furthermore, we commit ourselves to the stability and security of the Internet as a global facility and to ensuring the requisite legitimacy of its governance, based on the full participation of all stakeholders, from both developed and developing countries, within their respective roles and responsibilities."[67]

It is the UN General Secretary who was asked, under para. 72 of the Tunis Agenda, to not only convene the IGF, but also to review its operation and

65 Global Multistakeholder Meeting on the Future of Internet Governance, on the invitation of the government of Brazil, official website: www.netmundial.org. For the outcome see the NETmundial Multistakeholder Statement of April 24, 2014, with the "Internet Governance Principles" and a "Roadmap for the future evolution of the Internet Governance Ecosystem".

66 See the UN General Assembly Resolution 56/183 (21 December 2001) giving the ITU a leading role in the management of the World Summit. For more information see the website of WSIS available at: http://www.itu.int/wsis/basic/about.html.

67 Paras. 29–31 of the Tunis Agenda for the Information Society, 18 November 2005, available at: http://www.itu.int/wsis/docs2/tunis/off/6rev1.html.

to make recommendations regarding the extension of its mandate after five years. Nine IGF-meetings have taken place, meanwhile, around the world. As Janis Karklins, the Chair of the Multistakeholder Advisory Group (MAG) stated in his address to the ninth IGF meeting in Istanbul, more than 3000 participants from all continents representing different stakeholder groups (governments, private sector, civil society, technical community, and academia) came together. He explains why "so many government ministers and parliamentarians, CEOs and Internet entrepreneurs, civil rights defenders, scholars, engineers and other key stakeholders in the global Internet community devote one week of their time to engage in discussions about the future of the Internet" as follows:

"The answer is clear—all of these stakeholders care about maintaining a free, open, interoperable, stable, secure and trustworthy Internet within a multilateral, democratic, transparent and inclusive framework of multi-stakeholder governance as defined by the Tunis Agenda for the Information Society and endorsed by the World Summit on the Information Society (WSIS) in 2005. The IGF is a unique global forum for convening these multi-stakeholder discussions. It ensures the Internet continues to evolve in the global public interest consistent with these fundamental characteristics and objectives for the benefit of all Internet users".[68]

It is important to note the term "global public interest" used by the Chair, in this introduction, as guiding the future evolution of the Internet, and the self-conception of the IGF to serve this interest. And the global public interest, insofar, is understood to be articulated in a deliberative way at the IGF within a "multilateral, democratic, transparent and inclusive framework of multi-stakeholder governance". Given the openness of the discussions led in each session on specific topics at the IGF for active on-line participation from around the world, it is possible to conclude that at least the IGF gives voice to people at a global scale on issues of greatest general concern, and it so serves as a platform of a global public discourse. As participation is open and inclusive, everybody present off-line or on-line, connected through the Internet, has a voice and is respected as a participant with full rights. To some extent, thus, the "constitution" of Internet governance can be understood as an expression of what is required by the principle of human dignity.

68 Ambassador Janis Karlins, IGF 2014—the gateway for the future, available at: http://www.intgovforum.org/cms/blog-igf-2014.

The IGF does not take decisions, but innovations introduced at the ninth "edition" of the IGF in 2014 aim at "identifying more focused and concrete outcomes and the promotion of best practices on a range of important issues such as the multi-stakeholder model of Internet governance, child online protection, local content creation, ensuring security and combatting spam".[69] In addition, among the more specific key issues of the internet addressed at this edition are policies enhancing access, growth and development on the Internet, bridging the digital divide, freedom of expression, privacy, and cultural and linguistic diversity. The outcome of these discussions will certainly give some reference points for future principles and rules on these issues to be adopted in some way through other procedures at the international, regional and national level.

It is an open question whether or not at all, on the basis of another review presented to the General Assembly of the United Nations the mandate of the IGC will be extended in 2015 for another five or ten years. If so, it could also be amended so as to provide for procedures ensuring, on the basis of the clear recognition of the right to equal concern and respect of all participants, a more concrete outcome through conclusions or principles to be adopted by consensus of the participants present or connected to its meetings online.

4. Conclusion: Elements of a constitution of global governance

The EU is not a model for organising a system of democratically legitimate and effective governance at the global level, for it involves a too advanced degree of integration. Many of its characteristics, such as the recognition of the active European citizen as a fundament for the legitimacy of the EU policies,[70] are worth to be considered in the effort to design a system of global decision-making and regulation for matters of global concern. Also the UN and the WTO regulatory system of world trade, the Rio process and the development of internet governance from ICANN to the IGF offer elements that help institutionalizing a meaningful global public dis-

69 Ibid.

70 Highlighting the European citizenship in its democratic sense: Calliess/Hartmann, Zur Demokratie in Europa: Unionsbürgerschaft und europäische Öffentlichkeit, in particular 101–154.

course on what is in the global public interest. On top of platforms offering opportunities for people and organisations to contribute to this discourse there is a need for common institutions for democratically legitimate rule-making and compliance-control, a system of judicial review and dispute settlement as well as provision for the participation in the decision-making processes of the relevant stakeholders, if not the (global) citizens, and for the effective protection of fundamental rights.

If these conditions are met, global constitutionalism can exercise its function as a compensation[71] for democratic and efficiency deficits of national policies. It is clear, also, that a different concept of citizenship is required for a global system of governance open to a determining role to be played beyond state-centred institutions and processes. What Tully takes as

> "the classic democratic premise that people become citizens by actually exercising their civic capacities or *response-abilities* by participating in civic activities with fellow citizens for the sake of public goods in the webs of relationships of governance to which they are subject. People acquire the democratic form of subjectivity and intersubjectivity, as well as the complex arts of being a citizen, by engaging in public-oriented activities for the sake of public goods. This is the starting point for thinking of citizenship that accords with the dignity of self-governing persons and peoples",[72]

Tully conceptualizes on this basis what he calls "cooperative citizenship", it is not a status but rather an attitude and engagement that constitutes public spheres in a broad sense. Hard work of cooperative citizens over centuries, he points out, has produced representative governments, but the concept of cooperative citizen is not limited to the relationship of state institutions to the individual. If the institutions established for the common good do not deliver, the cooperative citizens may "take back their response-abilities of self-governing citizenship and exercise them themselves" by either reforming them, or by organising "democratic negotiation networks locally and globally around the relationship in question and around the way it causes a global problem", so exercising non-violent pressure through "activities such as protests, petitions, boycotts, non-cooperation, arguing and bargaining, alternative dispute resolution, and transformative justice",

71 See above, note 16.

72 Tully (note 26), 19.

or—"when the powers-that-be refuse to enter into such negotiations", Tully says—they

> "simply re-appropriate the capacities that they were exercising in the privatised activity that they find unjustifiable and they exercise these capacities themselves in their own organisations. They exercise powers of popular sovereignty directly—rather than delegating them to private or public corporations that exercise them in ways that harm public goods and evade democratic control".[73]

What is important in this concept for the present proposition are the dynamics and openness, in contrast to any statist state-related approaches. With the affirmation that "citizenship accords with dignity of the self-governing persons and peoples", who exercise, in case, "powers of popular sovereignty directly…", Tully puts the individual in the centre of what may be established progressively, in a process of trial and error, for effectively producing public goods, and this without evading democratic control. And if he emphasizes as the ethical basis of cooperative citizenship: "one should be the change" and not wait for modern governments to change the world,[74] this clearly demonstrates a new way of understanding how governance, from the local to the global level, can be undertaken and organised by individuals connecting for action in diverse forms, settings and levels. The European Union is but one of the examples, where supranational and intergovernmental structures have been established for better achieving goals that are beyond the reach of individual states, the Rio-Process and, within its scope, the Aarhus-System[75] and the emerging system of internet governance are other cases for the increasing participation of citizens and the civil society in norm-generating processes that are complementary to the classical forms of national legislation and international treaties.

---

73 Tully (note 26), 23 f. See also ibid., 25: "They simply re-appropriate and exercise democratically the relevant capacities of popular sovereignty that they are said to have delegated to states and corporations in modernisation theories".

74 Ibid., 27 et seq.

75 In particular for the functioning of the compliance mechanism under Article 15 of the Aarhus-Convention see: Bunge, Rechtsbehelfe in Umweltangelegenheiten: Vorgaben der Aarhus-Konvention und deutsches Recht, Natur und Recht, 605. Understanding the interaction of the global, European and national actors as a dynamic multilevel system: Pernice, "Umweltvölker- und europarechtliche Vorgaben zum Verbandsklagerecht und das System des deutschen Verwaltungsrechtsschutzes. Impulse zur Rechtsentwicklung im Mehrebenenverbund".

IV. Global constitutionalism and legitimacy

Experience from these and other models of rule-making in matters of common interest for the public good can be helpful for shaping institutions and procedures for regulation at the global level in a more or less democratic form. It allows further developing existing concepts for a new world order, for the constitutionalization of international law and the UN, or for global constitutionalism[76] that do not provide a satisfactory answer to the question of legitimacy. Granted, some legitimacy also for action at the international level follows from the representation of democratically elected governments negotiating agreements that are than ratified by national parliaments. The UN system, the WTO and many other international organisations are based upon this approach, though not all of their member states can be qualified as democracies. In addition, the work of the International Committee of the Red Cross, a private organisation, as well as the quasi-legislative activity of the tri-partite organs of the International Labour Organisation are examples for non-state actors of the civil society being involved in international normative processes and so adding to their legitimacy and giving the organisations a certain constitutional character.[77]

Constitutionalism however, as understood here, is beyond this indirect and very limited legitimation: It implies a direct relationship between people and institutions, both for the decision-making processes and for the binding effect of such decisions upon the individual. Constitutionalism requires that norms that directly impact rights or create obligations of the individual, within or beyond states, to be accepted as legitimate can be reconstructed as rooted in their own will. An example for this at a supranational level is the EU, even though there is a potential for improve-

76 For a critical overview see Kadelbach/Kleinlein, "International Law—a Constitution for Mankind? An Attempt at a Re-appraisal with an Analysis of Constitutional Principles", 303–347.

77 See Kadelbach/Kleinlein, (note 76), 324–327, where emphasis is given on the legitimacy based upon "the participation of NGO's on an institutional basis, so that it may claim to have incorporated a procedure of co-operation with interested groups and to have established a special standard of legitimacy" (ibid., 327).

ment.[78] Wherever a need for common global regulation is identified, it cannot be conceived as legitimate without constitutional structures and provisions ensuring people's political participation, democratic control and accountability, the respect of the rule of law as well as the protection of human dignity and other fundamental rights. People, their will and their rights need to be taken seriously.

Recent contributions to the discussion of global constitutionalism indicate a re-discovery of the individual for constituting legitimacy at the global level (infra 1.) and a specific role of the judiciary in the development of a general global law legitimized by the transnational cosmopolitan citizenry (infra 2.). For both approaches the internet seems to present a specific tool enhancing the impact of the thesis through the empowerment of citizens and stakeholders (infra 3.).[79]

1. Anne Peters: From bourgeois to citoyens

Anne Peters describes, in a remarkable clear manner, not only the contingence of the loss of the individual from the vantage point of international law in the 19th century, but also detects a return of the individuals' rights and obligations into the focus of international law during the last decades. She observes a "paradigm shift in international law in the sense that the integration of individuals in the international legal process, far beyond human rights, has become 'the basic axiom' of the international legal order". She concludes that:[80]

"From a constitutionalist perspective, the empowerment of individual beings is a core objective of any constitutional order… The constitutionalist interpretation of

78 Ingolf Pernice, Multilevel Constitutionalism and the Crisis of Democracy in Europe, lecture given at the Aristoteles University of Saloniki the 4th of December 2014, stream available at: https://www.youtube.com/watch?v=Do081tYopAE.

79 For another approach focussing on the individual regarding „global commons" see: Kotzur, "Völkerrecht von der Menschheit her denken", 43, talking about the globally "internetted" humanity. Constitutionalism, for him, is not dependent on states, but always a matter of people. Humanity, and so the global community of human beings, is conceptualised as a constitution-making power, related to the global commons (among which he also counts the internet as—potentially—humankinds' common resource of knowledge and information) or "concerns of all humankind", see ibid., 49, 55, 59.

80 Peters (note 14), 158.

Articles 6 Human Rights Declaration and 16 (2) IPCCR is that these provisions may not reasonably be limited to the domestic legal capacity, but that they enshrine a human right to have international legal personality".

Her account on already existing individual rights to participation in processes of global governance, developments towards individualized law-enforcement in international and national forums, the emergence of individual rights beyond human rights, individuals' role as "creditors of international responsibility" and subjects of obligations under international law allows her to conclude on a "trend towards *citoyenneté*" or "a transformation 'from subject of international law to international citizen", which is, as she posits,"part of the transformation of the international legal system from a Vattelian inter-state system into a universal constitutional democracy".[81]
Not far from the EU model of dual legitimisation (Article 10 TEU) Anne Peters pursues her approach in advocating for a "duality of global democracy" (the "*statist track*") rooted in the will of the peoples in their nation state as well in "direct democratic action on the supra-state level" (the "*individual track*").[82] For similar reasons as outlined above, she observes that "governance has become a multilevel process" and concludes that "a new design to enhance global democracy is needed".[83]

The problem is how to design democratic decision-making processes at the global level. A world parliament, as already advocated by Walter Schücking and proposed, more recently, by Jürgen Habermas,[84] is difficult to imagine as a meaningful representation of the diverse political interests in each part of the globe and would not bring people closer to the rule-making institutions. Anne Peters discusses alternative types of democracy, such as a deliberative, a participatory and a contestatory model. They all avoid the need for aggregation of will of "*demoi*" in pre-determined territories such as required for voting, and in some way substitute voice to voting. But she concludes that they "are no real substitute for formal democracy".[85]

Instead, Anne Peters spells out her "two-track" model of global democracy taken from EU experience: As states act as "democratic mediat-

81 Ibid., 178.

82 Peters, "Dual Democracy" (note 19), 264–5.

83 Ibid., 268.

84 Ibid., 320 Footnote 211, Habermas, Crisis (note 4), 54, 63–70.

85 Peters, "Dual Democracy" (note 19), 268–271.

ors", she pleads for the recognition of "a global constitutional prin-ciple of domestic democracy", coupled with a "transnational citizenship" to be the basis for a "Non-state democratisation of international governance" organised through "schemes of participation and representation that cut across nation states".[86] Not a uniform language, not homogeneity of a people is required in her view, but "a uniform space of communication".[87] Transnational referendums and consultations as well as the installation of a "global peoples' assembly" are considered, though she accepts that "true parliamentary powers, namely the adoption of global laws which would complement or replace inter-state treaties, are utopian".[88] Nevertheless she discusses parliamentary assemblies for the diverse organisations like WTO and, in particular, a "UN Parliamentary Assembly" as useful for the "typical mediating function of parliaments" creating transparency and organising interests.[89] More transparency, finally, is advocated as a "pre-requisite of accountability" and "a manifestation of constitutionalisation".[90]

The potential of the Internet is not addressed in this account, though it could well be the tool for organising the space of communication on issues of common concern—like Internet governance, but more than this. Could it not be the path towards "non-state democratisation of international governance", providing means to ensure transparency of political processes and decision-making and give people access to all relevant information and data, necessary to make their informed judgment on questions of global public interest? If a global parliamentary assembly with legislative powers is utopian and may be difficult to establish, a Global Governance Forum designed upon the experience with the IGF could be the more appropriate platform for an open discussion of the issues at stake, preparing for taking regulatory decisions by institutions to be vested with the powers needed.[91]

86 Ibid., 296–341. See also Habermas, Crisis (note 5), 58–59, 62, 65, using the terms "world citizens", "constituted world society" (68), or "cosmopolitan community" (69).

87 Peters, "Dual Democracy" (note 19), 308.

88 Ibid., 320.

89 Ibid., 324 f.

90 Ibid., 326–330, 329.

91 See infra V.2.

2. Cassese and von Bogdandy/Venzke: international courts

For Sabino Cassese there is another path towards the emergence of a new global legal order. In his view the judges, national and international, are progressively forming a network beyond national borders developing some common principles through which the diverse legal orders worldwide are linked together and receive a common basis. Cassese concretizes Anne-Marie Slaughter's concept of "A Global community of courts"[92] and concludes, on the basis of a number of striking cases, that through their judicial dialogue or conversation the judges are constituting a new global legal order. If the outcome were not to be a "diritto globale generale",[93] the judges nevertheless would seem to find rules of co-existence, "passarelles" or linkages among the legal orders—national, supranational, even private like the ICANN-system—that do not follow rules of legal hierarchy.[94] But he finds them surmounting fragmentation and constructing "a global system of legal orders".[95]

Cassese rightly raises the question of legitimacy, in particular since such activities of general impact may be considered "counter-majoritarian". For him, it is the special role of the judges whose competence is an essential part of the balance of powers as a guaranty for liberty, so the question of legitimacy appears as "un 'falso problema'".[96]

Armin von Bogdandy and Ingo Venzke, instead, look for a specific source of legitimacy. Their fascinating book with the telling title: "In wessen Namen. Internationale Gerichte in Zeiten globalen Regierens" describes the role of courts and, in particular, international courts not merely as dispute settlement bodies, but in a much broader sense as multifunctional actors of public authority and integral part of the system of global governance.[97] They are making law, exercising public authority, and therefore they need democratic legitimacy. The analysis shows that only the peoples and the individuals constituting the peoples can provide the democratic legitimacy as members of a transnational cosmopolitan citizen-

92 Harvard International Law Journal 44 (2002) 191.

93 Cassese, I Tribunali de Babele. I giudici alla recerca di un nuovo ordine globale, 42.

94 Ibid., 44.

95 Ibid., 93–101: "I giudici come costruttori del sistema globale degli ordini giuridici".

96 Ibid., 103–105.

97 Bogdandy/Venzke, In wessen Namen. Internationale Gerichte in Zeiten globalen Regierens.

ry.[98] This is why the authors conclude that international courts would take their decisions in the name of the peoples and the citizens[99] —a result, which is not far from the idea of double legitimacy we find in Article 10 TEU and in the propositions of Anne Peters and Jürgen Habermas already mentioned.

This account, however, remains abstract. There is no doubt that courts, national as well as international, are established by constitutional law, general law or international agreements ratified by parliaments. They consist of judges that are chosen through procedures establishing some link of legitimacy between democratically elected bodies and the courts. Courts have the task of interpreting and applying democratically adopted law so giving its provisions a normative reality. But their task is by no means only a mechanic one. In implementing their judicial function, they also have to develop the law in a creative manner, establish and develop general principles of law.[100] The European Court of Justice is an excellent example for this creative function that is crucial for the functioning of the European Union. It is part of the democratically established constitutional system of the EU.

Yet, these institutional and functional provisions alone would not suffice for establishing the legitimacy of judge-made law, neither at the national nor at the European, nor at the global level. Courts do not act in isolation, they cannot take their decisions "in the name of the people"—or of the citizens of the Union, or "of the peoples and the citizens" at a global scale, if their work is not embedded in a dialogue with the public: Colleagues, other courts, media, academia, the public sphere at large may applaud, consent or react critically, decisions may be subject to intense scrutiny in seminars and even in the political discourse—if the (constitutional) legislator does not correct the decision by an authoritative act. Judges cannot ignore this public reaction that triggers reconsideration of the courts' arguments or even of the rule established by a judgment in the next convenient case. In a longer perspective, "responsive jurisdiction" is a dialogue with the citizen, the legal and scientific communities and other

98 Ibid., 290.

99 Ibid., 291–2.

100 For their role in a "constitutional approach" to international law see Kadelbach/ Kleinlein (note 76), 324, 337–347.

stakeholders, a process of trial and error in search of solutions accepted as legitimate.[101]

3. The Internet: Empowerment of the citizens

What is new in the present context is the analysis of the exchange of views, cooperation and dialogue among constitutional and other courts not only at the European level,[102] but similarly at the global level. And it is the internet that can play a crucial role in not only facilitating the dialogue among courts but also in empowering the individual to participate actively in this conversation, so adding to the legitimacy of the judicial contribution in the making of a global rule:

- What Anne-Marie Slaughter describes as networks of constitutional courts[103] may develop to play a much more important role with the internet allowing to find most of the jurisprudence of other courts as well as comments and accounts of the follow-up, within seconds at any place in the world. This includes the communication with foreign and international judges directly, as appropriate, to exchange documents, to discuss in groups and have seminars without travelling. Easy access to comparative law and analysis, facilitated by the internet, will particularly promote the emergence of common principles in accordance with human rights recognised in international conventions, elements of a *ius commune globale* as a common reference, orientation and criterion also for legitimate exercise of executive and legislative powers at all levels.

101 For the judge-made law as the result of a communicative process in this sense see already Pernice, "Die Dritte Gewalt im europäischen Verfassungsverbund", 38–42.

102 See "Voßkuhle, Multilevel Cooperation of the European Constitutional Courts. Der Europäische Verfassungsgerichtsverbund", 175–198; see also Pernice, "La Rete Europea di Costituzionalità, Der Europäische Verfassungsverbund und die Netzwerktheorie", 51–71.

103 For the increasing readiness of courts to refer to judgments of courts in foreign countries or international courts see Benvenisti, "Reclaiming Democracy: The Strategic Uses of Foreign and International Law by National Courts", who establishes particularly the legitimacy of such references, ibid., 44–47; Slaughter, The New World Order, 65–103: "Judges: Constructing a Global Legal System", with particular emphasis on the role of networks of courts (ibid., summary, 100 ff.).

- With the internet, this dialogue is not limited to professional participants, not limited to powerful media and academics, but people generally are empowered to take stake and make their voice heard. Social networks, blogging, even twitter allow individual or massive reaction, where deemed appropriate, and this reaction is not limited to local or national issues but, as the effects of a ruling may cross borders or have even a global impact, point to court decisions that are taken anywhere in the world. Though in an un-coordinated way, common principles and, if so, a *ius commune globale* will emerge through the jurisprudence of the global network of courts communicating, through the internet, not only among each-other but also with—and under the control of—all relevant stakeholders including the general public.

Courts and their networks, after all, can play an important role in developing and giving effect to principles and rules having a global application in a legitimate way, if they are considered as a part of a system of global governance and open not only for the dialogue among each-other but also for the comments of the stakeholders and the general public. This seems to give the individuals, as global citizens, a stake in the development of a general global law by courts. This may include that, under the control of the global citizenry, courts take account—as appropriate in a given case—of principles emerging from discussions at global public forums such as the IGF, the NETmundial or the proposed GGF.

V. Enabling global constitutionalism

As the examples given above seem to indicate, the Internet has the potential to provide better conditions for constructing legitimacy for normative processes and regulation at the global level. It enhances the legitimising power of the individual as necessary in order to *take people seriously*. Seven constitutive elements of an internet-driven global constitutional framework will be identified and developed hereafter for further discussion: The "enabling" *basis* for meaningful participation in political processes at the global level is a free and open worldwide interoperable internet giving people equal access to "humankinds knowledge and information" (infra 1.). It presents an open *space* as needed to develop a public sphere with free access to communication, networks and platforms allowing a transnational public discourse and effective partici-pation of people in global political forums (infra 2.). This sphere would not emerge without an *institutional framework* at the "operative" level, where diverse opinions and interests are channelled and transformed into manageable normative propositions (infra 3.) following the *method* of a consensus-based multi-stakeholder standard-setting process leading to a still non-binding normative framework that serves as a reference for the policies of states, undertakings, civil society as well as for private enterprises and individuals (infra 4.). Such standards may, if appropriate, be *validated* as binding law through references in binding international agreements, in decisions of international organisations, in European or national legislation or the judiciary (infra 5.). Oversight through a *judicial* institution would ensure compliance, the settlement of disputes and the protection of individual rights as a matter of effectiveness and confidence of people (infra 6.). Extensive monitoring of the functioning and effects should, finally, be the basis of an inclusive *review* process providing people control and the opportunity to initiate reform, if deemed necessary, and adaptation to new developments (infra 7.).

1. The basis: knowledge, information, education

In an ever-shrinking world, where geographic and political borders have lost their categorical meaning and interpersonal relationships worldwide have reached a formerly unknown density, people in one part of the world are increasingly concerned by, and interested in legal systems, political processes and the conditions of life in other parts of the world. Reasons are not only the externalities of their respective policies, but also the security, humanitarian and economic issues there are becoming relevant here. Knowledge and dialogue about these conditions are of value. Having developed during the last twenty years the most dynamic and efficient tool for communication, information and social networking at a global scale, the Internet became the prominent tool for gathering information and exchanging experiences with people from other countries, and so adds to the merger of the fragmented national societies into one global society.

The internet gives people quasi unlimited access to news from all parts of the world, books, scientific insights and culture through electronic libraries, newspapers, blogs, education including massive open online courses etc., and it gives access also to the texts of constitutions, legislation, jurisprudence of highest courts worldwide. By means of the Internet, the promise of access to information and the transparency of public authorities can be made effective.[104] If knowledge is power, open access to information and knowledge resources from anywhere for everybody worldwide, thus, is about to transform the society, power structures and politics[105] and even the concept of "constitution" as a legal instrument of the society for organising itself politically, within and beyond national borders.[106]

The tradition of liberal constitutionalism suggests that individuals are ultimately the source of any legitimate public authority at any level. If the questions of accessibility in terms of hardware and software are successfully addressed, the internet, thus, may empower people in all parts of the world to have the information and tools necessary for defining themselves as global citizens, and it can be developed as the transmission mechanism in the formation of the political will in a society "constituting" itself at the global level.

To do this in a democratic and, thus, legitimate manner, a global public space is needed.

2. The "space": Public sphere and political participation

As a "digital market place" the internet has deeply changed the media-landscape and the public sphere, it has opened it potentially to everybody: The result is a global public space with no relevant barriers to access. While in former times the public sphere was characterised by a one-to-many communication through print media, radio or television, the internet provides "a new unbounded space for communicative interaction", as James Bohman notes, "as a *many-to-many* mode of communication", that has "lowered the costs of interaction with an indefinite and potentially

104 See more in detail Pernice, "Verfassungs- und europarechtliche Aspekte der Transparenz staatlichen Handelns", 17–34.

105 Pernice, Informationsgesellschaft und Politik. Vom neuen Strukturwandel der Öffentlichkeit zur Global Privacy Governance (Information Society and Politics: From the Structural Transformation of the Public Sphere to Global Privacy Governance).

106 Pernice, "Die Verfassung der Internetgesellschaft", 171, 179–182, 199–208.

large audience".[107] Contrary to times of aristocratic government, but also to national democratic arrangements, today with the Internet "participation in a democratic public is fundamentally open". Bohman describes, however, the particularity of what can be called "a global public":

> "...the only way to create a public sphere across a differentiated social space is through multiple communicative networks rather that an encompassing mass media, then the global public sphere should not be expected to mirror the cultural unity and spatial congruence of the national public sphere: as a public of publics, it permits a decentred public sphere with many different levels".[108]

This is not necessarily what Anne Peters says is "preconditional for global democracy, a uniform space of communication". But even if it is only possible to conceive a "distributive public sphere" composed of diverse more specific public spheres related to special issues,[109] and if communicators, agents or institutions are needed to create them, the internet offers a communicative space in which discourses can take place, and so creates opportunities for people to engage by understanding themselves as agents and not as mere 'users'.

The question is how to organise this space so to effectively allow democratic participation in the articulation of the global public interest, and in decision-making processes established for action on global challenges accordingly. This is the key question of global constitutionalism. If it is true that there are "countless public spheres", as Tully puts it,[110] a thematic public sphere with regard to global issues identified as matters of common concern is not impossible to be considered. It is not comparable to what we believe to exist within a nation-state, it will necessarily be fragmented and not representative for the entire world population, but the internet seems to make it possible for all desiring and able to participate.

Granted, a public sphere in and of itself, even if transnational in nature, does not make for democratic legitimacy per se. Truly democratic government rests on the mutual promise of individuals to recognize each other as free and equal comrades in a polity, a promise that must be institutionalized through procedures based on the principle of equal liberty. Truly democratic government on a global scale therefore calls for the partici-

107 Bohman (note 23), 73 f.

108 Ibid., 75.

109 Ibid., 77, 82, with the example of the Multilateral Agreement on Investment (MAI).

110 Tully (note 26), 19.

pation of individuals in such procedures on the basis of equal (positive) liberty. Transnational public spheres are not elected and do not represent a 'global people' in the strict sense.[111] They nevertheless may generate democratic legitimacy through their inclusiveness and openness, as forums for deliberation and contestation that engage individuals to get together on common issues to discuss, learn about differences, find common ground but also achieve to (peacefully) agree or accept disagreement. Public spheres thus may provide for a breeding ground for an emerging sense of global citizenship as a first step to closing the gap between the status of the individual as rights-bearer and a participant in a community at the global level, based upon the right to equal concern and respect.[112]

It may be questioned if the internet can provide for conditions of a public sphere similar to what we use to know as the room for democratic political processes, for a common discourse on shared concerns within a political community able to ensure integration and effective government. Does it not reflect just fragmented interests, is it not rather a virtual public of actors with a hidden agendas and unforeseeable, rather random impact on public opinion? To be sure, what "the public" really is, remains an open question. Is the public opinion, as we know it traditionally within the national context, not dominated by one or some opinion-leaders, newspapers, broadcasting companies etc.? Does the internet not, at least, offer alternative channels to participate in the discourses, give easier access to a broader range of newspapers and television chains, allow to consult alternative sources of information. It certainly broadens the sources and participatory tools for those who are interested in certain issues to have a

111 Cf. Brunkhorst (note 22), 158–9.

112 To conceive this as a democratic process, the description of Tully (note 26), 23,—though more general—seems to be most attractive: "In summary, in each of the previous cases—of questioning, dialogue, negotiation and cooperation—citizens are engaged in radically democratising the webs of relationships in which they are engaged from the ground up. They refuse to be governed in the way given to them. They treat the constrained freedom of participation within modern governance relationships as an opening to challenge, negotiate and transform them into partnerships under the shared democratic authority of all subject to them. They 'co-operate' the relationships. By bringing all those subject to a relationship into an ongoing dialogue and negotiation over it relative to public goods, and thus treating each other with democratic respect and reciprocity over time, they gradually make themselves into good interdependent governors and citizens. This is one of the oldest meanings of 'democracy'. It is the grass-roots form of democratisation of cooperative citizenship from below".

voice through blogs, social networks or individual websites.[113] It also facilitates direct communication between political leaders and people, organising political movements and demonstrations, inclusion and involvement of those who otherwise would stay aside.

The internet presents, in particular, new tools for discourses across borders, without limits also to the number of participants. The model of the IGF, to which NETmundial was meant to give new dynamics,[114] seem to be particularly appropriate for not only organising the public space regarding global internet governance, as a catalyser and focal point for people around the world interested to participate in the debate on equal terms and so to be respected and taken seriously. Sure, new power structures are emerging within the IGF, contrary to the idea of equal participation. The model should, thus, be further developed to ensure openness and equal access to all for the debate and elaboration of principles. It should be further developed to also cover other global issues, like climate change or the regulation of the global financial markets, so to inject new dynamics into political processes, which seem to have come to a halt. This could lead to the establishment of an inclusive Global Governance Forum (GGF) with various sections for specific issues to be established by the UN General Assembly, for channelling and structuring a global public discourse on matters having global priority.

3. Institutions: a framework for global rule-making

A parliament in a traditional sense, representing the world citizens (and peoples?) at the global level, taking decisions upon the global public interest and acting as a global legislator is difficult to imagine, for the size it would need, for the modes of functioning and, in particular, for the powers to be conferred on it. Such an institution may be understood as a threat to the sovereignty of the nation-states. Yet, the experience of global internet

113 An—yet debatable—example may be the internet campaigns against the SOPA and PIPA legislation in 2010, as analysed by Benkler/Roberts/Faris/Solow-Niederman/Etling, Social Mobilization and the Networked Public Sphere: Mapping the SOPA-PIPA Debate.

114 See the account of Hofmann, Inside NETmundial – Wie in Brasilien über die Zukunft des Internets diskutiert wird.

governance, namely of ICANN, IGF and others,[115] may help developing an alternative institutional framework for public spheres and political will formation that, finally, supports processes of democratically legitimate rule-making at the global level. Global internet governance[116] has developed as a multifaceted and multilevel multi-stakeholder process encompassing—in addition to the "hardware"-side of the net-transmission and -routing systems, lines, knots and computers—the setting up of technical codes and standards, of the system for domain names and ip-address distribution and management. But this initial range of subjects dealt is broadening so to include deliberation upon more general public policy issues like cyber-security, net-neutrality, the protection of intellectual property or personal data and privacy, end even the protection of human rights in the internet and through the internet generally.[117] It is open-ended, explorative and has no systematic institutional framework. Some of its elements, however, indicate not only that it is very different from traditional constitutional settings, but also that, nonetheless, it is neither ineffective nor undemocratic.

Particularly ICANN is an example for how a privately incorporated company has been accepted to evolve to a worldwide operation system for the internet without decisive involvement of states. Lars Viellechner has brilliantly analysed this development conceptualizing ICANN and, in particular, its Domain Name Dispute Resolution Policy (UDRP) as a case of "self-constitution" in a multi-stakeholder process.[118] In addition, the American government has announced that it will give up its regulatory and supervising rights regarding ICANN in favour of a multi-stakeholder solution. The first paragraph of the announcement of the NTIA in the US Department of Commerce in March 14, 2014 reads as follows:

115 See supra III.5.

116 For a comprehensive account see the contributions in: Radu/Chenou/Weber (eds.), The Evolution of Global Internet Governance. Principles and Policies in the Making.

117 See e.g. the Council of Europe, Report on "ICANN's procedures and policies in the light of human rights, fundamental freedoms and democratic values", presented to the IGF 2014 in Istanbul. See on the other hand the criticism of Salomon, Internet Governance Forum: A missed opportunity for human rights. The regional IGF-US forum addressed the questions in June 2014, see: Green, Reflecting on Human Rights and the Internet Governance Forum-USA.

118 Viellechner, Transnationalisierung (note 55), 257–264: "Eigenkonstitutionalisierung".

"To support and enhance the multistakeholder model of Internet policymaking and governance, the U.S. Commerce Department's National Telecommunications and Information Administration (NTIA) today announces its intent to transition key Internet domain name functions to the global multistakeholder community. As the first step, NTIA is asking the Internet Corporation for Assigned Names and Numbers (ICANN) to convene global stakeholders to develop a proposal to transition the current role played by NTIA in the coordination of the Internet's domain name system (DNS)".[119]

This can be understood as a clear acknowledgment of the proper functioning of the system, in particular because the announcement further insists on the multi-stakeholder approach in emphasising, that "NTIA will not accept a proposal that replaces the NTIA role with a government-led or an inter-governmental organization solution".[120] Proposals to bring internet governance under the control of the International Telecommunications Union ITU,[121] thus, seem to be settled.[122]

The question how to organise appropriate oversight in future was on the agenda of the 2014 IGF in Istanbul, the place where the multi-stakeholder community has its broadest gathering.[123] What has been discussed here will inform the work of ICANN when the stakeholders are convened for developing a proposal for the transition, as requested. It is important to note that ICANN is an example for a broad acceptance of a regulatory regime of highest importance as an infrastructure for communication and political life at large, to be not governed or controlled by public authorities. Its specific history from the origin explains not more than how it developed. It does not explain why governments accept it as such in spite of the crucial role the internet has taken early this century. The reason may be that governments simply would not reach agreement

119 NTIA Press Release, Announcement of Intention to Transition of Key Internet Domain Name Functions.

120 Ibid.

121 See Kaufmann, "What is the ITU? The Struggle for Internet Governance"; see also Viellechner, Transnationalisierung (note 54), 137.

122 See also Resolution Plen/3 (Dubai, 2012).

123 See the report by ICANN: "One of the most well-attended sessions of the week at the Internet Governance Forum in Istanbul was a joint discussion on the IANA functions stewardship transition and the parallel process reviewing ICANN's accountability, in light of the anticipated end of ICANN's current contractual relationship with the US Government to administer the IANA functions".

on the diverse technical codes and other regulations needed to make the system running as it does, at the global scale.

Public authorities, however, are not totally absent in the system. Regarding the development of the internet and so of ICANN the US-government played a role, for the IGF it was the UN-General Assembly to take the initial decisions and so to be the authority under which the IGF is working. Regarding NETmundial it is the government of Brazil that has organised this important event. And also in the operation of these institutions governments are stakeholders and participate side by side with other stakeholders and the general public.

The institutions mentioned are established not only for different missions in substance but also different in working methods and the form of outcome. It is possible to distinguish at least two characteristics: more deliberative and more action-oriented. While the IGF operates as an institution providing a public space for debates on internet governance in general, other bodies like ICANN, W3C and IETF are taking decision on concrete action like the setting of standards or defining the scope and operation of the domain name system.

For all, however, the multi-stakeholder approach has found broad acceptance for being both effective and sufficient inclusive and have a democratic function, though the procedures vary from case to case.

4. The method: Multi-stakeholderism and democracy

Multistakeholderism implies the participation of all interest groups, interested organisations, civil society and, in some cases, the public in the deliberation and decision-making processes on matters of common interest.[124] Richard Hill has recently described the various models.[125] At the 2005 World Summit on the Information Society (WSIS) the Tunis-Agenda was adopted and regarding the principles of internet governance the Agenda states:

124 See generally MacDonald, Global Stakeholder Democracy—Power and Representation beyond Liberal States, 85 ff., with a discussion about the broader and narrower strands of democratic stakeholderism.

125 Hill, "The internet, its governance, and the multi-stakeholder model", 27 f.

"that the Internet has evolved into a global facility available to the public and its governance should constitute a core issue of the Information Society agenda. The international management of the Internet should be multilateral, transparent and democratic, with the full involvement of governments, the private sector, civil society and international organizations. It should ensure an equitable distribution of resources, facilitate access for all and ensure a stable and secure functioning of the Internet, taking into account multilingualism".[126]

Paragraph 35 of the Agenda reaffirms that "the Internet encompasses both technical and public policy issues and should involve all stakeholders and relevant intergovernmental and international organisations"; insofar it recognises that:

"a) Policy authority for Internet-related public policy issues is the sovereign right of States. They have rights and responsibilities for international internet-related public policy issues.

b) The private sector has had, and should continue to have, an important role in the development of the Internet, both in the technical and economic fields.

c) Civil society has also played an important role on Internet matters, especially at community level, and should continue to play such a role.

d) Intergovernmental organizations have had, and should continue to have, a facilitating role in the coordination of Internet-related public policy issues.

e) International organizations have also had, and should continue to have, an important role in the development of Internet-related technical standards and relevant policies".[127]

The Agenda also recognises the contribution of the technical and academic communities with these stakeholder groups, and it concludes in paragraph 37 that "a multi-stakeholder approach should be adopted, as far as possible, at all levels". Yet, the Agenda does not detail out how this approach should work in practice. Also with regard to the IGF paragraph 73 states that "the Internet Governance Forum, in its working and

126 ITU Tunis Agenda for the Information Society, Booklet.
127 Ibid.

function, will be multilateral, multi-stakeholder, democratic and transparent."[128]

These statements leave room for a creative implementation and design of the processes of deliberation and decision-making. The question is, to what extent democratic principles prevail in the concrete bodies governed by the multi-stakeholder approach. As neither all governments, nor private companies, civil society organisations, all intergovernmental or international organisations, universities and technical communities can be called democratic, Hill concludes in his analysis that "it cannot be said that key current internet governance institutions are democratic in the conventional sense of the term".[129] This applies even if the term "democratic" would be applied not to each participant but to the multi-stakeholder model as a whole, so he comes to a negative result.[130]

Yet, neither the IGF nor other bodies of Internet governance are states. So the question needs to be asked—more so even as for the EU—whether the idea of democracy developed for states can be transposed to these institutions. "Self-rule of the people" would imply that there be a people, and that there is a rule. Democracy in the sense of ideals of Rousseau is not what we talk about here. Internet governance is different, and probably any analogy to the classical democratic nation-state would be inappropriate insofar, as for any other body of global governance. Nevertheless, certain elements of a democratic system are relevant also for a legitimate constitutional setting of multi-stakeholder arrangements beyond the state: Equal and open access to the deliberation and decision-making for all interested and potentially affected groups and people, non-discrimination of and equal respect for stakeholders, freedom of expression, decision by consensus or majority with a meaningful protection of the minorities, respect of the rule of law as well as the protection of individual rights. So, even if there is no *demos*, to the extent that people understand themselves to be global citizens interested in common global concerns and forming, with a view to put forward and pursue some regulatory goals striving to deal with the questions at stake, institutional arrangements and procedures could be used or established to achieve these goals, if the conditions mentioned above are met, in a way that can be called more democratic

128 On this see also Malcolm, Multi-stakeholder Governance and the Internet Governance Forum, 332 ff., 340 ff., 443.

129 Hill (note 125).

130 Ibid., 30.

than the present system of unbounded powers imposing the world their "laws" as facts.

It would be for another study to examine to what extent these and other requirements are met in the existing bodies of internet governance. Open access and inclusiveness, transparency, open deliberation, non-discrimination etc. seem to be common features, though in certain cases, like W3C, membership is required and only members have the right to submit initiatives for recommendations.[131]

Regarding other areas of global governance new bodies or institutions established would not be vested, at the present stage, with powers to make decisions or to legislate with legally binding effect. Whatever may be the outcome of their proceedings, such as common principles or recommend-dations for all stakeholders, would need to be validated by other democratically legitimated institutions in order to become legally binding. The practical effect of non-binding recommendations issued in a multi-stakeholder process after extensive debate and verification, however, should not be underestimated. Like in the area of technical normalisation, industry and consumers are used just to apply the norms that have been elaborated, without the public authorities being involved, and this system seems to work well.

5. Validation: Giving legal effect to principles and standards

If non-binding recommendations, standards and principles are the outcome of a multi-stakeholder process, whatever forum or body has produced them, there may be a need to give them legally binding effect. As long as there is no legislative body at the global level, it will be difficult to ensure global coverage of any of such rules. Nevertheless, there are a

131 See para. 11 of the proposed World Wide Web Consortium Process Document of August 1, 2014, available at: http://www.w3.org/2014/Process-20140801/#first-wd. Regarding participation the website (http://www.w3.org/participate/) announces: "W3C invites the public to participate in W3C via discussion lists, events, blogs, translations, and other means described below. Participation in Community and Business Groups is open to all. Participation in W3C Working Groups (and other types) is open to W3C Members and other invited parties. W3C groups work with the public through specification reviews as well as contributions of use cases, tests, and implement-tation feedback".

number of ways allowing the validation of the non-binding rules and norms so to make them binding law. One technique is the reference in national legislation to such norms incorporating them into national law. Another technique would be, likewise, to refer to them in international agreements or decisions of supra- or international organisations. The "new approach", adopted in the EU for the completion of the internal market, is an example for how such a system could work. A third way seems to be the effect national and international courts could give to principles and rules having found broad acceptance in global forums.[132]

There is room, however, for being more innovative with a view to establishing institutions at the global level vested with the power to validate rules that have been consented by multi-stakeholder bodies. Such institutions could be composed of representatives of governments or have a mixed composition so to include also members of national parliaments. They may decide by consensus or even in a majority mode, and the binding effect of such validation may be recognised having global reach, even if some governments did not vote in favour. EU experience with opt-out provisions or "emergency breaks" may serve as models for flexible solutions.

With regard to democratic legitimacy, the fact that such rules had gone beforehand through deliberation and approval in open, public and inclusive multi-stakeholder processes with broad online- und offline participation could be regarded as widely compensating a lack of parliamentary consent at the national level. Such conditions, however, would need to be spelled out in the "constitution" of the decision-making institutions competent to validate the rules in question. And different conditions may be relevant to norms of a more technical and administrative kind and other that are legislative and have an impact upon the liberties and rights of the individuals.

6. Judiciary: Dispute settlement and individual rights

Whether or not results of multi-stakeholder processes are validated or would find recognition to produce normative effects without validation, oversight on compliance, the settlement of disputes as well as the protec-

132 On the line of the reasoning developed supra, IV. 2.

tion of individual rights through judiciary bodies would not only make the system more effective but also support voluntary acceptance and confidence of people in its proper functioning.

The principles established by global forums such like the IGF or the proposed GGF may guide the work of this judiciary, and the general instruments of international law for the protection of human rights will have to be applied in any case. If the procedures are transparent and open for comments by stakeholders and the public, the jurisprudence of such courts could ultimately contribute to the emergence of a common global law that includes also the relevant constitutional elements.

7. Review: monitoring and Revisiting-processes

Monitoring and review-processes for the standards and rules established in the proposed system of multi-stakeholder-driven global norm-setting, based upon the internet and the experiences with internet governance, help to keep any regulation once achieved up to the dynamic developments of technology and society. More importantly, however, regular feed-back and continuous political control also of the effects of the regulation by the multi-stakeholder bodies which are at the origin of the standards and have established their guiding principles also may add to the (output-) legitimacy of the entire system. The system, thus, is a dynamically evolving system, it is a process, not a frozen structure set-up once for ever.

The review should be organised as a transparent and public process, with the internet as a tool for worldwide information and dialogue. It might be for the proposed Global Governance Forum (GGF) to discuss whether or not the actual measures taken by standardisation bodies or even a by global legislative institution are complying with the principles identified at earlier stages, and whether certain policies have to be revised, and in what direction. The GGF should be given the power to adopt—by broad consensus—not only principles and guidelines on matters of global common interest, but also recommendations to the other bodies to undertake the revision accordingly.

The GGF or similar bodies are the place where stakeholders and people can discuss individually and also engage as participants with equal rights in a continuously renewed consideration of the rules to be finally laid down with a view to deal effectively with global challenges. The internet allows that people do not need to elect representatives, but can participate directly in an open discourse and come to conclusions which, if followed by the norm-setting bodies, provide them with a special kind of legitimacy rooted in the will of "the" people taking responsibility as global citizens.

VI. Conclusions

The seven elements of the "constitution" of norm-setting at the global level outlined above remain necessarily vague and need further consideration and concretisation. And the present proposal is far from what is known as a constitution of a state. To invent this cannot be the goal, striving for a global state would not serve the self-determination of people. The present model is more modest, but guided by the values and principles of global constitutionalism rooted in the legitimising power of the individual. The respect of the other as equal participant in the process of regulation and of the others dignity as human being and holder of equal fundamental rights and freedoms is the fundament for designing and establishing a system that allows to locate decision-making power on matters of common global interest at the global level. Policies decided at that level have no externalities, by definition, instead they are a remedy avoiding externalities that would otherwise affect people who have no voice. Common regulation for all people concerned, by ensuring that all who are possibly affected can actually participate in the process of decision-making on equal terms, means self-rule of these people and, thus, *taking people seriously*.

As far as the principle of subsidiarity is respected, the regulatory powers conferred to global institutions would, therefore, not take away sovereignty or room for democratic self-determination from states, but add to the sovereign rights of the peoples in shaping their common future, if needed because of the global dimension of the problem, as a matter of common global public interest.

Some features of such a system are not unknown in European and international constitutional practice, but the present proposal combines experiences from the different supranational, international and governance-related models. Multistakeholderism is practiced, as shown, at the global level already in contexts like the Rio-process.[133] It is the underlying concept of the Aarhus-concept altogether. Yet internet governance is the area where it is practiced more extensively and systematically.[134] Multi-stakeholderism has a great democratic potential thanks to the opportunities offered by the internet, though this potential needs further consideration and development. It seems to be the appropriate mode for global standard-setting, namely on technical codes and requirements. Institutional arrangements for decision-making and validation by global institutions may rather follow the examples of the Council of the European Union, while the UN Security Council has a limited and differentiated membership and is less attractive as a model. Examples for oversight and monitoring are the secretariats and compliance mechanisms of international regimes or the European Commission, while for dispute settlement and the protection of individual rights the WTO bodies or the European Court of Justice offer plenty of experience. In each case transparency, dialogue and public participation in the proceedings through the internet would enhance the legitimacy of their decision-making.

Global constitutionalism and the internet, after all, can be related to each-other and be mutually supportive in various ways. On the one side, the internet is an important tool for developing a system of democratically legitimate regulation at the global level, giving people a voice, and so favours global constitutionalism, both for the space of communication and participation in politics, it offers, and for the models of multi-stakeholder processes it has developed. On the other side global constitutionalism, for the global level of what has been described as multilevel constitutionalism, provides the principles and conditions for the development of a "constitution" of internet governance. As the internet is becoming the most important infrastructure for worldwide communication, constitutionalising its governance is required in order to ensure its security and resilience as well as the protection of the individual rights of all people involved, including the freedoms of information and expression, of sciences and education, intellectual property rights and the protection of data and privacy as elementary aspects of human dignity.

---

133 See supra III. 3.

134 See supra III. 5.

Works Cited

Barlow, Jon Perry (8 February 1996): A Declaration of the Independence of Cyberspace, available at: https://projects.eff.org/~barlow/Declaration–Final.html.

Benkler, Yochai/Roberts, Hal/Faris, Robert/Solow-Niederman, Alicia/Etling, Bruce, Social Mobilization and the Networked Public Sphere: Mapping the SOPA-PIPA Debate, *Berkman Center Research Publication No. 2013–16*, available at: http://papers.ssrn.com/sol3/papers.cfm?abstract_id=2295953.

Benvenisti, Ayal (2008): Reclaiming Democracy: The Strategic Uses of Foreign and International Law by National *Courts*, *Tel Aviv University Law Faculty Papers, 59*, available at: http://law.bepress.com/taulwps/art59.

Besson, Samantha (2009): "Whose Constitution(s)? International Law, Constitutionalism, and Democracy", in: Dunoff, Jeffrey L. and Trachtman, Joel P. (eds.), *Ruling the World? Constitutionalism, International Law, and Global Governance,* Cambridge.

von Bogdandy, Armin (2003): "Demokratie, Globalisierung, Zukunft des Völkerrechts – eine Bestandsaufnahme", *Zeitschrift für ausländisches öffentliches Recht und Völkerrecht* (ZaöRV) 63, 853–877.

von Bogdandy, Armin/Venzke, Ingo (2014), In wessen Namen. Internationale Gerichte in Zeiten globalen Regierens, Berlin.

Bohman, James (2008): "The Transformation of the Public Sphere. Political Authority, Communicative Freedom, and Internet Publics", in: v. d. Hoven/Weckert (eds.), *Information Technology and Moral Philosophy*, Cambridge.

Braams, Beate (2013): *Koordinierung als Kompetenzkategorie*, Tübingen.

Brunkhorst, Hauke (2005): *Solidarity – From Civic Friendship to a Global Legal Community*, Cambridge.

Bunge, Thomas (2014): "Rechtsbehelfe in Umweltangelegenheiten: Vorgaben der Aarhus-Konvention und deutsches Recht", *Natur und Recht 36*, 605–614.

Búrca, Gráinne de (2010): "The European Court of Justice and the International Legal order After Kadi", *Harvard International Law Journal 51*, 1–44.

Calliess, Christian/Hartmann, Moritz (2014): *Zur Demokratie in Europa: Unionsbürgerschaft und Europäische Öffentlichkeit,* Tübingen.

Cass, Deborah Z. (2005): *The Constitutionalization of the World Trade Organization. Legitimacy, Democracy, and Community in the International Trading System,* Oxford.

Cassese, Sabino (2009): *I Tribunali de Babele. I giudici alla recerca di un nuovo ordine globale*, Rome.

Cohen, Jean L.(2012): *Globalization and Sovereignty. Rethinking Legality, Legitimacy, and Constitutionalism*, Cambridge.

Council of Europe, Report on "ICANN's procedures and policies in the light of human rights, fundamental *freedoms and democratic values"* (Monika Zalnieriute and Thomas Schneider), presented to the IGF 2014 in Istanbul, available at: http://www.coe.int/t/informationsociety/icann-and-human-rights.asp.

Delbrück, Jost (2002): "Prospects for a 'World (Internal) Law?': Legal Developments in a Changing International System", *Indiana Journal of Global Legal Studies 9*, 401–431.

Dreier, Horst (2013): "Article 1 I", in: id. (ed.) *Grundgesetz Kommentar*, vol. I, 3rd ed., München.

Dworkin, Ronald (1977): *Taking Rights Seriously*, Harvard.

Dworkin, Ronald (2011): *Justice for Hedgehogs*, Harvard.

Fassbender, Bardo (2009): *The United Nations Charter as the Constitution of the International Community*, Leiden/Boston.

Follesdal, Andreas (2009): "When Common Interests Are Not Common: Why the Global Basic Structure Should be Democratic", *Indiana Journal of Global Legal Studies 16*, 585–604.

Follesdal, Andreas (2013): "The principle of subsidiarity as a constitutional principle in international law", *Global Constitutionalism* 2, 37–62.

Green, Natalie (28 July 2014): "*Reflecting on Human Rights and the Internet Governance Forum – USA*", available at: https://www.publicknowledge.org/news-blog/blogs/reflecting-on-human-rights-and-the-internet-governance-forum-usa.

Habermas, Jürgen (2012): "Die Krise der Europäischen Union im Lichte einer Konstitutionalisierung des Völkerrechts – Ein Essay zur Verfassung Europas", *Zeitschrift für ausländisches öffentliches Recht und Völkerrecht* (ZaöRV) 72, 1–44.

Habermas, Jürgen (2012): *The crisis of the European Union. Response,* Cambridge.

Held, David (1995): *Democracy and the Global Order. From the Modern State to Cosmopolitan Governance*, Stanford.

Hill, Richard (2014): "The internet, its governance, and the multi-stakeholder model", *Emerald Insight Info 16*, 16–46.

Hofmann, Hasso (1993): "Die versprochene Menschenwürde", *Archiv des öffentlichen Rechts 118*, 353–377.

Hofmann, Jeanette (28 April 2014): "Inside NETmundial – Wie in Brasilien über die Zukunft des Internets diskutiert wird", *HIIG Blog*, available at: http://www.hiig.de/inside-netmundial-wie-in-brasilien-uber-die-zukunft-des-internet-diskutiert-wird.

Hofmann, Jeanette (2005): "Internet Governance: Zwischen staatlicher Autorität und privater Koordination", *Internationale Politik und Gesellschaft (IPG) 3/2005.*

Hofmann, Jeanette/Katzenbach, Christian/Gollatz, Kirsten (21 August 2014): "Between Coordination and Regulation: Conceptualizing Governance in Internet Governance", *HIIG Discussion Paper Series No. 2014.4*, available at: http://ssrn. com/abstract=2484463.

Hülsbömer, Simon (1.4.2013): "Vom Arpanet zum WWW. Zeitreise: So entstand das Internet", in: *PC Welt of 1.4.2013*, available at: http://www.pcwelt.de/ratgeber/Vom-Arpanet-zum-WWW-So-entstand-das-Internet-312786.html.

ICANN (2013): "Beginner's Guide to Participating in ICANN", available at: https://www. icann.org/en/system/files/files/participating-08nov13-en.pdf.

ICANN (2014): "Report", available at: https://www.icann.org/news/announcement-3-2014-08-25-en.

ITU (18 November 2005): "Tunis Agenda for the Information Society", available at: http://www.itu.int/wsis/docs2/tunis/off/6rev1.html.

ITU (2005): "Tunis Agenda for the Information Society – Booklet", in: *WSIS Documents ITU 2005*, available at: http://www.itu.int/wsis/outcome/booklet.pdf.

Kadelbach, Stefan/Kleinlein, Thomas (2007): "International Law – a Constitution for Mankind? An Attempt at a Re-appraisal with an Analysis of Constitutional Principles", *German Yearbook of International Law* 50, 303–348.

Karlins, Janis: "IGF 2014 – the gateway for the future", available at: http://www.intgovforum .org/cms/blog-igf-2014.

Kaufmann, Justin (4 June 2012): "What is the ITU? The Struggle for Internet Governance", *Public Knowledge Blogs.*

Kleinwächter, Wolfgang (2003): "From Self-Governance to Public-Private Partnership: The Changing Role of Governments in the Management of the Internet's Core Resources", *Loyola of Los Angeles Law Review 36*, 1103–1126, Los Angeles.

Kleinwächter, Wolfgang (2013): "Editorial", in: id. (ed.), *Internet und Demokratie, Multistakeholder Internet Dialog (MIND)* #5.

Kokott, Juliane/Sobotta, Christoph (2012): "The Kadi Case – Constitutional Core Values and International Law – Finding the Balance?", *European Journal of International Law* 23, 1015–24.

Kotzur, Markus (2014): "Völkerrecht von der Menschheit her denken, in: Alexander Blankenagel" (ed.), *Den Verfassungsstaat nachdenken. Eine Geburtstagsgabe*, Berlin.

Kumm, Matthias (2013): "The Cosmopolitan Turn in Constitutionalism: An Integrated Conception of Public Law", *Indiana Journal of Global Legal Studies 20*, 605–628.

Lawrence, Jessica (2013): "Contesting constitutionalism: Constitutional discourse at the WTO", *Global Constitutionalism* 2, 63–90.

Lessig, Lawrence (2006): *Code Version 2.0,* New York.

MacDonald, Terry (2008): *Global Stakeholder Democracy – Power and Representation beyond Liberal States*, Oxford.

Mahlmann, Matthias (2012): "Human Dignity in Modern Constitutional Orders", in: Michel Rosenfeld & Andras Sajó (Eds.), *The Oxford Handbook of Comparative Constitutional Law,* Oxford.

Malcolm, Jeremy (2008): *Multi-stakeholder Governance and the Internet Governance Forum*, Perth.

Mayer, Franz (2001): "Review Essay. The Internet and Public International Law – Worlds Apart?", *European Journal of International Law* 12, 617–622.

McCrudden, Christopher (2008): "Human Dignity and Judicial Interpretation of Human Rights", *European Journal of International Law* 19, 655–724.

Milan, Stefania/Hintz, Arne (19 September 2014): "In Multistakeholderism We Trust: On the Limits of the Multistakeholder Debate", available at: http://www.global.asc.upenn.edu/in-multistakeholderism-we-trust-on-the-limits-of-the-multistakeholder-debate.

Milewicz, Karolina (2009): "Emerging Patterns of Global Constitutionalization: Toward a Conceptual Framework", *Indiana Journal of Global Legal Studies 16*, 413–436.

Morozov, Evgeni (2011): *The Net Delusion: How Not to Liberate the World*, Penguin.

Müller, Thomas (2014): "Global constitutionalism in historical perspective: Towards refined tools for international constitutional histories", *Global Constitutionalism* 3, 71–101, Cambridge. National Telecommunications and Information Administration (NTIA), *Press Release* "NTIA Announces Intent to Transition Key Internet Domain Name Functions", available at: http://www.ntia.doc.gov/press-release/2014/ntia-announces-intent-transition-key-internet-domain-name-functions.

NETmundial: "Multistakeholder Statement of 24 April 2014", available at: http://netmundial.br/wp-content/uploads/2014/04/NETmundial-Multistakeholder-Document.pdf.

Neyer, Jürgen (2012): *The Justification of Europe. A Political Theory of Supranational Integration*, Oxford.

Paulus, Andreas L. (2009): "The International Legal System as a Constitution", in: Jeffrey L. Dunoff and Joel P. Trachtman (ed.), *Ruling the World? Constitutionalism, International Law, and Global Governance*, Cambridge.

Pernice, Ingolf (1996): "Die Dritte Gewalt im europäischen Verfassungsverbund", *Europarecht* 31, 27–43.

Pernice, Ingolf (1998): "Constitutional Law Implications for a State Participating in a Process of Regional Integration. German Constitution and „Multilevel Constitutionalism", in: Eibe Riedel (ed.), *German Reports on Public Law Presented to the XV. International Congress on Comparative Law*, Bristol.

Pernice, Ingolf (2000): "Der Europäische Verfassungsverbund auf dem Wege der Konsolidierung. Verfassungsrechtliche Ausgangslage und Vorschläge für die institutionelle Reform der Europäischen Union vor der Osterweiterung", in: Peter Häberle (ed.), *Jahrbuch des Öffentlichen Rechts der Gegenwart.* Neue Folge/Band 48, Tübingen.

Pernice, Ingolf (2006): "The Global Dimension of Multilevel Constitutionalism: A Legal response to the Challenges of Globalisation", in: Pierre-Marie Dupuy, Bardo Fassbender, Malcolm N. Shaw and Karl-Peter Sommermann (eds.), *Common Values in International Law. Essays in Honour of Christian Tomuschat*, Kehl-Strasbourg-Arlington.

Pernice, Ingolf (2010): "La Rete Europea di Costituzionalità. Der Europäische Verfassungsverbund und die Netzwerktheorie", *Zeitschrift für ausländisches öffentliches Recht und Völkerrecht* (ZaöRV) 70, 51–71.

Pernice, Ingolf (2012): "Informationsgesellschaft und Politik. Vom neuen Strukturwandel der Öffentlichkeit zur Global Privacy Governance" (Information Society and Politics: From the Structural Transformation of the Public Sphere to Global Privacy Governance), available at: http://papers.ssrn. com/sol3/papers. cfm?abstract_id=2222046.

Pernice, Ingolf (2013): "Solidarität in Europa. Eine Ortsbestimmung im Verhältnis zwischen Bürger, Staat und Europäischer Union", in: Christian Calliess (ed.), *Europäische Solidarität und nationale Identität – Überlegungen im Kontext der Krise im Euroraum*, Tübingen.

Pernice, Ingolf (2014): "Die Verfassung der Internetgesellschaft", in: Alexander Blankenagel (ed.), *Den Verfassungsstaat nachdenken. Eine Geburtstagsgabe,* Berlin.

Pernice, Ingolf (2014): "Multilevel Constitutionalism and the Crisis of Democracy in Europe", lecture given at the Aristoteles University of Saloniki the 4th of December 2014, stream available at: https://www.youtube.com/watch?v=Do0 81tYopAE.

Pernice, Ingolf (2014): "The EU – A Citizens' Joint Venture. Multilevel Constitutionalism and Open Democracy in Europe", in: José M. Magone (ed.), *Routledge Handbook of European Politics*, New York.

Pernice, Ingolf (2014): "Umweltvölker- und europarechtliche Vorgaben zum Verbandsklagerecht und das System des deutschen Verwaltungsrechtsschutzes. Impulse zur Rechtsentwicklung im Mehrebenenverbund", in: Ekkehard Hofmann (ed.), *Demokratisch-Funktionale Analyse der Öffentlichkeitsbeteiligung im Umwelt- und Infrastrukturrecht*, Workhop Saloniki 4–6 December 2014 (forthcoming).

Pernice, Ingolf (2014): "Verfassungs- und europarechtliche Aspekte der Transparenz staatlichen Handelns", 2. IFG-Tagung Berlin am 6./7. September 2012, in: Alexander Dix et al. (eds.), *Informationsfreiheit und Informationsrecht. Jahrbuch 2013,* Berlin.

Pernice, Ingolf (2015): "Das Völkerrecht des Netzes. Konstitutionelle Elemente eines globalen Rechtsrahmens für das Internet", in: Giovanni Biaggini (ed.), *Festschrift für Daniel Thürer zum 70. Geburtstag*, forthcoming, Baden-Baden.

Peters, Anne (2006): "Compensatory Constitutionalism: The Function and Potential of Fundamental International Norms and Structures", *Leiden Journal of International Law* 19, 579–610.

Peters, Anne (2009): "Dual Democracy", in: Jan Klabbers, Anne Peters, Geir Ulfstein (eds.), *The Constitutionalization of International Law,* Oxford.

Peters Anne (2009): "Membership in the Global Constitutional Community", in: Jan Klabbers, Anne Peters, and Geir Ulfstein (eds.), *The Constitutionalization of International Law*, Oxford.

Peters, Anne (2009): "The Merits of Global Constitutionalism", *Indiana Journal of Global Legal Studies* 16, 397–411.

Peters, Anne/Förster, Till/Koechlin, Lucy (2009): "Towards non-state actors as effective, legitimate, and accountable standard setters", in: Anne Peters et al (eds.), *Non-State Actors as Standard Setters,* Cambridge.

Petersmann, Ernst-Ulrich (ed.) (2005): Reforming the World Trading System: Legitimacy, Efficiency and Democratic Governance, Oxford.

Petersmann, Ernst-Ulrich (2006): Human Rights, "Constitutionalism and the World Trade Organization: Challenges for World Trade Organization Jurisprudence and Civil Society", *Leiden Journal of International Law* 19, 633–667.

Platon, Sébastien (2014): "The 'Equivalent Protection Test'. From European Union to United Nations, from Solange II to Solange I (with reference to the Al-Dulimi and Montana Magegement inc. V. Switzerland Judgment of the European Court of Human Rights)", *European Constitutional Law Review* 10, 226–262.

Radu, Roxana/Chenou, Jean-Marie/Weber, Rolf H. (eds.) (2013): *The Evolution of Global Internet Governance.* Principles and Policies in the Making, Berlin.

Rawls, John (1972), *Theory of Justice,* Oxford.

Salomon, Josefina (5 September 2014: "Internet Governance Forum: A missed opportunity for human rights", *LIVEWIRE, Amnesty's global human rights blog*, available at: http://livewire.amnesty.org/2014/09/05/internet-governance-for um-a-missed-opportunity-for-human-rights.

Sifry, Micah L. (2014): *The Big Disconnect: Why the Internet Hasn't Transformed Politics (Yet)*, New York.

Slaughter, Anne-Marie (2003): "A Global Community of Courts", *Harvard International Law Journal* 44, 191–219.

Slaughter, Anne-Marie (2004): *The New World Order,* Princeton.

Tully, James (8 May 2010): *A Dilemma of Democratic Citizenship*, Paper delivered at the University of Victoria.

Uerpmann-Wittzack, Robert (2008): "Multilevel Internet Governance Involving the European Union, Nation States and NGOs", in: Andreas Follesdal, Ramses A. Wessel and Jan Wouters (eds.), *Multilevel Regulation and the EU. The Interplay between Global, European and National Normative Processes,* Leiden.Boston. UN General Assembly, Resolution 56/183 (21 December 2001). UN Sustainable Development Knowledge Platform, "Announcement for the Expert Group Meeting on the role of the high-level political forum on sustainable development in post-2015 development framework", 30 April-1 May 2014, available at: http://sustainabledevelopment.un.org/index.php?page=view&nr=667&type=13&menu=1556.

US Department of Commerce: "Memorandum of Understanding between the U.S. Department of Commerce and Internet Corporation for Assigned Names and Numbers", available at: https://www.icann.org/resources/unthemed-pages/ic ann-mou-1998-11-25-en.

Tietje, Christian/Nowrot, Karsten (2009): "Das Internet im Fokus des transnationalen Wirtschaftsrechts: Normative Ordnungsstrukturen für den E-Commerce", *Archiv des Völkerrechts* 47, 328–366.

Viellechner, Lars (2012): "Constitutionalism as a Cipher: On the Convergence of Constitutionalist and Pluralist Approaches to the Globalization of Law", *Goettingen Journal of International Law* 4, 599–623.

Viellechner, Lars (2013): *Transnationalisierung des Rechts,* Weilerswist.

Voßkuhle, Andreas (2010): "Multilevel Cooperation of the European Constitutional Courts. Der Europäische Verfassungsgerichtsverbund", *European Constitutional Law Review* 6, 175–198.

Walker, Neil (2009): "Reframing EU Constitutionalism", in: Jeffrey Dunoff and Joel Trachtman (eds.), *Ruling the* World? Constitutionalism, International Law and Global Governance, Cambridge.

Wiener, Antje/Lang, Anthony F./Tully, James/Maduro, Miguel Poires/Kumm, Mattias (2012): "Editorial – Global constitutionalism: Human Rights, democracy and the rule of law", *Global Constitutionalism* 1, 1–15.

World Wide Web Consortium (1 August 2014): "Process Document", available at: http://www.w3.org/2014/Process-20140801/#first-wd.

Notes on Contributors

Rainer Hofmann, Professor of Public Law, European Law and Public International Law at Frankfurt University; Member of the Executive and Management Board of the EU Fundamental Rights Agency; Hofmann has published widely on issues of public international law, in particular human rights, national minorities' and refugee law.

Michael Bothe, Professor emeritus of Public Law and Public International Law at Frankfurt University; former Member and President of the International Humanitarian Fact-Finding Commission (2001–2011); Bothe has published widely on issues of general public international law, humanitarian law and environmental law.

Stefan Kadelbach, Professor of Public Law, European Law and Public International Law at Frankfurt University; Member of the Board of the Cluster of Excellence "Formation of Normative Orders"; Co-Rapporteur, International Law Association Committee on Human Rights; Kadelbach has published widely on issues of public international law and European Law.

Martti Koskenniemi, Professor of International and Director of the Erik-Castrén-Institute for International Law and Human Rights, University of Helsinki; former Member, UN International Law Commission; Koskenniemi has published widely on issues of public international law, including its theoretical foundations and historical development.

Joseph H.H. Weiler, President, European University Institute, Florence, and Professor of European Law, New York University; formerly Professor of International and European Law at the Universities of Michigan and Harvard and New York University; Weiler has published widely on fundamental issues of European Law, in particular its *sui generis* character, the role of the European Court of Justice and the theoretical foundations of European integration law.

Ingolf Pernice, Professor of Public Law, European Law and Public International Law and Director of the Walter-Hallstein-Institute for European Constitutional Law,

Humboldt-University, Berlin; Pernice has published widely on issues of public international and European law, in particular on EU institutions and human rights.